John M. Curran

The Geology of Sydney and the Blue Mountains

a popular introduction to the study of geology

John M. Curran

The Geology of Sydney and the Blue Mountains
a popular introduction to the study of geology

ISBN/EAN: 9783337287832

Printed in Europe, USA, Canada, Australia, Japan

Cover: Foto ©Andreas Hilbeck / pixelio.de

More available books at **www.hansebooks.com**

GEOLOGY OF SYDNEY

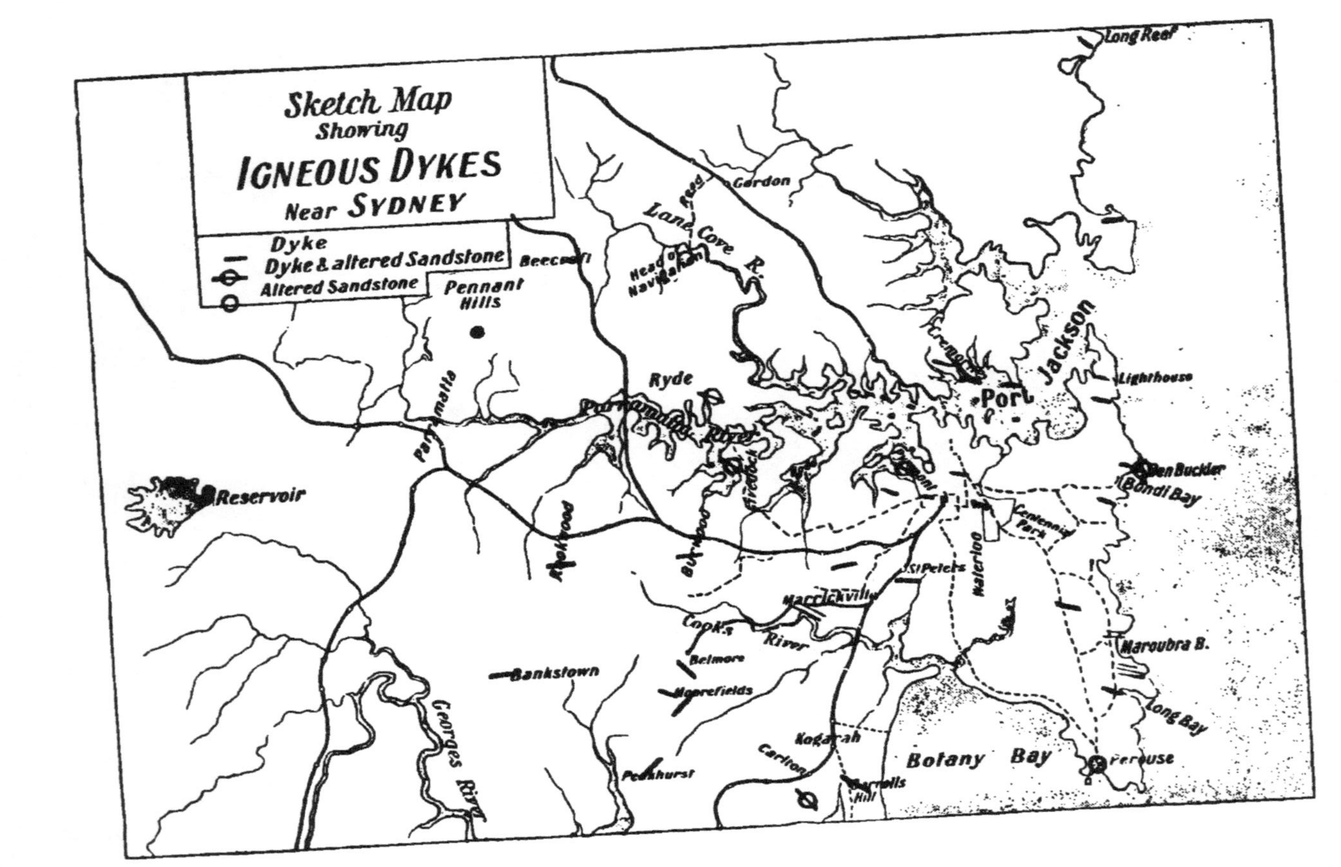
Sketch Map
Showing
IGNEOUS DYKES
Near SYDNEY
Dyke
Dyke & altered Sandstone
Altered Sandstone
Long Reef
Gordon
Lane Cove R.
Pennant Hills
Ryde
Port Jackson
Lighthouse
Bondi Bay
Reservoir
Rookwood
St Peters
Waterloo
Cook's River
Belmore
Bankstown
Georges River
Maroubra B.
Long Bay
Kogarah
Carlton
Botany Bay
Peakhurst

THE

…Y OF SYDNEY

…BLUE MOUNTAINS

…INTRODUCTION TO THE
…OF GEOLOGY

1899

TO

FREDERICK BRIDGES, Esq.,

Chief Inspector of Schools

Department of Public Instruction

who

as the First Superintendent of

Technical Education

Fostered the teaching of Geology

in New South Wales.

PREFACE

> "Il n'y a que ceux qui ne font rien quine se trompent pas."—FAVRE.

THIS little book is a practical reply to a number of persons who repeatedly ask the writer for some information on the Geology of Sydney and the Mountains. The only possible reply has hitherto been to refer them to a number of reports buried away in Blue Books, or to scientific papers scattered through the proceedings of various learned societies. Many of these papers and reports are now out of print. As stores of scientific knowledge, they are invaluable, but they have not proved inviting to the public generally.

In the chapters now presented to my readers, I have done little more than collect some of the scattered information referred to; but I may claim that the method of presenting the subject is my own. Primarily, I have considered the needs of the general reader, at the same time bearing in mind the wants of the student. The book, small as it is, would be impossible were it not for the labours of three eminent geologists, now alas! no longer amongst us—Clarke, Wilkinson, and Tenison-Woods. I have also drawn on the writings of Mr. Robert Etheridge, junr., Curator of the Australian Museum, Professor David, of the University of Sydney, and Mr. Pittman, the Government Geologist.

Considerable care has been taken with the illustrations. They are, with a few exceptions, reproduced from my own photographs. In the case of fossils, reference is made in foot-notes to the original figures. Most of them have been re-drawn, but I fear they have suffered somewhat from the difficulty of rendering the original lithographs into line work. I am indebted to Mr. Charles Hedley, of the Australian Museum, for some of these drawings, and also for valued advice in preparing the work. To Mr. Cathels is due the credit of admirable reproductions of some of my own sketches. I must also express my indebtedness to two of my students, Miss Elsie English and Mr. Carl A. Sussmilch; the former read the proof-sheets and compiled the index, the latter verified many references in the list of fossils, and worked out the section (fig. 46) at Bundanoon.

Finally, I may say that the book, as it leaves my hands, falls very far short of my ideal. I can only hope that perhaps its very shortcomings will induce someone with resources more ample than mine to take the matter in hand, and give us a work altogether worthy of the subject.

J. M. C.

Technical College,

17th October, 1898.

PREFACE TO THE SECOND EDITION.

THE first edition of this book was sold out in a few months. This may be taken as a proof that the work, which was published with some diffidence, has met with the approval of the public. It was my endeavour to introduce the student to a practical method of studying Geology—by handling specimens, and examining rocks along the cliff and on the hillside in "Nature's roofless school." Without sacrificing simplicity, I have, when possible, given references to reliable sources of information, thus in a manner helping the student to continue his study on a higher grade.

Reference is made repeatedly in the text to the late Professor de Koninck's Atlas of New South Wales Palæozoic Fossils, published at Brussels in 1873. This work is now available in English, with all the original beautiful lithographic plates.[1]

I have added two new maps, and made several new photographs to supply fresh illustrations. In studying the country west of Mount Victoria I received considerable help from Mr. H. G. Rienits, who walked over much of the ground with me. When most of my notes were made I learned that a map had already been prepared, quite independently, by Mr. C. L. Ball. This gentleman, who is intimately acquainted with the

1. Descriptions of the Palæozoic Fossils of New South Wales, by L. G. de Koninck. Translated from the French by T. W. Edgeworth David, Mrs. David, and W. S. Dun. W. Applegate Gullick, Government Printer, Sydney, 1898.

district, very kindly placed his work at my disposal. The geological map now added to this volume is therefore the joint work of Mr. Ball, Mr. Rienits, and the present writer. The district coloured was selected as being an area easily accessible to the student, and one in which the rocks vary considerably in age and character. The map facing the title page shows the position of a number of igneous dykes around Sydney of which no record has hitherto been published.

Some friendly critics have found fault with the disposition of the illustrations, pointing out that the figures are not always on the same page as the text referring to them. Geological pictures of general interest, illustrating many principles may, I think, be distributed *with their explanatory legend,* through a volume such as this.

I would express my indebtedness to Professor David, of the University, for reading through the book, making some corrections, and giving me many valuable suggestions which are embodied in this edition. For information and assistance generally I have to thank Mr. John Mitchell, Mr. David Wiley, Mr. J. M. Taylor, LL.B., Mr. A. G. Hamilton, and Mr. W. J. Enright.

J. M. C.

CONTENTS.

CHAPTER I.

GEOLOGY, A HISTORY OF THE WORLD BEFORE HUMAN HISTORY BEGAN.

CHAPTER II.

EXAMINATION OF ROCKS.

CHAPTER III.

FOSSILS.

CHAPTER IV.

ROCKS.

CHAPTER V.

GEOLOGICAL SEQUENCE OF ROCKS.

CHAPTER VI.

RECENT DEPOSITS AND PLEISTOCENE.

CHAPTER VII.

THE TRIASSIC ROCKS.

CHAPTER VII.—(*Continued.*)

THE FOSSIL PLANTS.

CHAPTER VIII.

THE PERMO-CARBONIFEROUS.

CHAPTER IX.

DEVONIAN.

CHAPTER X.

THE SILURIAN ROCKS.

CHAPTER XI.

BASALT, GRANITES, AND DIORITES.

CHAPTER XII.

ORIGIN OF THE MOUNTAINS.

CHAPTER XIII.

PLACES OF GEOLOGICAL INTEREST.

APPENDICES.

ILLUSTRATIONS

In the photographs of the Igneous Dykes the undecomposed basalt comes out black, as in fig. 15. When the basalt is decomposed the photographs show the dykes in a lighter shade than the surrounding shales.

For the information of readers not familiar with the topography of the mountains and some other districts named, it may be well to say that—

Mount Hay, Mount Tomah, and Mount King George are prominent basalt-capped hills, which may be seen in the distance from Mount Victoria and Katoomba.

The Canoblas is a mountain of andesitic basalt, and an ancient volcano, about seven miles from Orange, and about one hundred and ninety miles west from Sydney.

Mount Victoria is seventy-seven miles from Sydney on the main Western line. A line of coaches runs from here to the Jenolan Caves daily.

Molong is a town on a branch of the Western railway line, two hundred and sixteen miles from Sydney.

CHAPTER I.

GEOLOGY A HISTORY OF THE WORLD BEFORE HUMAN HISTORY BEGAN.

AUSTRALIA HAS A HISTORY FAR MORE ANCIENT THAN ANY WRITTEN BY MEN—TO READ THIS HISTORY IS ONE OF THE OBJECTS OF GEOLOGY—RECORDS PRESERVED IN THE GREAT STONE-BOOK OF NATURE.

NOT long ago some strange-looking impressions were discovered on a block of shale at St. Peters, near Sydney. The block was dug from a band seventy feet below the surface. The impressions were evidently made by a living animal walking over the partially-hardened shale, when that shale band was the surface of the land. After the creature left its foot-print several hundred feet of newer shales were deposited. There is convincing evidence to show that these foot prints were made when the Blue Mountains were still beneath the waters, and before the Alps or the Himalayas were lifted to their proud eminence. But by what manner of creature were these foot prints left? The impressions did not look as if they could have been made by any animal that living man had ever set eyes upon.

Some time before, the remains of a wonderful "extinct monster" were unearthed in the same quarry.

There is nothing like it living now on earth. Even the natural order to which it belonged is quite extinct. This ungainly creature was a shovel-headed Salamander which pottered about like Falstaff in his old age, "with much belly and little legs." But it measured ten or fourteen feet in length, and was as large as an ox in girth—a huge Batrachian, not separated very much from the frogs and newts. Transverse sections of its teeth show a wonderful labyrinthine pattern, from which these animals have been called Labyrinthodonts.

In the shales alongside are found very clear impressions of ferns that grew while the shale was being formed layer above layer. One of these ferns, *Macrotæniopteris*[1] (Fig. 4), was a stately plant, but nowhere can it be found living to-day. Here, then, we have evidence of animals and plants—and be it noted highly-organised animals and plants, differing completely from those now existing—having peopled the world before the forms around us came into existence. We have proof of amphibians wandering by ancient lakes, and leaving the impress of their huge bulk on the muddy flats. Highly-organised plants flourished on the edges of these lakes. There are ripple-marks on the shale also, left by the lapping of tiny waves. All this is buried down so deep that vast ages must have elapsed since these ferns grew, and since that great reptile lived. This passing

1 Gk. *Macros*, great; *tænia*, a ribbon; *pteron*, a wing, a fern-frond

glance into those far-off days shows us that even in that distant past the sun shone for the growing plants, the winds blew, and rain fell, and animals peopled the earth. Long afterwards rumblings could be heard, the result of great earth movements, and the rocks at more than one point burst upwards, letting loose floods of lava that cooled and hardened

FIG 1.—Bondi, near Sydney (after Scholl).
A wave-beaten sea-cliff, much carved by the sea.

into the blue-black compact rock we call basalt. But the volcanic fires are long since cooled, the great ribbon-fern no longer lives, and no *Labyrinthodont* can be found on earth to-day.

Without going one step further, we see Australia has therefore a history far older than that preserved in written records. The oldest written information takes us back hardly more than a few hundred years.

And our existence, as a people in a new country, practically begins with the century. The pages of the great stone-book of Nature take us far back into the childhood of the world. By piecing together the fragments of "strange markings" on the rocks, we are able to picture the conditions that prevailed long before a block of sandstone existed where Sydney now stands. The sandstone cliffs, forming the gates to Port Jackson, attract the attention of every observer. The giant walls of sandstone on the Blue Mountains are sublime in their magnificence. But these giant walls were not *always* on the Mountains. The sea did not *always* send its rolling billows through the Port Jackson heads. There was a day, long ago, when there was no sea there to roll, and no cliffs to form headlands. There was a time when the highest tops of the mountains were depressed beneath the troubled waters of a great estuary. And when they finally rose in their grandeur to their present height or higher, volcanic fires lighted up the scene of Nature's mountain-building. Mounts Hay, Tomah, and King George are the remnants of a one-time continuous sheet of lava. This lava rose through the neck of a volcano, and was poured out just as fiery streams are seen to issue from Vesuvius or Etna to-day. Surely these are glimpses of a past history, more ancient than any written by man. But it will be asked on what *proven facts* do these statements rest? The question is best answered by an examination of the materials—the rocks themselves.

Meanwhile we wonder where the book may be found wherein all this history is recorded? When did those giant reptiles, and graceful ferns, come into and begin to live on this earth? When did the rivers that scored the mountain's side first run to the sea? What

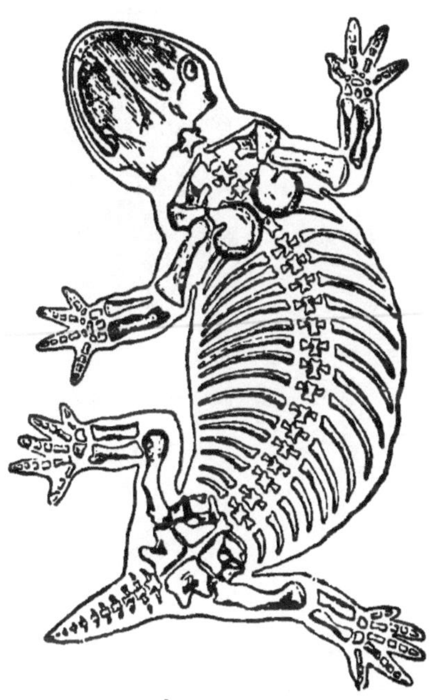

FIG. 2.-- *Labyrinthodon* restored, ventral aspect; found in Triassic Rocks around Sydney.

manner of beings were those whose remains are imbedded, in countless myriads, in the various rocks? The sedimentary rocks are one vast sepulchre; can we decipher the curious legends engraven on these tombs? When were those volcanic fires first lighted? "There is no volume of man's making in which an answer may be found; no library could contain the thousandth part of it; but it is inscribed on the rocks around us and beneath our feet. They constitute the volume you wish to read, every word of which is written by

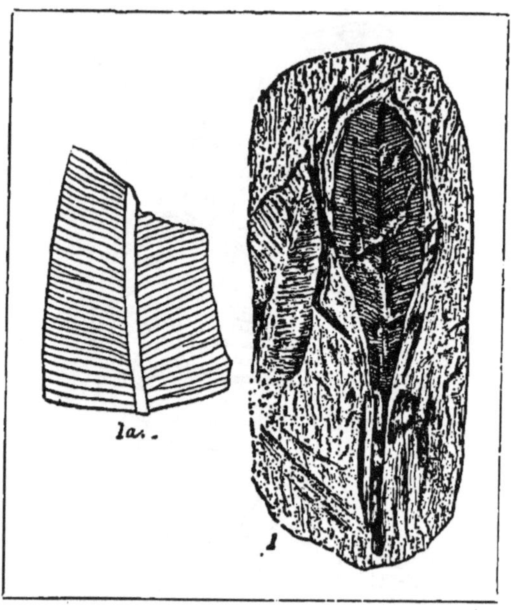

FIG. 3.—*Oleandridium.*[1] A fossil plant from the Hawkesbury Sandstone. 1*a*.—Enlarged portion of same showing venation

Nature's own hand. She has kept a record of all her doings—kept with wonderful accuracy her diary; and we may read her own statement of facts more wonderful than the fictions of Arabian fancy. All unconsciously the fiery volcano has traced its turbulent

1 Record of Geol. Sur. of N. S. Wales, Vol. IV., Plate viii.

history with a burning pen; the coral and the sea-weed, the fishes, reptiles, birds, and beasts of the olden time have written their life-story in the plastic rock, for us to read. All is recorded in them that has been done to bring the world from the original rude state in which it existed to the condition of life and beauty that crowns it to-day."

CHAPTER II.

EXAMINATION OF ROCKS.

PRINCIPLES OF GEOLOGICAL STUDY—MUCH MAY BE LEARNED FROM AN INDOOR STUDY OF ROCK SPECIMENS —NO STUDY OF ROCKS COMPLETE WITHOUT AN EXAMINATION IN THE FIELD—PRINCIPLES UNDERLYING GEOLOGICAL SCIENCE—THE EARTH SUBJECT TO CHANGE—THE SOLID LAND ELEVATED AND DEPRESSED—CONTINUED SLIGHT MOVEMENTS OF THE EARTH'S CRUST.

THE study of a rock is not at first sight very inviting. On a close examination it will be found that most rocks can be made to tell much of their own history. Ruskin has written that "there is no natural object out of which more can be learned than out of stones. They seem to have been created especially to reward a patient observer. Nearly all the other objects in Nature can be seen, to some extent, without patience, and are pleasant even in being half seen. Trees, clouds, and rivers are enjoyable even by the careless. But the stone under the foot has nothing for carelessness but stumbling; no pleasure is to be had out of it, nor food, nor good of any kind; nothing but symbolism of the hard heart and the unfatherly gift. Yet do but give it some reverence and watchfulness, and there is bread

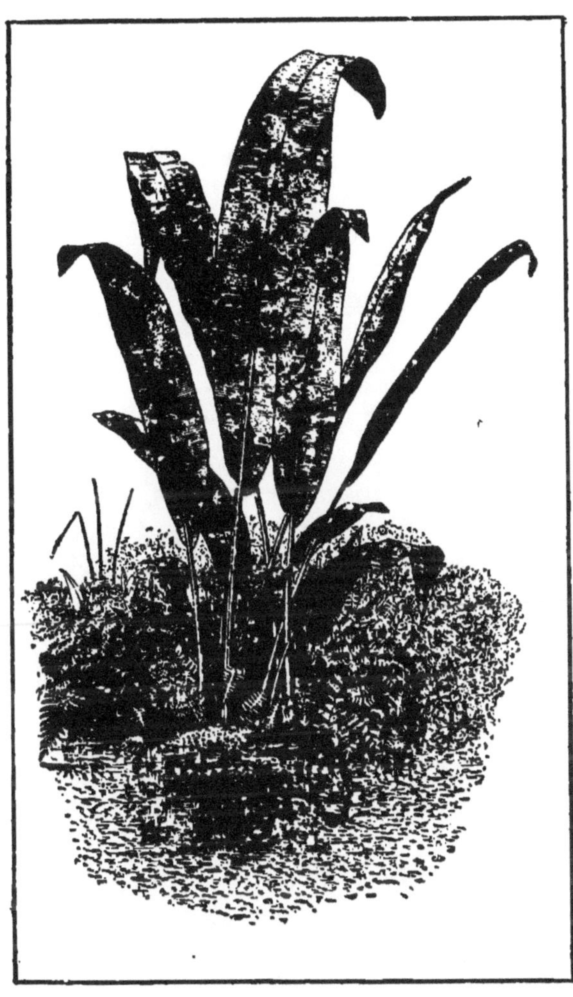

Fig. 4.—*Macrotæniopteris*[1] restored. A fossil fern found in the Wianamatta Shales around Sydney.

---

1 Bull. of the U S Geol. Sur. No. 85, Plate viii.

of thought in it more than in any other lowly feature of all the landscape. For a stone, when it is examined, will be found a mountain in miniature." We can even go further and say that by the use of the microscope it is possible to discover much concerning the minute structure of rocks, and from that structure to learn a good deal as to their mode of origin. When Sorby first cut thin slices of rock for the microscopes, he was

FIG. 5.—Hawkesbury Sandstone near Sydney, showing the effects of Marine Erosion.

met with the reproach that it was impossible to look at a mountain through a microscope. In the same way it is often said that it is hardly possible to learn much from hand specimens of rocks. We shall see further on what may be learned from the bare examination of a piece of sandstone. In referring to the more minute structures in rocks, Sorby says: "Some geologists only accustomed to examine large masses in the field may, perhaps, be disposed to think the objects so minute as to be quite beneath their notice, and that all attempts at accurate calculations from such small data are quite inadmissible. What other science, however, has prospered by adopting such a creed? What physiologist would think of ignoring all the invaluable discoveries that have been made in his science with the microscope merely because the objects are minute? . . . With such striking examples before us, shall we physical geologists maintain that only rough and imperfect methods of research are applicable to our own science? Against such an opinion I certainly must protest; and I argue that there is no necessary connection between the size of an object and the value of a fact, and that, though the objects I have described are minute, the conclusions to be derived from the facts are great."[1]

The study of a rock indoors can never be altogether satisfactory. We must, if possible, see the rock in the cutting, ravine, or cliff. We must learn its relation to surrounding rocks. Not until we have done this may we say that we are in possession of sufficient *facts* to gather together the history of that rock, by deductions based on these facts.

The principle underlying all geological study is that this earth is subject to change. The crust of the earth is now subject to disturbance and dislocation. The interior of the earth is probably solid, with no doubt lakes of molten matter. Some authorities hold for a liquid interior. But the one thing beyond dis-

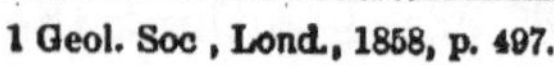

1 Geol. Soc, Lond., 1858, p. 497.

pute is that the interior of the earth is intensely hot. In either case the central mass continues to cool and therefore to contract. One result of this is, that the crust is thrown into folds, or vast masses of the crust may break off and sink below the rest.

We are accustomed to speak of the ocean as a type of instability, and to refer to the eternal hills as typical of the unchanging. If there is one conclusion more than another that geologists are agreed upon it is that the crust of the earth is not stable and unchanging. On the contrary, the hills are worn down by rain, winds, and frost; streams and rivers cut for themselves channels, the eroded materials are transported as sediments to lakes and seas, and there spread out in strata. Vast quantities of this eroded material are sometimes spread over alluvial plains by flood waters.

The sea itself is encroaching on the land, in many places at an alarming rate. The breakers are sawing into the cliffs around the dry land. The overhanging rocks are undermined and topple over, in the course of time. These, hurled back by the waves against the cliff, help in the work of destruction, so that, as someone has remarked, the cliffs of the world supply an artillery to destroy themselves.

Then there are the known movements of the earth's crust, some portions being elevated, and some portions being slowly submerged. Many of these earth movements are so gradual as to be hardly appreciable in a century. On the other hand, sudden and violent catastrophes are far from uncommon, and modify the earth's surface over large areas. Callao is the northern limit of a stretch of country, 2,400 miles long, that has been considerably elevated since the advent of man. Old sea beaches are found here from 60 to 1,000 feet above the sea level. We have, besides, in every quarter of the globe, active volcanoes sending forth masses of molten rock, and showers of dust and ashes.

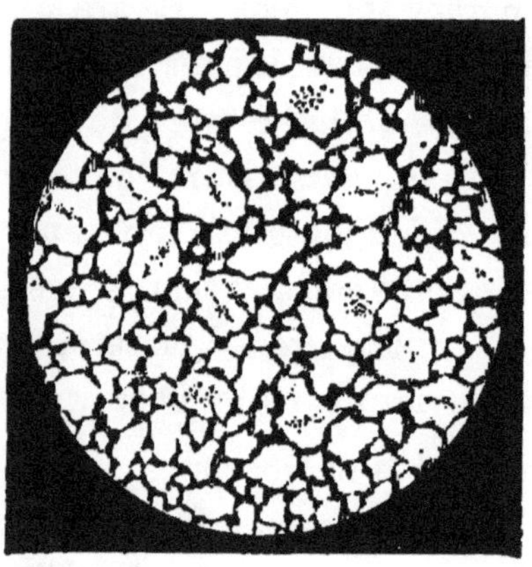

FIG. 6.—Microscopic structure of Sandstone.

Professor Shaler says: "The notion that the ground is naturally steadfast is an error,—an error which arises from the incapacity of our senses to appreciate any but the most palpable, and at the same time most exceptional, of its movements. The idea of terra firma belongs to the ancient belief that the earth was the centre of the universe. It is, indeed, by their mobility that the continents survive the increasing assaults of the ocean waves, and the continuous down-wearing which the rivers and glaciers bring about." Professor Milne, a great authority on earthquakes, has noticed slight swayings of the earth which, though occupying a short time—from a few seconds to a few hours—are still too slow to produce a shock of any kind. These he calls "earth pulsations." They have been observed by means of delicate spirit levels, the bubbles of which move with very slight changes of level at either end of the instrument. At present only a few experiments of this kind have been made; but they tell us that the surface of the earth (which is apparently so firm and immovable) is subject to slight but frequent oscillations. Some think that they depend upon changes in the weight of the atmosphere. If this is so, the balance between the forces at work below the earth's surface and those that operate on its surface must be very easily disturbed. Still we cannot see that this is a serious objection; on the contrary, there is much reason to think that any slight extra weight on the surface such as might be caused by an increase of the pressure of the atmosphere, and still more by the accumulation of the vast sedimentary deposits on the floor of the ocean, may be quite sufficient to cause a movement to take place. Moreover, Mr. G. H. Darwin has shown that the earth's crust daily heaves up and down under the attraction of the moon, in the same kind of way that the ocean does; so that we must give up all idea of the solid earth being fixed and immovable, and must look upon it as a flexible body, like a ball of india-rubber.

Slight movements of rather a different kind have been noticed, to which the name of "earth-tremors" has been given. These are very slight jarrings or quiverings of the earth, too slight to be observed by our unaided senses, but rendered visible by means of very delicate pendulums and other contrivances. Now, wherever such observations have been made, it has been discovered that the earth is constantly quivering as if it were a lump of jelly. In Italy, where this subject has been very carefully studied, the tremors that are continually going on are found to vary considerably in strength; for instance, when the weather is very disturbed and unsettled, the movements of the pendulum are often much greater. Again, before an earthquake, the instrument shows that the tremors are more frequent and violent.

Another way of observing these curious little movements is by burying microphones in the ground. The microphone is a little instrument invented of late years, which is capable of enormously magnifying the very slightest sounds, such as our ears will not detect. By its means one can hear, as someone said, "the tramp of a fly's foot," if he will be so obliging and walk over it. It has thus been proved in Italy that the earth sends forth a confused medley of sounds caused by little crackings and snappings in the rocks below our feet.[1]

The facts referred to so far will convince most people as to the instability of the so-called solid crust.

1 Hutchinson. "Story of the Hills," p 193.

In the light of Geology the highest mountains are but of yesterday, and mountain ranges whose summits once pierced the clouds and seemed immovable and indestructible, have been worn down by the unceasing effects of disintegration and denudation.

> "The hills are shadows, and they flow
> From form to form, and nothing stands;
> They melt like mists, the solid lands,
> Like clouds they shape themselves and go."

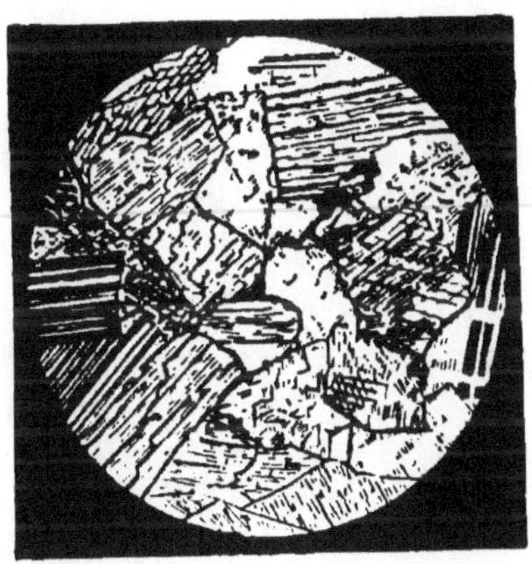

FIG. 7.—Microscopic structure of Diorite.

Further on we shall see that rocks now far away from the sea, and many hundred feet above sea level, were actually formed beneath the waters of an ocean. The changes now in operation in sea and on the land will help us to understand how these rocks have been lifted from the quiet depths of the ocean, and afterwards carved, into their present outlines of hill and dale, by running water and atmospheric agencies.

The principles of this new cycle of change are very clearly summarized as follows by Dr. Molloy.[1]

It may be asked how the various strata of aqueous rocks which constitute the chief portion of the earth's crust have been lifted up above the level of the sea; for, according to our theory, they were at first deposited under water. This is a question that must inevitably occur to the mind of every reader, and geologists are ready with an answer. They tell us that, from the

FIG. 8 —Microscopic structure of Basalt, Bald Hills, Bathurst.

earliest ages, the crust of the earth has been subject to disturbance and dislocation. At various times and in various places it was upheaved, and what had been before the bed of the ocean became dry land; again it sunk below its former level, and what had been before dry land became the bed of the ocean. Thus, in the former case, a new stratum which had been deposited

1 "Geology and Revelation," p. 18.

at the bottom of the sea, with all its varied remains of a bygone age, was converted, for a season, into the surface of the earth, and became the theatre of animal and vegetable life; while in the latter case, the old surface of the earth, with its countless tribes of animals and plants—its fauna and flora, as they are called—was submerged beneath the waters, there to receive in its turn broken-up fragments of a former world, deposited in the form of mud, or sand, or pebbles, or minute particles of lime. Nor is this all; it is but a single link in the chain of geological chronology. We are asked to believe that, in many parts of the globe, this upward and downward movement has been going on alternately for unnumbered ages: so that the very same spot which was first the bed of the ocean was afterwards dry land; then the bottom of an estuary or inland lake; then, perhaps, once more the floor of the sea, and then the dry land again; and, furthermore, we are assured that thousands and thousands of years may have rolled away while it remained in each one of these various conditions.

But, from what source does that mighty power come, which can thus upheave the solid earth, and banish the ocean from its bed? We are told, in reply, that this giant power dwells in the interior of the earth itself, and is no other than the subterranean heat of which we have already spoken. This vast internal fire acts with unequal force upon different parts of the shell or crust of the earth, uplifting it in one place, and in another allowing it to subside. Now it is violent and convulsive, bursting asunder the solid rocks, and shaking the foundations of the hills; again, it is gentle and harmless, upheaving vast continents with a scarcely perceptible undulation, not unlike the long, silent swell of the ocean. So it has been from the beginning, and so it is found to be even now, in this last age of the geological calendar. For, even within historic times, vast tracts of land have been permanently upraised by the convulsive shock of the earthquake; and many parts of the earth's crust have been subject to a slow wave-like movement, rising here and subsiding there, at the rate of perhaps a few feet in a century. Sometimes, too, the fiery liquid itself has burst its barriers, and poured its destructive streams of molten rock far into the peaceful, smiling valleys.

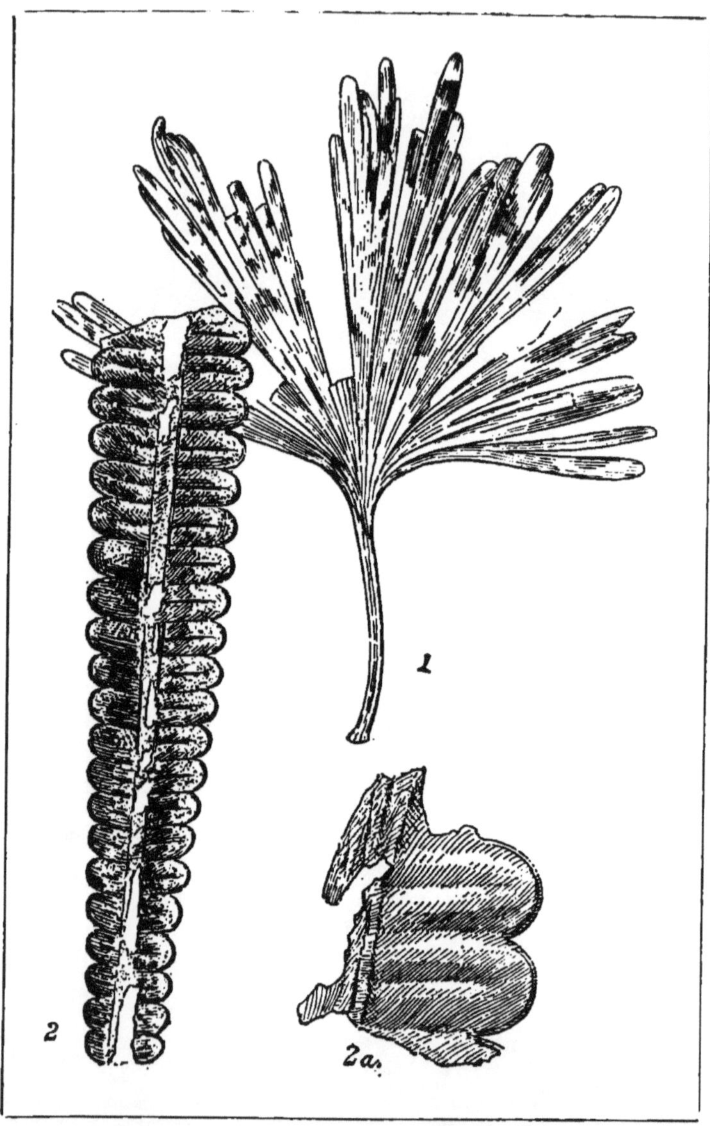

Fig 9.—1. *Jeanpaulia palmata*[1], from the Wianamatta Shales. 2. *Cycadopteris scolopendrina*[2], half nat. size, from the Wianamatta Shales. 2*a*. Pinnules[2a] enlarged, showing the border.

---

1 Proc. Linn. Soc. N. S. Wales. Vol. I. (2nd series), Plate xvii.
2 & 2a ,, ,, ,, ,, ,, ,, ,, ,, xvi.

CHAPTER III.

FOSSILS.

WHAT ARE FOSSILS?—WHAT DO THEY TEACH?—PRESERVATION OF FOSSILS—EVIDENCES OF LIFE IN AGES THAT ARE GONE—EVIDENCES OF THE MARINE OR FRESH-WATER ORIGIN OF ROCKS.

A FOSSIL may be described as the remains, or the traces of the remains, of any animal or plant which has been entombed in rocks. Each successive formation in the long history of the earth is characterized by fossils peculiar to itself. Dr. Page says shells, fishes, and other animals, are buried in the mud or silt of lakes and estuaries; rivers also carry down the carcases of land animals, the trunks of trees and other vegetable drift; and earthquakes submerge plains and islands, with all their vegetable and animal inhabitants. These remains become enveloped in the layers of mud and sand and gravel formed by the waters, and in process of time are petrified, that is, are converted into stony matter, like the shells and bones found in the oldest strata. Now, as at present, so in all former time, must the remains of plants and animals have been similarly preserved, and, as one tribe of plant is peculiar to the dry plain, another to the swampy morass; as one family belongs to a temperate, another to a tropical region, so, from the character of the imbedded plants, we are enabled to arrive at some knowledge of the conditions under which they flourished. In the same manner with animals, each tribe has its locality assigned it by peculiarities of food, climate, and the like; each family has its own peculiar structure, for running, flying, swimming, plant-eating, or flesh-eating, as the case may be; and by comparing fossil remains with existing races, we are enabled to determine many of the past conditions of the world with considerable certainty.

It is a well-ascertained fact that each period in the world's history was marked by the existence of an animal and a vegetable creation peculiar to itself, and so characteristic of certain formations are certain fossils that the geologist can very often determine the exact age of, and place in its geological sequence, a formation he has never seen, provided a collection of its fossils is placed before him. When a geologist finds a specimen of *Glossopteris*, for instance (fig. 38), in New South Wales, he can safely conclude that the rocks he is investigating are newer than Devonian, and older than Triassic, and that they belong to the series that contain the workable coal seams of the colony. *Macrotæniopteris* (fig. 4) characterizes beds lying above the productive coal measures. It tells of a formation that accumulated on the land, and not in the sea. *Thinnfeldia* (fig. 30) is peculiar to a formation still higher up in the series. The fossil figured on page 203 is evidently a sea-shell, and therefore characterizes a marine formation. These fossils are never mixed. A single frond of any one of them is sufficient to decide the relative position of the beds containing them.

We have already referred to fossils from the shales near Sydney. In case of the footprints, the fossils were preserved merely as impressions. Writing of similar impressions in New England, Winchell says:

FIG. 10.—Microscopic structure of Granite.

"It is a solemn and impressive thought that the footprints of these dumb and senseless creatures have been preserved in all their perfection for thousands of ages, while so many of the works of man which date but a century back have been obliterated from the records of time. Kings and conquerors have marched at the head of armies, across continents, and piled up aggregates of human suffering and experience to the heavens, and all the physical traces of their march have totally disappeared, but the solitary biped which stalked along the margins of an inlet before the human race was born pressed footprints in the soft and shifting sand which the rising and sinking of the continent could not wipe out."

Sometimes not merely impressions but the whole skeletons of animals long since extinct are preserved as fossils. Almost complete skeletons of the extinct giant marsupial *Diprotodon* were found in great abundance at Lake Mulligan[1]. Fossils are preserved in somewhat different methods. (1) In rare instances the original substance may be preserved. In the case of coal the carbon present is the carbon of which the plants were formed. (2) The forms of shells are sometimes preserved as casts and moulds. (3) The substance may be entirely lost, and the form preserved completely in another material. The so-called "petrified shells" come under this heading. Also "wood turned into stone"—silicified wood of geologists. In the case of silicified wood, the whole substance has been changed from wood into stone, but every structure and fibre, as well as the rings of growth, are perfectly preserved.

It is, says Jukes, "as if a house were gradually rebuilt brick by brick, or stone by stone, a brick or a stone of a different kind being substituted for each of the former ones, the shape and size of the house, the forms and arrangements of rooms, passages, and closets, and even the number and shape of the bricks and stones remaining unaltered." Sir Charles Lyell has also dealt with this most interesting question, and thus explains

1 Lake in Central Australia, but in South Australian territory.

Fig. 11.—Basaltic Dyke cutting through Wianamatta Shales, near Beecroft Railway Station.

the change of say a piece of wood to stone. "If an organic substance is exposed in the open air to the action of the sun and rain, it will in time putrefy, or be dissolved into its component elements, consisting usually of oxygen, hydrogen, nitrogen, and carbon. These will readily be absorbed by the atmosphere to be washed away by rain, so that all vestiges of the dead animal or plant disappear. But if the same substances be submerged in water, they decompose more gradually, and if buried in the earth, still more slowly, as in the familiar example of wooden piles or other buried timber. Now, if as fast as each particle is set free by putrefaction in a fluid or gaseous state a particle equally minute of carbonate of lime, flint, or other mineral is at hand and ready to be precipitated, we may imagine this inorganic matter to take the place just before left unoccupied by the organic molecule. In this manner a cast of the interior of certain vessels may first be taken, and afterwards the more solid walls of the same may decay and suffer a like transmutation."

Silicified wood appeals directly to the observer, its original woody condition being so apparent. Specimens are common enough in basaltic country, being evidently derived from the drifts underlying the basalt. Blocks of silicified wood are also strewn in great abundance about Milparinka, and from there across to the South Australian border.

The divisions of geological history are founded entirely on the animals and plants which characterize the different periods and which are preserved for us as fossils. Fossil plants are indicative of dry land. Stratified rocks containing marine fossils were undoubtedly formed in the sea. Other fossils point conclusively to the fact that the rocks containing them were laid down in fresh water.

Summed up, fossils are evidences of life in times gone by. By their aid we construct the divisions of geological time, and they tell us of the conditions under which rocks were deposited.

"The existence of fossil remains is, then, a fact. Go where you will through the civilized world, and every chief town has its museum, into which they have been gathered by the zeal and industry of man; descend where you can into the crust of the earth—the quarry, the mine, the railway cutting—and there, notwithstanding the plunder which has been going on for two centuries and more, you will find that the inexhaustible cabinets of Nature are still teeming with these remains of ancient life.

"When we are brought, for the first time, face to face with these countless relics of a former world, we are impressed with a sense of wonder and bewilderment. That the skeletons before us, though now dry and withered, were once animated with the breath of life; that the trees now lying shattered and prostrate and shorn of their branches, once flourished on the earth, we cannot for a moment hesitate to believe. But, beyond this one fact, all is darkness and mystery.

These gaunt skeletons, these uncouth monsters, these petrified forests, are silent, lifeless, as the rocks within whose stony bosoms they have lain so long entombed.

FIG. 12.— Wentworth Falls, Blue Mountains, showing stratified rocks of Triassic age.

Had they speech and memory, they could tell us much, no doubt, of that ancient world in which they bore a part, of its continents, and seas, and rivers and mountains; of the various tribes of animals and plants by which it was peopled, of their habits and domestic economy, how they lived, how they died, and how they were buried in those graves, from which, after the lapse of we know not how many ages, they now come forth into the light of the day. As it is, however, we can but gaze and wonder. We have nothing here but the relics of death and destruction; there is no feeling, no memory, no voice, in these dry bones; no living tenant in these hollow skulls, to recount to us the history of former times.

"So thinks and reasons the ordinary observer. But far different is the language of the geologist. These dry and withered bones, he tells us, are gifted with memory and speech; and, though the language they speak may seem at first unfamiliar and obscure, it is not on that account beyond our comprehension. Like the birds, reptiles, fish, and other symbols, inscribed on the obelisks of ancient Egypt, these bones and shells stored up in the crust of the earth, have a hidden meaning which it is the business of Science to search out and explain. They are Nature's hieroglyphics, which she has impressed upon her works to carry down to remote ages the memory of the revolutions through which our Globe has passed; and, when we come to understand them aright, they do unfold to us the story of that ancient world to which they belonged."[1]

1 Molloy, "Geology and Revelation," p. 235.

v

Fig. 13.—Fissure left by a previously existing Volcanic Dyke, Bondi, near Sydney.

CHAPTER IV.

ROCKS.

WHAT IS A ROCK?—MATERIALS OF ROCKS—HOW TO STUDY ROCKS—CLASSIFICATION OF ROCKS—ROCKS OF SYDNEY AND THE BLUE MOUNTAINS.

A ROCK is the constituent of the earth's surface, and, though it may consist of a single mineral, it is generally a mechanical mixture of two or more minerals. Rocks are then, for the most part, aggregates of minerals.

A *mineral*[1] is a natural inorganic substance, which has a homogeneous structure, definite chemical composition and physical properties, and usually a definite crystalline form.

A mineral may consist of a single element, or more than one element.

A mineral is made up of the single undecomposable substances, called by chemists elements.

These elements, in turn, form minerals, and minerals form rocks.

The number of known minerals makes a long list, and this list is constantly increasing. The minerals, however, entering to any extent into the

---

1 Coal is usually classed with minerals, although of organic origin, and having no definite crystalline form.

composition of the rocks we have to deal with, are not many.

1. **QUARTZ.**—Quartz is an oxide of silicon; in other words, it is a substance made up of the two elements Oxygen and Silicon.

The milk-white stone of a quartz reef, the clear glass in pebble spectacles, and the grains of sand on the sea-shore, or the grains that go to make up the Hawkesbury Sandstone, are chemically one and the same substance.

Quartz is very hard; cannot be scratched with a knife, but quartz scratches glass easily. It is a most insoluble substance, but is attacked slowly by heated caustic alkalies, and by hydrofluoric acid. The reddish-looking quartz in some quartz reefs is due to staining by oxide of iron Amethyst, a gem stone we prize considerably, is quartz colored by oxide of manganese. Cairngorm is also a colored quartz. Chalcedony, Opal, Agate, Flint, Jasper, are all varieties of quartz.

2. **FELSPAR.**—The varieties of felspar are many, but they are all slicates of alumina with potash, soda, or lime added. The felspars decompose rather easily, giving rise to Kaolin. The finest pottery is made from Kaolin, Kaolin itself being merely a decomposed felspar.

The lath-shaped crystals seen in thin slices of Basalt from Bathurst are felspars. The glistening rectangular crystals in the Bowral Syenite (Trachyte of the builders) are also felspars.

3. **MICA**.—The shining scales found in river sands are usually one of the micas. All micas have a very perfect cleavage. The thin leaves or plates of mica are flexible and elastic. A plate of mica shows its elastic properties when slightly bent, as it springs back to its former position. Plates and scales of Talc, which somewhat resemble mica, show no elasticity, and when slightly bent remain bent. The two more important varieties of mica are Muscovite and Biotite. Muscovite is usually of a silvery-white color, while Biotite is usually black or dark green. Partly decomposed

FIG. 14.—Microscopic section showing flow-structure of lath-shaped Felspars in Basalt.

and altered Muscovite, such as is found in river sands, is of a golden yellow color.

4. **HORNBLENDE**.—Hornblende is one of the constituents of Diorite, and an important rock-forming mineral. It is nearly, but not quite so hard as felspar. Its color is usually a greenish-black.

To distinguish between quartz and felspar is very often a beginner's difficulty. The general reader may be so far interested as to desire to recognise felspar as a constituent of granite, or even to separate that mineral from quartz. The following tabular statement may prove a help.

QUARTZ	FELSPAR
is very hard ;	is not so hard as quarts ;
it easily scratches glass ;	does not easily scratch glass ;
is not scratched by a knife ;	is barely scratched by a knife ;
shows on breaking *no flat* and *lustrous faces*, due to cleavage ;	on breaking shows *flat* and *lustrous* faces, due to cleavage ;
is infusible ;[1]	fuses with difficulty ;
is insoluble ;	decomposes into Kaolin ;
does not easily decompose ;	has rather a pearly than glassy look ;
is glassy looking ;	breaks with flat faces ;
breaks with rounded faces ;	is translucent, but usually somewhat turbid ;
is usually transparent ;	has a non-metallic lustre.
has a non-metallic lustre.	

5. AUGITE.—Augite is not far removed from Hornblende. It is a very abundant and important rock-forming mineral. In color it is green to black, and although an essential constituent of Basalt, is not often visible to the unaided eye. In some basaltic districts, crystals of augite are found amongst the decomposed rock material in short prisms.

As Mica is the third constituent of Granite, and Hornblende is also a constituent of most Australian

1 Infusible in an ordinary blowpipe flame without any flux. With carbonate of soda as a flux, quartz fuses before the blowpipe

granites, the following table may prove of use:—

MICA	HORNBLENDE
is usually in thin lustrous leaves or plates;	does not occur in thin leaves and plates;
is mostly transparent;	is not elastic or flexible;
is elastic and flexible;	is usually found with crystalline faces in granites and diorites;
the thin leaves can be split up into thinner leaves;	is scratched with difficulty by a knife;
Muscovite is silvery-white mica;	is usually greenish-black, black or brown;
Biotite is a dark green or black mica;	not transparent or translucent.
the plates can be very easily scratched by a knife;	
some decomposing micas in river sands are golden-yellow.	

6. **OLIVINE.**—Olivine is also a constituent of Basalt, and may oftentimes be noted in that rock with the unaided eye, as rather glassy-looking crystals of a very dark olive-green, sometimes almost black. When Olivine is transparent, it is used as a gem stone, and is then known as Chrysolite.

7. **CALCITE.**—Calcite is a most abundant mineral, and the only *common mineral* that is rapidly attacked even by cold and weak acids. When acids act upon calcite, carbon-dioxide escapes with effervescence. When calcite is pure it is known as Iceland Spar, and is then transparent.

The cleavage of calcite is very perfect, the mineral breaking up into crystals always showing two or more perfect faces of a rhombohedron.

Nearly all natural waters hold some carbon-dioxide in solution, and in that condition these waters can dissolve limestones.

The vast masses of limestone that occur in the crust of the earth consist, for the most part, of Calcite or carbonate of lime.

Iron Pyrites is a compound of Sulphur and Iron.

Barite is a compound of the element Barium and Sulphuric acid.

Gypsum is a compound of the element Calcium and Sulphuric acid and some combined water.

Limestone is a compound of Lime and a gas—Carbon dioxide.

Lime is a compound of the element Calcium and a gas—Oxygen.

8. **MAGNETITE.**—Magnetite is the black oxide of iron. It is widely diffused through rocks in grains, veins and beds. The mineral is strongly magnetic. A magnet passed through clays, arising from the decomposition of basalt, will usually collect some grains of magnetite.

9. **HÆMATITE.**—Hæmatite is known as ferric oxide. Its color is black or steel grey, but the mineral is always red or reddish when finely powdered. In other words, hæmatite gives a red streak. The ironstone bands in the Hawkesbury Sandstone are mostly impure hæmatite.

10. LIMONITE.—Limonite is sometimes known as brown hæmatite. It is softer than hæmatite, and in color is yellow or brown.

The three more common iron-minerals can be compared as follows:—

MAGNETITE	HÆMATITE	LIMONITE
is magnetic; *streak is black;* is very hard; is not scratched by a knife; is black; is mostly in crystals; is a constituent of basalt.	is not usually magnetic; *streak is red or reddish;* not as hard as magnetite; is brown or brown-red; sometimes in crystals; never a constituent of basalt	not magnetic; *streak yellow;* very soft; yellowish in color; never in crystals; never a constituent of basalt; gives off water when heated in a glass tube.

We can now turn to the rocks composed as they are of the minerals described. In order to spend any time profitably in the study of rocks we must begin by seeing and handling the rocks themselves. This is essential. There should be no difficulty in procuring

1. A piece of sandstone.
2. A piece of granite.
3. A piece of basalt.
4. A piece of limestone.

The specimens need not be more than one inch square; but, if possible, they should be in convenient cabinet size, say 4½ by 3 by 1 inch.

Take a specimen of Sandstone, Granite, Basalt, and Limestone, and place these rocks side by side. Examine them carefully, using a pocket lens if necessary. At first sight, possibly, a beginner may think that there is very little to distinguish one stone from the other. But he soon discovers that the rocks before him differ in many ways in their characters, and that certain qualities observable in one are absent from others. For instance, they differ in *hardness, color, texture,* and in their *composition* and *mode of origin.*

In order to classify rocks, we must decide on some BASIS OF CLASSIFICATION. It has been found that no serviceable classification can be based on the color or the texture of rocks. The specimen of sandstone is white, but sandstones are often grey and red. Basalt is black or blue-black, and some limestones are also black. Neither does a classification depending on texture serve any useful purpose, as sandstones, basalts, and granites vary much in texture. We, therefore, fall back on the *composition* and the mode of *origin* of rocks to give us a basis of classification.

A student will, with very little trouble, note the following characters in the sandstone :—

1. Sandstone is made up of numbers of small grains.
2. The grains are held together by a cementing material.
3. The grains are seen to be rounded and worn, not angular and sharp.

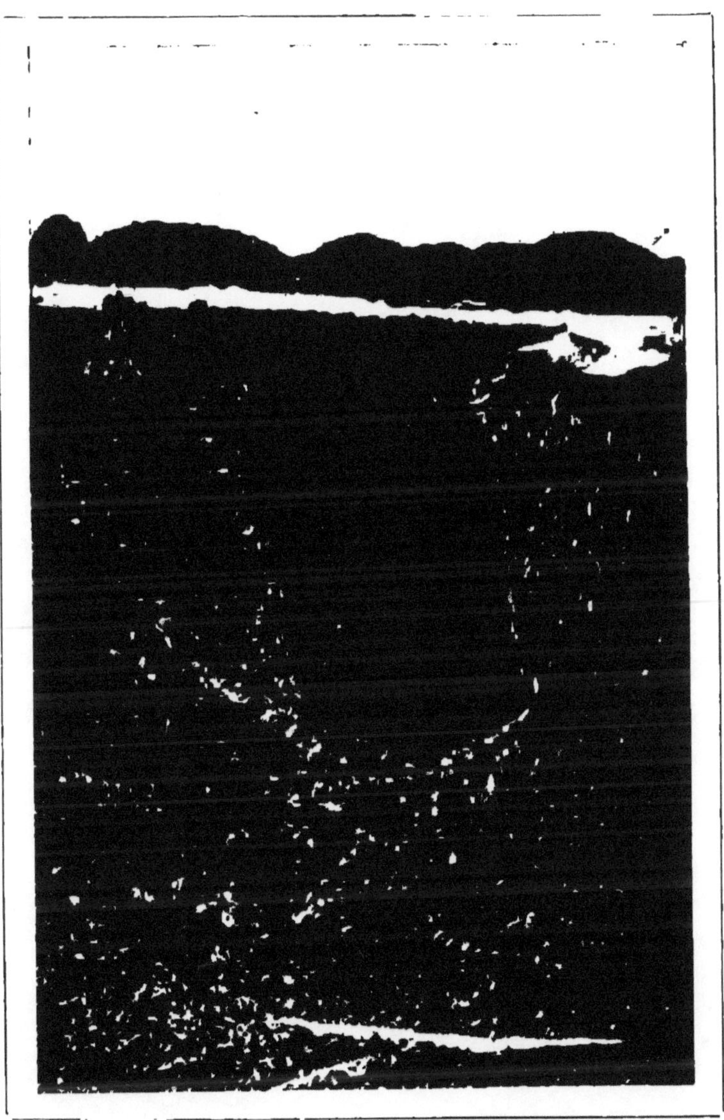

Fig. 15.—Excavation showing a Basaltic Dyke, at Canterbury, near Sydney.

4. When separated from the rock the rounded grains differ in no way from grains of sand.
5. Sandstones will often show other minerals besides sand grains. Silvery spangles of a mineral called mica can be detected.
6. Sand is nothing more than broken particles of rock, mostly quartz, worn or abraded so as to become more or less rounded.
7. When this sandstone is examined in a railway cutting or in a cliff, it is found to rest in layers, and the rock splits easily along these layers.
8. If the sands of a river-bed or of the sea-shore were hardened into a solid mass, this would differ in no way from our sample of sandstone.
9. Geologists can prove that sandstones were once sand, and that this sand was carried by running water to the sea, and settling down, layer above layer, on the sea bottom, became hardened into sandstone.
10. The sandstone before us was broken by a geologist from a mass of work many hundred feet above the level of the sea. As this sediment, now hardened into sandstone, was once spread out over the bottom of the sea, it will be for us to inquire into those movements of the crust of the earth that have lifted a portion of the country from below sea level to a position many hundred feet above the sea.
11. Without any further examination we are able to say that—**Sandstone is a rock made up of rounded particles of other rocks or**

minerals. It was formed under water,[1] and when massive is seen to be arranged in layers more or less parallel.

Now take the piece of granite. Note how very different it is from the sandstone, both in texture and in the kind of minerals it is composed of. We find that—

1. Granite contains no rounded grains.
2. There is no cementing material, the various minerals being compressed and knitted together.
3. If a piece of granite is ground level on one side, or if a polished slab is examined, three and often four separate and very different minerals can be seen as the materials that go to form granite.
4. These minerals are all angular, are not arranged in any definite order, and evidently were originally formed just where we see them.
5. The minerals that form granite are—

   Quartz, which is seen as clear, glassy grains, but too hard to be scratched by a steel point.[2]

   Felspar, which lies in fairly well defined rectangular, grey-white or flesh-colored crystals, and which reflect light from their faces. Felspar can be scratched by a steel point.

   Mica is seen in lustrous plates which easily split into very thin leaves. Mica is in color often silvery-white. One species is a deep and shining black, but which changes to a brass-yellow when altering or decomposing.

1 There are sandstones other than those formed under the sea. Some sandstones were laid down on the bed of great inland lakes, or in the waters of an estuary. Blown sand and volcanic dust form rocks on dry land resembling ordinary sandstone.

2 The point of a penknife blade may be made to act as a steel point.

Hornblende is a constituent of many Australian granites. This is a blackish-green mineral, which may be distinguished from the mica in the same rock by its *not* splitting into thin leaves.

6. When granite is examined in the field it is seen to have intruded dykes, veins, and tongues of its own material into the rocks above and around it. This proves a former liquid or plastic condition. There is abundant evidence to show that this former condition of granite was altogether due to heat.

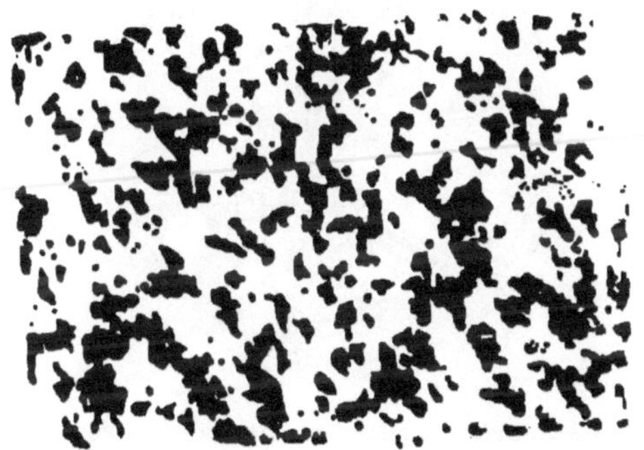

FIG. 16.—Texture of ordinary Granite.

7. Getting results together, we are able to say that **Granite is a fire-formed rock made up of three distinct crystalline minerals, quartz, felspar and mica, with a fourth mineral, hornblende, often present.**

The student must not conclude that because granite was in a molten condition water could not also be present. Dry heat, such as we see in furnace operations, has left proof of its effect upon rocks. Geologists, however, recognise heat of another kind—that is, heat in the presence of moisture or superheated steam under great pressure—as having played a more important part in the making of rocks.

When the piece of basalt is examined in the same way as the sandstone and granite, a very decided difference is apparent. Few, if any, individual minerals can be seen without the help of a lens. The contrast in this respect with the other rocks is in itself characteristic. If a piece of basalt is polished, or if a thin slice is cut and examined under the microscope, quite a number of minerals are seen to make up the

FIG. 17.—A thin slice of granite as seen under the microscope. The rectangular crystals are felspar, the clear mineral is quartz, and the shaded portions represent mica.

mass, but *quartz*, which was so prominent in sandstone and granite, is absent. One can hardly help noting the almond-shaped cavities common in basalt, and these resemble in more ways than one the steam cavities we find in lava. On comparing our specimen with a lava from Vesuvius or Mt. Etna, for example, the resemblance is so complete we at once conclude that basalt is a lava. When basalt is studied in the field, we learn that it *flowed* into the position it now occupies. When, as often happens, it cuts up in wall-like masses, through granite, slate, sandstone, or

FIG. 18.—Mount Victoria Pass, Blue Mountains, showing how the stratified sandstones are cut under by Atmospheric agencies.

beds of coal, we observe that it leaves traces of its fiery origin by baking the adjoining sandstones, and burning the coal it comes in contact with in its upward course. There can be no doubt basalt was once molten, and that it flowed from some old and perhaps long extinct volcano. We are now able to say that **Basalt is a fire-formed or igneous rock, which welled up through some crack in the earth's crust or flowed from a volcano, and is an intimate aggregate of several minerals.**

We take the limestone next, and may bear in mind that we are dealing with one of the most interesting and important of all rocks. Limestone is a greyish or bluish rock, sometimes white, sometimes black or brown. The texture is fine and close grained, but may show a crystalline structure not unlike loaf-sugar. On examining a number of specimens you are sure to find embedded in the stone some remains or traces of sea-living animals. As a rule, a general examination will tell us nothing more. The chemist and the geologist come to our assistance here, and we are told that chalk, marble, and common limestone are mere varieties of the same stone, and that they are of the same chemical composition as sea shells and coral.

Let the student now take a piece of coral or a sea shell, and note that both can be scratched with a knife, giving a white powder. Lift a drop of strong hydrochloric acid[1] on a glass rod and carefully transfer the acid to the shell. Observe that the acid effervesces

1 Hydrochloric acid must be handled with caution and kept in a glass-stoppered bottle, labelled poison. It is very destructive to clothes, and a valuable lesson will be learned by trying the effect of a few drops of the acid on a worn out coat.

Fig. 19.—Basaltic Dyke cutting through Wianamatta Shales, near Belmore Railway Station.

or "boils up" freely. Place a drop of the acid on granite; there is no effervescence. Place a drop of the acid on your specimen of limestone, and see that it effervesces just as in the case of the shell.

There must be something in common then between shells, coral, and limestone. The fact is, that all three are composed of *calcite*.

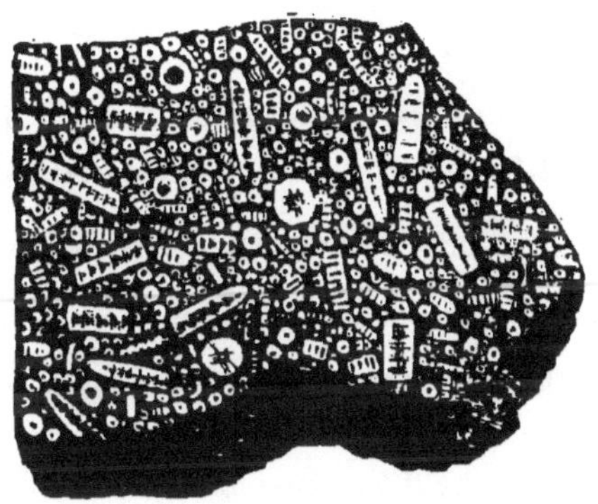

FIG. 20.—A piece of limestone made up almost entirely of the remains of marine animals. Rocks of this kind are common in Australian Silurian Limestones, as at Cave Creek, Orange, New South Wales.

From a geological standpoint calcite is a mineral of the first importance, being the sole essential constituent of all limestones. Calcite is the *only common* mineral effervescing freely with *cold* hydrochloric acid, and limestone is the *only rock* that will *effervesce freely* with cold hydrochloric acid. This behaviour with hydrochloric acid is a geologist's rough test for limestone, marble, and calcite. Why these rocks effervesce with the acid is simple enough. Chemically, limestone or calcite is a compound of lime and carbonic acid gas. The hydrochloric acid seizes on the lime so eagerly that the other constituent is set free and escapes as bubbles of gas.

Coral reefs are vast masses of limestone now in course of formation. A piece of compact limestone taken from a coral reef would answer to each of our tests given above. There can be no doubt, therefore, that limestones are formed, under water, for the most part by the agency of living things, and limestone is therefore said to be an aqueous rock of organic origin.

We can summarize our knowledge in this way :—

Sandstone,

is made up of rounded grains, and shining spangles of mica.

the grains are held together by a cement.

the grains are quartz and do not differ from ordinary sand.

the rock is arranged in layers or strata.

the sandstone once formed a sediment at the bottom of the sea, and is therefore said to be a Sedimentary rock.

Granite,

is not made up of rounded grains.

is a fire-formed or igneous rock.

is made up of angular and partly crystalline particles of quartz, felspar, mica, and often hornblende.

these minerals are interlaced and imbedded in each other, and hold together without a cement.

Basalt,

is an intimate and compact mixture of many minerals.

is a rock without any quartz grains.

does not differ from the lava now poured out by some volcanoes.

has abundant vesicles caused by steam while yet molten.

an examination in the field shows that basalt flowed down old valleys as a lava stream.

it charred wood, and baked sandstones and burnt coal.

many cooled and hardened streams of basalt can be traced to the mouths of old and extinct craters.

Limestone,

is fine grained.

is a water formed and Aqueous rock.

will effervesce with acids.

is made up of the same material as coral, and the shells of sea creatures.

is often a mass of shells cemented together by a base or matrix of shells ground up more finely.

We are now in a position to utilize the facts we have learned for the purposes of classifying rocks. It is at once apparent that there are two great classes of rocks—the Aqueous and the Igneous. Later on we shall learn that geologists are acquainted with a third class of rocks which originally might have been Igneous or Aqueous, but at present are so altered from their original condition, that they are termed Metamorphic.

AQUEOUS ROCKS.—Rocks of Aqueous origin are divided into classes accordingly as they were formed by

(*a*) the mechanical power of moving water;
(*b*) the intervention of some chemical agency; or
(*c*) by the help of plants or animals.

Rocks formed by the *mechanical force* of moving water are simply consolidated deposits of mud, sand, gravels, or shingle. These deposits were brought down by a river to an estuary or sea, or were produced by the action of the sea in wearing away a coastline. The denuded material is swept away into less troubled waters, where it is laid down to form rock. In the course of time pressure alone, or pressure aided by chemical action, will consolidate the sand to sandstone, and the loose gravel to conglomerate, while the finer materials will settle down and form a shale or a slaty claystone.

Aqueous rocks that owe their origin to some form of *chemical action* are exemplified in many of our limestones, particularly in the "formations" seen in limestone caves. Bands of ironstone that are seen in stratified rocks are also due to chemical reactions. Water holding carbonic gas in solution (most natural waters hold this gas dissolved) is able to dissolve limestone. This carbonate of lime or limestone will be held in solution only so long as the requisite carbonic acid gas is present. Directly the carbonic acid gas, from any cause, passes off, the carbonate of lime is dropped down as a fine white precipitate. Some

Fig. 21.—Stalactites, Jenolan Caves, New South Wales, showing a cavern formed in limestone by the solvent action of water, and the deposition of carbonate of lime (stalactites) from solution.

springs, rising from great depths, contain a large quantity of mineral matter in solution. A considerable part of this material (carbonate of lime chiefly) is deposited when the water reaches the surface. If by any means the carbonic acid gas is removed or broken up, a further quantity of the dissolved carbonate of lime is deposited, and, if the water should evaporate, the whole of the dissolved materials will remain and settle down on the bottom, layer upon layer. Fresh-water limestones are formed in this way near Bungonia, and near Cooma, New South Wales. Stalactites, that form so marked a feature in limestone caverns, are familiar examples of Aqueous rocks formed by chemical agency. Water with carbonate of lime in solution drops from the roof of a limestone cave. Each drop, as it falls to the floor, partially evaporates, and leaves a thin crust of limestone, which grows a little with every drop, so that in time a column of this carbonate of lime or limestone rises from the floor to meet a pendant of the same material, formed in a similar way on the roof of the cavern.

A third class of Aqueous rocks is formed from the fragments of plants and animals, and is therefore said to be *organic*. Coal is a rock composed for the most part of vegetable remains. Chalk, which occupies great areas in Europe, is made up almost entirely of foraminiferal shells, so minute as to be visible only under the microscope. A common variety of limestone has been formed by the continuous growth of corals, cemented into a solid rock by fragments of broken coral, shells, and mud washed into the interstices between the growing branches. Coral reefs are really great beds of limestone now in course of formation. Vast beds of limestone are found in Australia, and also in the old world, consisting almost entirely of the calcareous joints of marine creatures known as crinoids or sea-lilies. See Fig. 20.

IGNEOUS ROCKS.—If one great group of rocks had an aqueous origin, it is equally certain that another great group of rocks was formed by fire, and is therefore called *Igneous.* Some of the fire-formed rocks cooled and hardened deep down in the earth, "or sometimes, perhaps, under a certain weight of superincumbent ocean."[1] These are known as Plutonic rocks. Other fire-formed rocks were forced from the interior of the earth to the surface, and were poured out for the most part as great molten streams of lava from the craters of volcanoes. Basalt, usually called "blue metal," is a type of volcanic rock very common in Australia. Great sheets of basalt are found all along the flanks of the dividing range, from Mount Kosciusko to Cape York, and every sheet is an ancient lava stream that poured as a river of molten rock from the fiery crater of some long extinct volcano.

The Igneous rocks owe their origin to heat, they being at one time in a state of fusion. When this molten matter cooled deep down in the earth the result was a rock of a crystalline structure resembling granite, and rocks of this class are called *Plutonic.*[2] Often the

1 Lyell's Elements of Geology, p. 7.
2 From Pluto, the ruler of the regions of fire.

molten matter is forced to the surface along cracks and fissures, and may be poured out as a lava stream from the mouth of a volcano; such rocks are on that account called *Volcanic*. Igneous rocks do not occur in any particular order, and are not confined to any particular age. Wall-like masses of Igneous rocks are found in Aqueous rocks of all ages. They are known as dykes, and represent fissures or lines of weakness, along which the molten matter was forced from below. Some of these great cracks may have been produced by the alternate subsidence and elevation of the land.

METAMORPHIC ROCKS.—There is yet another group of rocks called *Metamorphic* that go to make up the crust of the earth. These are rocks that resemble the Aqueous, inasmuch as they show some signs of stratification, while in their internal structure they resemble the Plutonic Igneous rocks. Modern research has shown that the Metamorphic rocks were originally either Igneous or Aqueous, but have, since they were first formed, undergone changes that altered their structure. In this way some rocks that were formed under water have been so altered by heat that they show some features characteristic of Igneous rocks, and rocks of undoubted igneous origin are found occasionally to have developed a bedded and banded structure suggestive of stratified Aqueous rocks.

The rocks, then, which go to make up the crust of the earth may be divided, according to their origin, into three groups—the Aqueous, the Igneous, and the Metamorphic. The Aqueous rocks were formed under water either by ocean currents or rivers carrying along sediments and depositing them in layers, or by some chemical reactions, or by the intervention of organic life. In tabular form the divisions stand thus :—

Rocks of Aqueous origin.	I. Sedimentary	Clay, shale, flagstone. Sandstones. Conglomerates.
	II. Organic	Limestones. Coal.
	III. Chemical	Rock-salt, some limestones. Flint. Gypsum, &c.
Rocks of Igneous origin.	I. Volcanic.	Lavas, Basalt, Volcanic Ashes, &c.
	II. Plutonic.	Diorite. Granite.
Metamorphic. Rocks of Aqueous or Igneous origin.		Marbles. Some slates. Various kinds of schists. Gneiss, &c.

In the districts referred to in this book the following rocks occur :—

IGNEOUS ROCKS	Basalt : Dykes about Sydney. Dolerite : at Prospect. Basalt : Mount Hay, Mount Tomah, and Mount King George, Bathurst and Orange.

IGNEOUS ROCKS.	Diorites: near Jenolan Caves, near Locksley, Lagoon Road, Bathurst, T. Delaney's farm six miles west of Mt. Victoria. Andesites: Canoblas, near Orange. Trachyte: Canoblas, near Orange. Syenite: Bowral. Granite: Cox River, Bathurst, Locksley, Tarana. Porphyrite: Cowra. Gabbro: Carcoar. Porphyritic Granite: White Rock, near Bathurst, Locksley. Felsite: T. Delaney's farm near Mt. Victoria, Sunny Corner, Carcoar Railway Station.
AQUEOUS ROCKS.	Sandstones: Sydney and the Mountains. Shales: near Sydney. Slates: Jenolan Caves, Orange, Newbridge (true slates, such as roofing slates, not known). Limestone: Jenolan Caves, Limekilns, Molong. Conglomerates: the Mountains, and in the Coal Measures.
METAMORPHIC ROCKS.	Hornfels: Bathurst. Serpentine: near Orange. Schists: Cow Flat, near Bathurst. Marble: Jenolan, Belubla River, Cow Flat, Rockley, Limekilns. Talcose Slate: Rockley. Kaolin: Bathurst.[1] Quartzite: Bald Hills, Bathurst. Altered Sandstones near Sydney, Mt. Lambie.

1 It is open to question whether Kaolin may be classed as a Metamorphic rock.

A MORE COMPLETE LIST OF ROCKS OF AQUEOUS ORIGIN IS AS FOLLOWS:—

LIST OF MECHANICALLY FORMED ROCKS.

Arenaceous or Sandy.	Gravel and Rubble when loose; Conglomerate and Breccia when compacted. Sand and Silt when loose; Sandstone, Flagstone and Gritstone when compacted.
Argillaceous or Clayey.	Mud, Clay, Marl, and Loam when soft; Shale, Mudstone, Clay-rock and Slate when indurated.

LIST OF ORGANICALLY FORMED ROCKS.

Carbonaceous.	Peat, Lignite, Coal, Anthracite, Graphite.
Calcareous or Lime-bearing.	Limestone and its varieties — Compact, Crystalline, Chalky, Oolitic, some Dolomites, and Globigerina ooze.
Siliceous or Quartz-bearing.	Radiolarian rocks, Chert and Diatomaceous rocks.

LIST OF CHEMICALLY FORMED ROCKS.

Siliceous.	Flint, Chert,[1] Sinter.
Calcareous.	Travertine, Stalactites, Stalagmite, Calcareous nodules, and concretions.

1 Fine-grained argillaceous sedimentary rocks occurring in the Coal-Measures are sometimes called cherts.

CHAPTER V.

GEOLOGICAL SEQUENCE OF ROCKS.

THE ROCKS NOT IN CONFUSED MASSES—THEY OCCUR IN A DEFINITE ORDER—OLDEST ROCKS OF THE MOUNTAINS —THE TRUE SEQUENCE OF THE STRATIFIED ROCKS.

UP to the present we have been considering of *what materials* rocks are made, as well as, *how* these materials were brought together. We now touch on the question *when* and in what order they were formed. The stratified rocks are not a confused mass; on the contrary, they occur in a definite series, and it is proved satisfactorily that this order does not vary, although one or more members of the complete series may be wanting.

Imagine a dozen copies of the same historical volume scattered about a room. Each volume, let us suppose, is imperfect. Chapters are missing here and there; they have been torn out, or perhaps were never bound up with the volume. Although a chapter is absent now and again, the order of the chapters does not vary. Chapter X. always comes after Chapter IX., or, if the ninth chapter is missing, after Chapter VIII. In the same way Chapter XX. always follows Chapter XV., even though more than one chapter may be wanting between. By a diligent comparison, however, of the different volumes, a correct and continuous history can be made out. The parts absent from one volume will be found present in another. Just in the same way—although nowhere on earth are the whole chapters of the geological record present in a continued succession—we can, by comparing the succession shown in various parts of the world, construct one complete record. Strata are missing here and there, but the order of the chapters does not vary in the great stone book of Nature. In Fig. 22 we have a sequence of the stratified rocks, with some of the best known of our formations, placed in their true position.

At Burragorang, Permo-Carboniferous rocks are found resting directly on Granite; the Devonian, Silurian, and Cambrian being absent.

Around Sydney, Triassic rocks form the surface of the country, and representatives of the Jurassic, Cretaceous and Tertiary periods, which should be present to complete the series upwards, are absent. Near Wilcannia, Cretaceous rocks rest directly on Devonian sandstones, Jurassic, Triassic, Permian and Carboniferous being all absent. The succession, however, never varies, and having decided this order or succession, we divide the whole series of Stratified rocks into three great groups.

As each great group has fossils peculiar to itself, we are thus enabled to recognize identical formations, even when they are many miles apart. We can do this by observing the similarity of the contained fossils.

As an illustration, it may be safely said that if a geologist discovers the fossil fern shown in Fig. 40, he

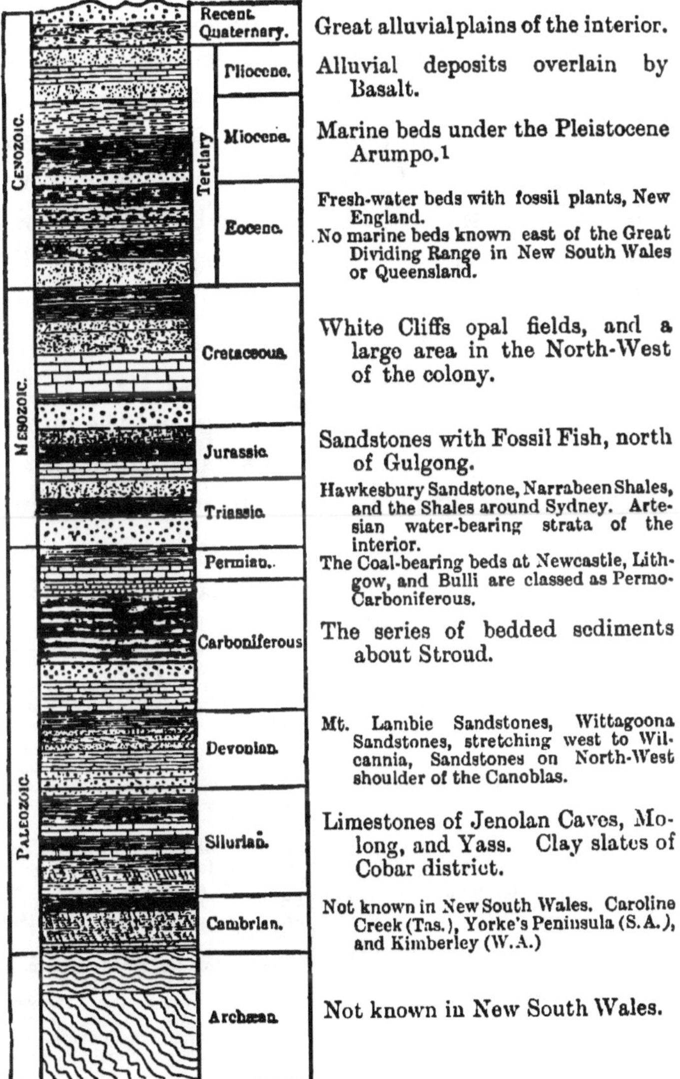

FIG. 22.—Succession of Stratified Rocks in New South Wales.

---

1 Geologists are not unanimous in deciding whether these beds are Eocene or Miocene.

at once concludes that the rocks around him are Carboniferous. And if he found the fossil, represented as it appeared when growing, in Fig. 4, he would feel certain the rocks around him were Mesozoic, and probably Triassic. In the same way the presence of the Spirifers shown in Figs. 56 and 57 would point to Devonian beds. Finally, no geologist finding the fossil fern shown in Fig. 38 would for a moment doubt, in New South Wales at any rate, that he was dealing with Permo-Carboniferous rocks.

We now come to see the meaning and the importance of *characteristic fossils*, any one of which is almost sufficient to identify the formation in which it occurs.

Principal Australian Sedimentary Formations, with some Characteristic Fossils.

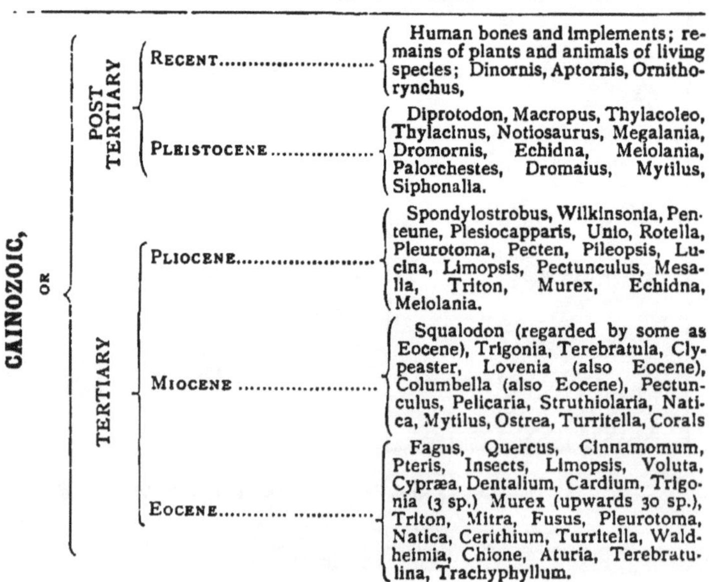

CAINOZOIC, OR	POST TERTIARY	RECENT	Human bones and implements; remains of plants and animals of living species; Dinornis, Aptornis, Ornithorynchus,
		PLEISTOCENE	Diprotodon, Macropus, Thylacoleo, Thylacinus, Notiosaurus, Megalania, Dromornis, Echidna, Meiolania, Palorchestes, Dromaius, Mytilus, Siphonalia.
	TERTIARY	PLIOCENE	Spondylostrobus, Wilkinsonia, Penteune, Plesiocapparis, Unio, Rotella, Pleurotoma, Pecten, Pileopsis, Lucina, Limopsis, Pectunculus, Mesalia, Triton, Murex, Echidna, Meiolania.
		MIOCENE	Squalodon (regarded by some as Eocene), Trigonia, Terebratula, Clypeaster, Lovenia (also Eocene), Columbella (also Eocene), Pectunculus, Pelicaria, Struthiolaria, Natica, Mytilus, Ostrea, Turritella, Corals
		EOCENE	Fagus, Quercus, Cinnamomum, Pteris, Insects, Limopsis, Voluta, Cypræa, Dentalium, Cardium, Trigonia (3 sp.) Murex (upwards 30 sp.), Triton, Mitra, Fusus, Pleurotoma, Natica, Cerithium, Turritella, Waldheimia, Chione, Aturia, Terebratulina, Trachyphyllum.

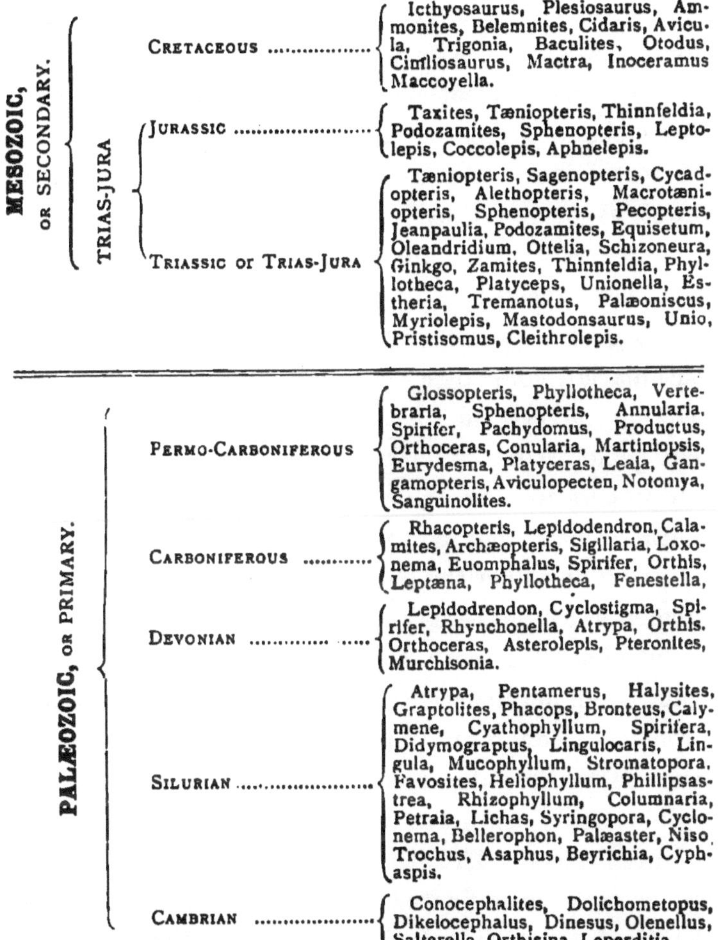

Era		Period	Fossils
MESOZOIC, OR SECONDARY.		CRETACEOUS	Icthyosaurus, Plesiosaurus, Ammonites, Belemnites, Cidaris, Avicula, Trigonia, Baculites, Otodus, Cimliosaurus, Mactra, Inoceramus Maccoyella.
	TRIAS-JURA	JURASSIC	Taxites, Tæniopteris, Thinnfeldia, Podozamites, Sphenopteris, Leptolepis, Coccolepis, Aphnelepis.
		TRIASSIC or TRIAS-JURA	Tæniopteris, Sagenopteris, Cycadopteris, Alethopteris, Macrotæniopteris, Sphenopteris, Pecopteris, Jeanpaulia, Podozamites, Equisetum, Oleandridium, Ottelia, Schizoneura, Ginkgo, Zamites, Thinnteldia, Phyllotheca, Platyceps, Unionella, Estheria, Tremanotus, Palæoniscus, Myriolepis, Mastodonsaurus, Unio, Pristisomus, Cleithrolepis.
PALÆOZOIC, OR PRIMARY.		PERMO-CARBONIFEROUS	Glossopteris, Phyllotheca, Vertebraria, Sphenopteris, Annularia, Spirifer, Pachydomus, Productus, Orthoceras, Conularia, Martiniopsis, Eurydesma, Platyceras, Leaia, Gangamopteris, Aviculopecten, Notomya, Sanguinolites.
		CARBONIFEROUS	Rhacopteris, Lepidodendron, Calamites, Archæopteris, Sigillaria, Loxonema, Euomphalus, Spirifer, Orthis, Leptæna, Phyllotheca, Fenestella,
		DEVONIAN	Lepidodrendon, Cyclostigma, Spirifer, Rhynchonella, Atrypa, Orthis. Orthoceras, Asterolepis, Pteronites, Murchisonia.
		SILURIAN	Atrypa, Pentamerus, Halysites, Graptolites, Phacops, Bronteus, Calymene, Cyathophyllum, Spirifera, Didymograptus, Lingulocaris, Lingula, Mucophyllum, Stromatopora. Favosites, Heliophyllum, Phillipsastrea, Rhizophyllum, Columnaria, Petraia, Lichas, Syringopora, Cyclonema, Bellerophon, Palæaster, Niso Trochus, Asaphus, Beyrichia, Cyphaspis.
		CAMBRIAN	Conocephalites, Dolichometopus, Dikelocephalus, Dinesus, Olenellus, Salterella, Orthisina, Leperditia.

It should be plain now, why it is that geologists strive so earnestly to become possessed of fossils, and also why it is that, notwithstanding all the refinements of laboratory methods, the hammer, after all, typifies the true vocation of the geologist. The views of a modern writer—Dr. Norman Steele—in this connection, are very suggestive. He remarks:—" Each formation possesses its peculiar fossils. This similarity obtains in a great degree over the entire world. Thus, the identification of fossils is the identification of formation. We can, therefore, understand with what eagerness they are gathered and preserved. Fragments, which the ignorant would spurn from his feet, are invested with as high an interest as the obelisks of Egypt or the sculptures of Nineveh. The antiquarian pores over these with intense enthusiasm, seeking to read the history of a few thousand years. The geologist bends with equal delight over the forms and impressions on the rocks, seeking to gather information with regard to a past, compared to the duration of which the chronology of man is but as the moments of yesterday. The print of a leaf, a petrified shell, a tooth, the fragment of a bone, a fish-scale even, may serve to unriddle the most puzzling problem. Rough and mutilated though the fragments may be, to the educated eye they embody a tale as legible as any sculpture or hieroglyphics, and far more comprehensive. That tiny stem, a mere discoloration on the rock, once floated as sea-weed on the waters; that reed once luxuriated in a primeval marsh; that delicate rock impression was a fern that once waved in the sunshine; and that simple leaf, now only a film of coal-like matter, sparkled with the dew of heaven as certainly as the tender herb is cherished by the dew to-day, or existing verdure grows to beauty in the sunlight. Every trace then becomes a letter, every fragment a word; every perfect fossil a chapter

Fig. 23.—Natural section near Jenolan, New South Wales, showing horizontal stratification of Permo-Carboniferous rocks.

in the world's history. Each tells of races that lived, multiplied and died, of the lands that were tenanted, and waters thronged with life—so oft-repeated, again and again, that the mind, at first excited by the marvels, at last grows weary and loses itself in the contemplation of the works of the Infinite Creator."

Glancing at the succession of strata as shown in Fig. 22, it will be seen that the oldest rocks on the Mountains are the Silurian slates and limestones. Next in order of age come the Devonian sandstones of Mount Lambie, and the Canoblas. The Permo-Carboniferous are seen to be newer than the Devonian, and newer still are the Hawkesbury Sandstones, these last being of Triassic age. Much more recent than the sandstones is the basalt that caps Mount Hay, Mount Tomah, and Mount King George. This basalt was poured out subsequent, of course, to the formation of the sandstone, and before any of the Blue Mountain gorges were eroded. The basalt is therefore, geologically speaking, comparatively recent. So that between the formation of the sandstones and the out-pouring of the basalt there are many chapters of the geological record missing. In other words, no traces of Cretaceous, Eocene, Miocene, or Pliocene rocks remain on the Blue Mountains, if they ever existed.

The succession of strata, as illustrated in Fig. 22, refers to New South Wales only. The geology of New South Wales cannot, however, be separated from the geology of Australia, and therefore I think it well to introduce here a table showing the general succession of Australian stratified rocks.

TABLE.

SHOWING THE GENERAL SUCCESSION OF AUSTRALASIAN STRATA.

PERIOD.	SYSTEM.	SOME TYPICAL EXAMPLES.
Post Tertiary.	RECENT.	Gravel, sand, loam and mud now accumulating.
	PLEISTOCENE.	Alluvial flats and great plains of the Interior. Raised beaches of the N.W. coast, Tasmania. Large area in the south-east of South Australia.
Cainozoic or Tertiary	PLIOCENE.	Limestone Creek, Western Victoria. Upper volcanic, Queensland. Marine limestones, Croyden Bore, Adelaide.
	MIOCENE.	River Murray Cliffs, Corio Bay, Victoria. Hallett's Cove, near Adelaide. County of Wentworth (under Pleistocene), New South Wales. Lower volcanic, Queensland.
	EOCENE.	Coralline Limestones of Shark's Bay, West Australia. Carbonaceous beds, Cape Otway. Muddy Creek beds, Victoria. Great Australian Bight. Aldinga, South Australia. Table Cape beds, Tasmania. Plant beds near Emmaville, New South Wales. *No Marine beds of Eocene, Miocene, or Pliocene age are known east of the main Dividing Range in New South Wales or Queensland.*
Mesozoic or Secondary.	CRETACEOUS.	Upper Cretaceous.—Desert sandstone of Queensland. Lower Cretaceous.—Rolling Downs formation of Queensland. Artesian water bearing beds of north-western New South Wales. Kennedy Range and Gascoyne River, West Australia.
	JURASSIC.	Beds with fossil fish, Talbragar River, New South Wales. Oolitic limestone of Champion Bay District, West Australia.
	TRIASSIC OR TRIAS JURA.	The Hawkesbury Sandstones and associated shales of New South Wales. Lower Mesozoic Rocks of the Clarence River. The Ipswich and Burrum Beds of Queensland with *Tæniopteris*. The upper Coal Measures of Tasmania, and the Collie Creek Coal Measures of West Australia are considered to be of Mesozoic age.
	Pending a fuller knowledge of our secondary rocks, some geologists merely divide them into Upper and Lower Mesozoic.	

	Period	Localities
Palæozoic or Primary.	PERMO-CARBONIFEROUS.	Coal Measures of New South Wales, Newcastle, Illawarra, and Lithgow, with *Glossopteris*. Upper and Middle Bowen River formations, Queensland. Collie River and Irwin River, West Australia. Tasmanite beds, Mersey and coast about the estuary of the Derwent, Tasmania
	CARBONIFEROUS.	Port Stephens District, New South Wales. Gympie, Lower Bowen, and Star formations, Queensland. Also the lower Coal Measures of Tasmania
	DEVONIAN.	Mt. Lambie sandstones, Rydal, New South Wales. Avon River and Mt. Tambo beds, Victoria. Burdekin beds, Queensland. Sandstones and grits, Kimberley, West Australia. Fingal slates, Tasmania.
	SILURIAN.	Highly-inclined clay slates and talcose slates, New South Wales, South Australia, and West Australia and Victoria. Graptolite beds of Victoria Yass and Molong limestones. New South Wales. "Larapintine" limestones, Macdonnell Ranges. Queen River schists and slates, and the Gordon River Group, Tasmania.
	CAMBRIAN.	*Olenellus and Salterella* beds of Kimberley, West Australia. Ardrossan beds of South Australia. Magog and Caroline Creek groups, Tasmania. Yorke Peninsula series, South Australia. Kimberley, West Australia. Heathcote, Victoria.
	PRÆ-CAMBRIAN.	Quartzite and some metamorphic rocks of Tasmania. Mount Lofty Ranges, South Australia.

[The statement (page 90) that Cretaceous rocks are the source of artesian water in north-western New South Wales is allowed to stand in deference to the generally accepted views of local geologists, as recorded in the publications of the Department of Mines of this colony. The present writer is of opinion, however, that the artesian supply is derived entirely from Triassic or Trias-jura beds which underlie the Cretaceous, and that the Cretaceous beds are not the source yielding artesian water in New South Wales.]

CHAPTER VI.

RECENT DEPOSITS AND PLEISTOCENE.

MARINE DEPOSITS NOW FORMING—WIND-FORMED ROCKS —SAND DUNES—ALLUVIAL DEPOSITS—TERTIARY.

RECENT deposits are conveniently divided into:—

(1). Marine or sea-formed deposits.

(2). Æolian or wind-formed deposits.

(3). Alluvial or river-formed deposits.

No recent marine deposits are known near Sydney or on the New South Wales Coast. Not that such deposits have not been laid down, but there has been no elevation of the land, in recent times, to lift these deposits so as to form dry land. There is no mistaking the signs of upheaval, if upheaval there had been in recent times. The country between the mouth of the River Murray and Cape Bridgewater is a good instance—over two hundred miles in length—of a land tract raised from beneath the sea in Recent times. For twenty miles inland on this coast there are a series of raised beaches, with sea-shells and sea-cliffs. Almost anywhere beneath the soil one can find masses of marine organisms—shells, corals, polyzoa, &c. It might be argued that, although these are true marine deposits, yet the elevation did not take place in *Recent* times; it might, perhaps, have happened in Cretaceous or in early Tertiary times. The reply is direct, and, I think, convincing. We believe the elevation to have taken place in Recent times because the fossils referred to, although now many miles from the sea, are *all* the remains of existing species, and in no way differ from what is now living in the adjacent seas.

Nothing at all like this condition of things is known about Sydney. In the absence of any evidence pointing to elevation, there is a presumption that the land may be undergoing depression. But, so far, little or no direct evidence has been discovered in proof of any recent depression of our Coast.

Attention has been drawn to a submerged forest at Shea's Creek. In the absence of any more satisfactory explanation, this points to a relative change in the level of the sea or land.

Æolian.—The sand-hills about Kensington, on Cronulla beach, and between Bondi and Port Jackson, are the best illustrations of wind-blown formations near Sydney. Altogether these wind-blown sand-hills cover a large extent of country from Port Hacking to Sydney. They can be observed in many places burying fences, trees, and even houses. The encroachment of moving sand-hills about Newcastle was at one time a source of considerable trouble and expense.

Fulgurites, or tubes of fused silica, are not uncommon in these sand-hills. They are caused by lightning striking the sand, and in its passage fusing it. The fulgarites are found in the form of irregular tubes varying from one-quarter of an inch to three inches in diameter. These tubes give off smaller tubes as they descend, and are invariably coated on the inside with a perfect enamel of fused quartz. With a hand lens the enamel is seen to be quite full of vesicles evidently due to the conversion of the water that was present into steam or perhaps its constituent gases.

Alluvial.—The low-lying lands anywhere about Sydney are recent deposits of alluvium. Better examples can be found on the Nepean River from Penrith to Richmond. The Richmond Flats and the rich plains around Penrith are deposits left by rivers, but of course older than the deposits now forming by the river silting up in places. High floods are still adding fresh deposits to these plains down to the present day. The material laid down in this way supplies a lesson on denudation and the transporting power of rivers. Pebbles and boulders of granite, quartz, and porphyry can be found in the alluvial deposits near Penrith that must have travelled from the upper reaches of the Cox River, forty miles or more away, as the river runs.

In the Cliffs at Long Bay a layer of mould, three feet below the surface, has been recognised as an old land surface. Human remains with some stone implements have been found on this old land surface. Stone implements were also found in the deposits covering the submerged forest at Shea's Creek.

PLEISTOCENE.

Alluvial Flats may be seen on the banks of the Nepean, evidently formed by flood waters, never reached by the highest floods of the present time. They are believed to be of the Pleistocene age. In this connection it is interesting to note that geologists are

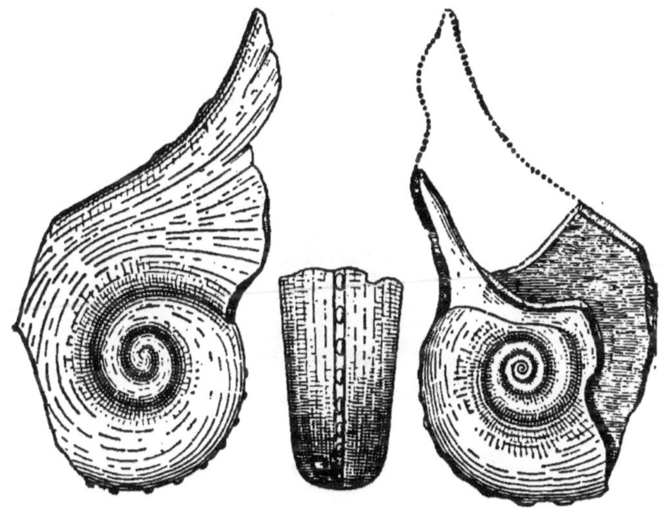

FIG. 24.—*Tremanotus Maideni*[1] Eth. fil. A fossil shell from the Hawkesbury Sandstone, Biloela, Sydney.

fairly agreed that the rainfall of the Pleistocene period in Australia was much greater than it is now. The existence of the gigantic *Diprotodon* which roamed in herds over the plains of the interior is one proof of this. They could hardly have existed in such numbers, without a luxuriant vegetation, such as only a semi-tropical and very moist climate would make possible.

1. Ann. Rep. Dept. Mines, N. S. Wales, 1886, Appendix N., p. 174.

TERTIARY.

We have no notable developments of Eocene, Miocene, or Pliocene rocks within the area we are dealing with, and beds of marine origin belonging to either of these periods are not known. This absence of marine beds of Tertiary age is remarkable, as there is a great development of marine Tertiary deposits in Victoria, South Australia, and Tasmania. The country around the Great Australian Bight, and for one hundred and

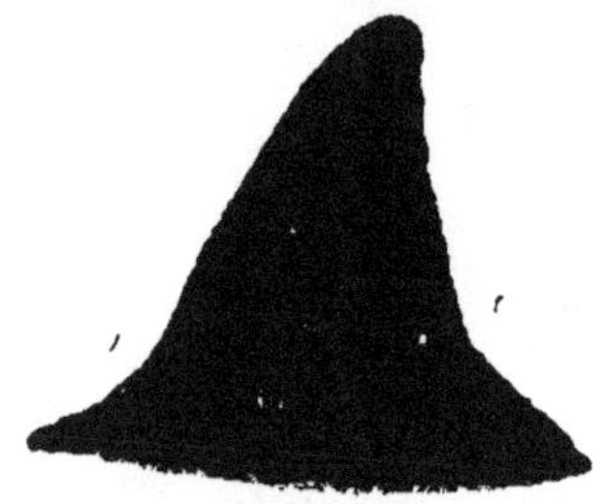

FIG. 25.—*Myriolepis Clarkei*[1], Egerton. A dorsal fin reduced.

fifty miles inland, consists of marine formations of Tertiary age. The absence of any similar beds on the New South Wales coast points to the fact that our coastal district stood above the sea as dry land during the vast length of time that the marine deposits referred to were accumulating.

The material at our disposal justifies us in picturing this portion of New South Wales as dry land, while the Tertiaries of South Australia, Victoria, and

1 Woodward's Fossil Fish of the Hawkesbury Series at Gosford, Plate ii.

Tasmania were slowly accumulating beneath the sea. The waters of this Tertiary sea spread many miles to the north of the Murray River, and covered a large area of Victoria, its shore-line sweeping around to the east of the Great Australian Bight.

The climate on the dry land must have varied considerably during a part of the period. We find in many parts of New South Wales fossil leaves of lower Tertiary age, and they tell us that the cinnamon was a rather common tree in early Tertiary times, while oak, beech, and laurel also flourished. In fact, the extinct flora that clothed our hills in the early Tertiary was not widely different from the flora of the same age in the Northern Hemisphere. It is not improbable, therefore, that the unique and peculiar flora that separates Australia from every other land to-day, has been characteristic of this country only since the later Tertiary.

CHAPTER VII.

THE TRIASSIC ROCKS.

ORIGIN OF THE NAME—A THREE-FOLD DIVISION—THE HAWKESBURY-WIANAMATTA SERIES—THE SANDSTONES—THE SHALES—THE IRONSTONES—THEIR FOSSIL CONTENTS—THE SANDSTONES AND SHALES BELONG TO THE SAME GEOLOGICAL PERIOD.

THE beds known as Triassic are so called from the fact that in Germany rocks of Triassic age are made up of three distinct groups:

1. Keuper or
   Marl group.
2. Muschelkalk or
   Mussel-chalk.
3. Bunter or
   Coloured Sandstone

Curiously enough, the Triassic beds of the coastal districts of New South Wales admit of a like three-fold grouping. The three groups are:—

1. Wianamatta Shales.
2. The Hawkesbury Sandstones.
3. Narrabeen Shales,

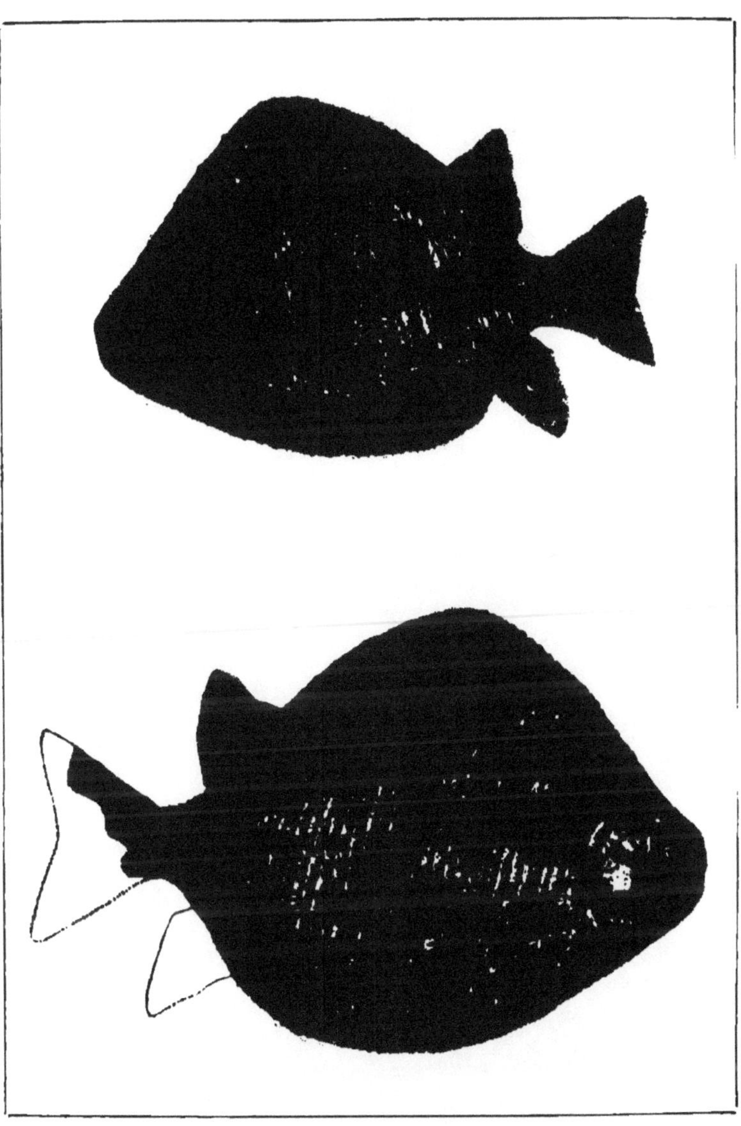

FIGS. 26 & 27.—*Cleithrolepis granulatus*[1], Egerton. A fossil fish from Triassic Rocks, near Gosford.

---

1 Woodward's Fossil Fish of the Hawkesbury Series at Gosford, Plate vii.

The first and second of these divisions cannot, however, be separated by any hard and fast lines. It is convenient, however, to retain the division, bearing in mind at the same time that there is no essential difference between the fossils of the Sandstones and the Shales. The Hawkesbury-Wianamatta Series is a convenient term embracing the two.

In the British Islands, Triassic rocks are known as the New Red Sandstones. This is to distinguish them from the other and much older Red Sandstones made famous by Hugh Miller. The New Red Sandstones sometimes overlie productive Coal Measures, and in that case there is a possibility of finding coal below. Some of the Old Red Sandstones are, physically, not unlike the New Red Sandstones, but as the Old Red are below the Coal Measures, there is no hope to find coal by boring through them. Where the series is complete, the rocks referred to occur in the following manner :—

1. New Red Sandstones, Triassic.
2. Permian.
3. Carboniferous.
4. Old Red Sandstones, Devonian.

In Europe, Triassic rocks are remarkable as having introduced to the world the age of reptiles. Here also are met for the first time in the geological record the internal bones of cuttle-fish, known as *Belemnites,* and more commonly when found fossil as thunder-bolts.

Some very remarkable fish teeth were found in Triassic rocks near Bristol, to which Agassiz gave the name *Ceratodus*. The teeth were the only portions of the creature known. Strange to say, long afterwards a fish was discovered living in Queensland rivers with similar teeth. It is known as Ceratodus or mud-fish. This unexpected discovery of the living animal throws much light on its distinguished English ancestor of Triassic times. The survival in Australia of this remnant of ancient life is full of interest to the geologist. But it is not the only instance of the kind known. A survival of forms, allied to creatures that lived in Secondary times, is not at all uncommon here. Indeed, Australia has been called (in a geological sense) the land of living fossils.

The Port Jackson shark (Cestracion) is an equally remarkable living fossil. It is the sole survival of a group of sharks remarkable for the pavement of crushing teeth which line the mouth. Sharks of this type were extremely common in the European seas of the Secondary period. Buckland first drew attention to the fact that in far-off geological times these sharks lived side by side with the *Trigonias*, and it is a fact of surpassing interest to see "the same comradeship kept up on the distant coast of Australia."

It may not be generally known that the beautiful *Trigonia* shell of our harbour is a genus originally known as extinct. The first descriptions were published from fossil forms. It was a welcome discovery for science to find the *Trigonia* still surviving in Australian seas. There are only about five species living to-day, and even these are not too plentiful. In the Secondary period, however, they must have been extremely abundant, and they swarmed in Oolitic seas.

"Quite recently another link connecting the present fauna of Australia with that of Secondary Europe has been discovered. For a considerable time a peculiar group of herrings (Diplomystus) characterised by having a row of scutes on the back, resembling those found in other types on the opposite aspect of the body, have been known from Cretaceous and early Tertiary rocks, their range including Brazil, Wyoming, the Isle of Wight, and the Lebanan. Till the other day these doubly-armoured herrings were considered to be totally extinct, but now, lo and behold! they have turned up alive in certain rivers of New South Wales."[1]

THE SANDSTONES.

It would be superfluous on the writer's part to describe the Sandstones, when excellent descriptions have already been given by Darwin, Clarke, and Wilkinson. The last-named author writes:—

"In the picturesque cliffs around Sydney Harbour, and especially in those facing the ocean for some miles to the north and south of the Heads, may be

1 Lydekker, Life and Rock, p. 161.

seen all the leading characteristics of the Hawkesbury series. This formation underlies nearly the whole of the Sydney district, and consists of thick and thin horizontal beds of white and brownish yellow sandstone, passing occasionally into grits and conglomerates, with a few interstratified lenticular beds of shale resembling the Wianamatta shales. These shale-beds were formed in small saucer-like hollows, and may be considered as miniature precursors of the Wianamatta formation which filled a wide depression caused by the elevation of the surrounding portions of the Hawkesbury formation."

The character of the Sandstones on the Mountains differs very little from the rock as seen round Sydney, that is, as far as its composition and intimate structure are concerned. The cementing matter holding the grains together is the same. The materials of the grains themselves—quartz—are the same. The beds are divided by bands of shale, but naturally there is a very great difference in the cohesion of the various beds of sandstone. A bed may be found quite friable or so divided into layers by "cross-stratification" as to be useless for a building-stone. Examples of this cross-stratification are very characteristic of the sandstones, and localities where the structure is very pronounced are too numerous to mention. The cliffs north of Bondi Bay furnish some very good examples. But, as a matter of fact, a pleasure trip in any direction, even to Manly, will discover abundant instances of this false bedding or cross-stratification. Immediately under a bed rendered worthless by this structure, we often find a bed up to forty feet in thickness of magnificent freestone show-

FIG. 28.—(1) *Pristisomus latus*,[1] lateral aspect, wanting tail.
(2) *Pristisomus latus*, lateral aspect, wanting head.
Fossil Fish from Beds of Triassic Age, near Gosford.

ing the merest trace of a disposition to break in any one direction. It is, therefore, a perfect freestone. If proof were wanting of its perfect suitability even for the refinement of the builder's art, we can point

1 Woodward's Fossil Fish of the Hawkesbury Series at Gosford, Plate ii.

to the noble buildings that adorn our city. Saunders' Quarry, at the foot of Harris-street, is, perhaps, the most accessible locality to see these beds of sandstone *in situ*, and to see monoliths quarried that might build a pyramid.

But, although the structure and intimate composition of the sandstone may be the same around Sydney and on the Blue Mountains, there the resemblance ends. The sandstones on the Mountains are weathered and scored by Nature's sculptors—rain and rivers—to an extent that remains geologically impossible along the coast. A glance at Fig. 31 will show why this should be so. It will be seen that on the Mountains the sandstones are lifted quite two thousand feet above sea-level, whereas at Sydney the sandstones are for the most part below sea-level. In the battle between the warring elements of Nature, the Mountain sandstones are exposed to the full fire of the enemy; nearer Sydney, their lines are safely entrenched below sea-level. Their pillars and battlements of rock, which, like ruined fortresses, stand up from every valley in the Mountains, tell a tale of destruction such as the concentrated hurricanes of fire and steel, that ploughed the earth at Plevna, could not effect in a thousand years. A description of one of these valleys by Charles Darwin will be read with interest, more particularly if we anticipate a little, and take for granted that these valleys are entirely due to atmospheric agencies.

"In the middle of the day we baited our horse at a little inn called the 'Weatherboard.' The country here is elevated 2,800 feet above the sea. About a mile-and-a-half from this place there is a view exceedingly well worth visiting. By following down a little valley and its tiny rill of water, an immense gulf is unexpectedly seen through the trees which border the pathway, at the depth of perhaps 1,500 feet. Walking on a few yards, one stands on the brink of a vast precipice, and below is the grand bay or gulf (for I know not what other name to give it) thickly covered with forest. The point of view is situated as if at the head of a bay, the line of the cliff diverging on each side, and showing headland behind headland, as on a bold sea coast. These cliffs are composed of horizontal strata of whitish sandstone; and so absolutely vertical are they, that in many places a person standing on the edge and throwing down a stone can see it strike the trees in the abyss below. So unbroken is the line that it is said, in order to reach the foot of the waterfall formed by this little stream, it is necessary to go a distance of sixteen miles round. About five miles distant in front, another line of cliff extends, which thus appears completely to encircle the valley; and hence the name of bay is justified as applied to this grand amphitheatrical depression. If we imagine a winding harbour, with its deep water surrounded by bold cliff-like shores, laid dry, and a forest sprung up on its sandy bottom, we should then have the appearance and structure here exhibited. This kind of view to me was quite novel and extremely magnificent."

The Rev. W. B. Clarke thus describes the Hawkesbury Sandstones:—"Over the uppermost workable Coal Measures, which are of considerable thickness, is deposited a series of beds of sandstone, shale, and conglomerate, oftentimes concretionary in structure and very thick-bedded, varying in composition, with occasional false bedding, deeply excavated, and so forming deep ravines with lofty escarpments, to the upper part of which series I have given the name of Hawkesbury rocks, owing to their great development along the course of the river-basin of that name. These beds are not less in some places than from 800 to 1,000 feet in thickness, containing patches of shale occasionally with fishes, with fragments of fronds and stems of ferns, a few pebbles of porphyry, granite, mica, and other quartziferous slates, and assume in surface outline the appearance of granite, from the materials of which and associated old deposits they must in part have been derived."

THE SHALES.

The shale-beds of the Hawkesbury-Wianamatta Series are much in evidence about Sydney, if only for their economic importance. Brick and pottery works make a large industry, materials for which are entirely derived from the Wianamatta Shales. It must not be forgotten, though, that shales occur at various levels, or, as geologists express it, on various horizons in the sandstones. The thickest beds of shales, however, are those that lie above the sandstones forming most of the surface of the country from Sydney to Penrith. Professor David writes thus of the Wianamatta Shales:—"Of this formation, which probably at one time covered a considerable area on the Blue Mountains, only a small portion is left undenuded. The western-most extension of these shales is probably at a point about half-way between Linden and Faulconbridge. At Springwood the shales attain a thickness of about eighty feet, and further eastwards are completely denuded at intervals, until the monocline at the top of Lapstone Hill is reached. They form a thin capping near the top of the monocline and thicken out rapidly at its base in the valley of the Nepean. They occupy almost the whole of the surface area between Penrith and Sydney, and extend northwards at least as far as the Kurrajong Heights, and southwards beyond Sutton Forest. The Rev. W. B. Clarke estimated their maximum thickness at eight hundred feet; he called them Wianamatta Shales, from Wianamatta—the native name for South Creek. The junction of these shales with the underlying Hawkesbury Sandstone is frequently marked by contemporaneous erosion. The shales are dark grey to bluish-grey at a depth, owing to the presence of iron, probably as protoxide, and carbonaceous material. Near the surface where they have been weathered, they have become bleached through the aggregation of the iron into segregation veins and nodules of hæmatite and limonite, and the removal of some of the carbonaceous material. Bands and nodules of clay ironstone occur on certain horizons, especially near the base of the series, and thin seams of coal have been described in the upper beds of these shales. Mr. Clarke states that one of these seams with its clay bands, at South Creek, has an aggregate thickness of four feet."[1]

The promising appearance of some of the coal referred to, when seen in hand-specimens, has sometimes led to the belief that these beds belong to the true Coal Measures—a very obvious mistake which was more than once pointed out by geologists long before the Cremorne bore proved that the true Coal Measures are quite three thousand feet deeper down.

ORIGIN OF THE SANDSTONES AND SHALES.

With one notable exception, geologists are agreed in the opinion that the Hawkesbury Sandstones are a sedimentary formation. It is not, however, quite obvious whether the sandstones were deposited under marine conditions, in brackish water, or in fresh water. Of course, we look to the fossils to settle this point, although it is questionable whether we have sufficient material at our disposal to make a final judgment. New fossils may be discovered any day that would settle the question. The fossils at present

1 Address to Roy Soc., N.S.W., 1896.

Fig. 29.—Scene in Triassic times, showing the aspect of country where Sydney now stands. The drawing shows *Labyrinthodont*. and such fossil plants as *Macrotæniopteris*, *Thinnfeldia*, and *Phyllotheca* restored.

known are for the most part plants—land plants, or such as would grow in lagoons or marshy places. The magnificent fronds of *Thinnfeldia* found in the sandstones could never have been drifted very far, and must have grown quite close to were the fossil imprints are found. Of course, fish remains have also been discovered, but they are such as might easily have lived in brackish or estuarine waters. The late Rev. J. E. Tenison-Woods at one time held that the sandstones were all of Æolian origin, but in later years he abandoned that theory. From my standpoint, there seems to be no room for doubt that the Hawkesbury Sandstones were for the most part laid down under water. At the same time, there are minor features which are strongly suggestive of the sands being subjected to the action of wind previous to consolidation. There is presumptive evidence, too, that the sand might have been re-distributed and bedded by wind over small areas.

No one doubts but that the shales were laid down in water—in shallow lakes or lagoons. These lakes must, it goes without saying, have been surrounded by dry land. Now, beds of shale are found at different levels in the sandstones, and, therefore, were formed at various levels, as the sandstones themselves were formed. Evidently, then, the still unconsolidated sands formed the dry land surrounding the lagoons. Under these conditions, it is more than probable that sand-dunes were formed locally. A general depression of the land was in progress, and the shales already formed in the lagoon, as well as the wind-swept sandhills, were depressed beneath the waters and fresh sedimentary deposits laid down above them.

The absence of coarse grit in much of the shale requires an explanation. The troubled waters rushing down from the hills brought grit and pebbles without a doubt, but these were kept back by the water having to find its way to the lagoon by filtering through a thick undergrowth of reeds and fern. This is not a mere assumption—you can see reeds and ferns thickly imprinted on this block of shaley sandstone, and, as is well known, the shales are carbonaceous, and could only have derived this carbon from a dense vegetation surrounding and partly filling the lagoons. We shall see now how this might account for the deposition of extremely fine sediments that form our shales. A process not at all dissimilar is yet going on in the interior of this colony. The Macquarie is slowly filling up the flat country beyond Cannonbar and the marshes further down. I have noticed, no matter how coarse the sediments are, that the river carries swiftly past Dubbo and Warren, yet the sediments laid down on the plains far away from the river are invariably fine. Back from the river, the water flowing gently through the grass is perfectly limpid, having deposited its load of sediment—being filtered, in fact—in finding its way through the thickly-growing grass. I have seen perfectly limpid and crystal-clear water "backing up" through the long grass on the lower Macquarie, from the turbid and flooded river more than a mile away. It was certainly somewhat in this way, the undergrowth around the ancient Triassic lagoons that are now beds of shale, more or less cleared the waters of the coarser materials and allowed the finer sediments to pass on.

The speed of the running water is checked also in flowing through a thick undergrowth of vegetation, and the heavier materials that are being carried along are at once dropped to the bottom. The finer particles held in suspension are not deposited until the waters cease to flow on reaching a lake or lagoon.

It has been stated, in passing, that Tenison-Woods himself abandoned the theory as to the Æolian origin of the Hawkesbury Sandstone. Personally, I am inclined to the opinion that the theory, though not accepted by geologists, was, in the words of Professor Liversidge, "a valuable and suggestive paper, and one of the most interesting brought before the Royal Society on geological matters for a long time." And, after all, it may yet be discovered there was a germ of truth in the views of Tenison-Woods. Writing on this subject, Dr. Taylor says: "I hold that this theory of Tenison-Woods, whether ultimately proved or not, is a gain to speculative science. I have long thought that Solar denudation has not been sufficiently taken into effect in Physical Geology. Twenty years ago it was the fashion to give the sea the predominance as a denuding agent. That was in the geologically conservative times. We laughed when poor old Colonel Greenwood published his quaint book entitled 'Rain and Rivers,' wherein he showed that it was the earth's atmosphere, and not the sea, which did all the wearing-and-tearing work. But geologists don't think so now—and Colonel Greenwood is dead!"

So far we have been speaking of *how* the sandstones and shales were deposited. It is quite another question to discuss where the material was brought from. On this point our knowledge is not very complete. The making of the Hawkesbury Sandstones means the denudation and wearing down of an equal amount of country elsewhere. It would take a fair-sized mountain range to give the stones, so to speak, required to build up this formation. As far as geologists are aware, this high land stood away to tho south-west, and it was the rivers flowing from that direction that brought down the sediments, as mud, sand, and shingle, to make the sandstones and shales. These were afterwards re-distributed and spread out in layers in a sea so shallow that portions could become dry land, support a vegetation, and contain the lagoons in which the shales were deposited.

ORIGIN OF THE IRONSTONE BEDS.

Iron in some form or other is one of the most widely diffused of the metals. All plants and soils contain iron. Clays and rocks, with very few exceptions, are coloured by iron compounds. "Iron is

Nature's universal dye. Without it the soil would be a dirty white—the colour of snow in the time of thaw. Instead of the pretty, lively colour of sand and pebbles, we should see the dull and sombre hue of ashes, and, instead of the glittering sand of the sea and lake-shore, a plain drab or gray, which no wealth of sunshine or of spray could turn to beauty. The slates used for roofing have a warm, rich tint; oxide of iron puts vermilion into them, as it does into our bricks, which else would be only a plain pepper and salt. The ruddy hues of brown now seen in ploughing sandy fields, contrasting so richly with the green of woods and meadow, would be, without the iron, only the cold repulsive gray of clayey soils. Many marbles, too, are coloured with the same familiar dye. The violet veinings and variegations of the marble of Sicily and Spain, the glowing orange and amber of Sienna, the blood-red colour of precious jasper that enriches the temples of Italy, are all painted with iron-rust."

The actual amount of iron, however, present in even highly-coloured rocks is so small indeed that it could never be extracted with profit. It is only when ironstones are concentrated, as it were, in beds, veins, and lodes that the ore is rich enough to pay for the extraction of metallic iron.

How comes it that, as in the case of the Hawkesbury Sandstones, the ironstones occur in beds? Why is it that a considerable thickness of Wianamatta Shales should be practically devoid of iron, while immediately below there should be a bed of ironstone? It will be remembered that one of the essentials of a good clay for porcelain is the absence of iron. Also one of the essentials of a good brick clay is a low percentage of iron. It is only the clay that contains practically no iron that will burn white in a kiln. Brick clays, even when colourless, burn red. This is due to the fact that these clays contain iron as a *protoxide,* and this protoxide is converted on burning into the *peroxide* which gives the brick its red colour.

It is then a matter of the highest importance, from an economic standpoint, that shales should be free from iron. And it is equally important that in places ironstone beds should be segregated, so to speak, rich enough in iron to render them fit for the extraction of the metal for manufacturing purposes.

We will now follow the process by which ironstones were formed in beds. I must, to make the matter clear for the general reader, premise that the following facts are familiar :—

1. The iron in rocks is for the most part combined with oxygen.
2. This gives rise to two oxides, the *Protoxide* and the *Peroxide.*
3. The Protoxide is soluble in carbonated waters.
4. Peroxide is insoluble in carbonated waters.
5. The combinations of protoxide of iron are bluish, greenish, or colourless; for example, brick clays.

6. The combinations of peroxide of iron are reddish-brown, for example, iron-rust, and ordinary burnt brick.
7. Rain waters become carbonated on falling through the atmosphere, or on filtering through beds of decomposing vegetable matter.

With these ascertained facts before us we can see for ourselves beds of ironstone in the course of formation. Carbonic acid is given off everywhere in swampy thickets, from layers of fallen leaves, from decaying timber and tangled undergrowths. Vast quantities of the same gas are given off by volcanoes, and by mineral springs, such as the Soda Springs near Cooma. The carbonic acid so abundantly available is taken up by water. Here, then, we have a solvent able to penetrate the pores, cracks, crevices, and joints of rocks, and seize upon all the protoxide of iron it meets in its passage. Laden now with its invisible load in solution, the water oozes from the soil, untli it collects in some lagoon or ditch. Soon a film of the water in the lagoon, in contact with the air, absorbs additional oxygen from the atmosphere. The result is that the soluble and invisible protoxide becomes converted into a peroxide, which is both visible and insoluble. This shows itself as an iridescent scum floating on the water, not unlike a film of oil. But being a peroxide of iron and insoluble, it quickly sinks to the bottom of the lagoon as a reddish mud. A fresh quantity of protoxide now comes in contact with the air, to be in its turn converted into peroxide. This also sinks, as another layer of ironstone. The process continued gives us a bed of iron ore.

Perhaps a fern frond, or a tiny leaf, lies below. It is soon buried in the accumulating iron mud, and this shows how the impress of fossil leaves are found in these ironstones.

This explanation, it may be said, is satisfactory enough in theory, but how does it work in practice? Perfectly. Go to any fresh-water lagoon in swampy country. You will soon discover the iridescent scum I have described. Water in these lagoons has an inky taste from the dissolved protoxide of iron. Standing by the water you are looking on one of the most beautiful, and for ages past, hidden processes that Nature has made use of through all time, to separate ironstone into beds. We are not concerned with theory, as a matter of fact, some of the best Swedish steel is being manufactured from such deposits of iron ore, now forming in Swedish lakes.

It only remains to add that the iron diffused in rocks and collected by carbonated waters need not necessarily be in the form of soluble protoxide. Nature has another simple and silent reaction unceasingly in operation, which is forcibly removing a portion of its oxygen from the insoluble peroxide, and so converting it into the soluble protoxide.

FIG. 30.—*Thinnfeldia odontopteroides*,[1] Morris. A characteristic fossil plant from the Hawkesbury Sandstones.

1 Feistmantel's Coal and Plant-bearing Beds of Eastern Australia and Tasmania, 1890. Plate xxiv.

Dr. Sterry Hunt, who explains these reactions, points out that, as the decomposition of vegetable matter is required for the deposition of ironstone, then every bed of ironstone is as perfect a record of vegetable growth as is a bed of coal. "We find," he continues, "in the rock formation of every different age beds of sediments which have been deprived of iron by organic agencies, and near them will generally be found the accumulated iron. Go into any coal region, and you will see evidences that this process was at work when the coal beds were forming. The soil in which the coal-plants grew has been deprived of its iron, and, when burned, turns white, as do most of the slaty beds from the coal-rocks. It is this ancient soil which constitutes the so-called fire-clays, prized for making bricks, which, from the absence of both iron and alkalies, are very infusible. Interstratified with these, we often find, in the form of ironstone, the separated metal; and thus from the same series of rocks may be obtained the fuel, the ore, and the fire-clay."

From what I have said, it will be understood that great deposits of iron ore generally occur in the shape of beds, although waters holding the compounds of iron in solution have in some cases deposited them in fissures or openings in the rock, thus forming true veins of ore. I wish now to insist upon the property which dead and decaying organic matters possess of reducing to protoxide, and rendering soluble the insoluble peroxide of iron diffused through rocks; and

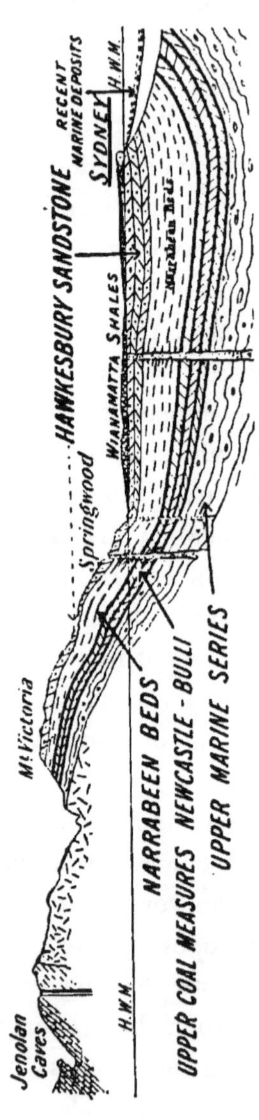

FIG. 31.—Section from the Blue Mountains to Sydney. (After Prof. David)

reciprocally the power which this peroxide has of oxidizing and consuming these same organic matters, which are thereby finally converted into carbonic acid and water. This last action, let me say, in passing, is illustrated by the destructive action of rusting iron bolts on moist wood, and the effect of iron stains in impairing the strength of linen fibre.

We see in the coal formation that the vegetable matter necessary for the production of the iron-ore beds was not wanting; but the question has been asked me, where are the evidences of the organic material which was required to produce the vast beds of iron ore found in the ancient crystalline rocks? I answer that the organic matter was, in most cases, entirely consumed in producing these great results, and that it was the large proportion of iron diffused in the soils and waters of these early times, which not only rendered possible the accumulation of such great beds of ore, but oxidizised and destroyed the organic matters which in later ages appear in coal.

There is just one matter that may be made clear at this point for the benefit of the general reader, and that is the difference—the great difference—between material held *in suspension* by water, and material held *in solution*. As a rule, matter held in suspension can be separated by filtration, while matter held in solution cannot be separated in this way. The finely-divided rock, that makes flooded rivers muddy, is held in suspension, and is not dissolved or in solution. If some fine sand is stirred up in a glass of water, we have a mixture. If a spoonful of salt is stirred up with water in the same way, we have a solution. Salt in solution disappears from view, and will not fall down on letting the water stand. Carbonated waters flowing in rapid torrents through limestone country affect the rock in two ways. The streams carry some of the finely ground-up limestone in suspension as a mere *mixture* of sand, or mud and water. But the water also *dissolves* a quantity of the limestone, which will appear again only by some chemical action, by being separated with the help of some living organism, or by the water drying up. The materials held in suspension will settle down partly on the speed of the current being arrested, and completely when the water comes to rest in a lake or lagoon.

FOSSILS.

It is well to bear in mind, when speaking of the fossils of the Hawkesbury series, we are speaking of all that is left to us of the animals and plants that peopled and clothed the earth in Triassic times. There is a danger of looking on fossils as geological specimens merely. But, in truth, is this shattered bone merely a specimen? Piece it together; find the next bone which should join it, and gradually a thing of life takes shape, of which these dried bones are the mere frame-work. The beautiful impressions of ferns found in our shales are valuable specimens, but their great lesson is lost if we cannot in the mind's eye picture them as they lived. The geologist can conjure back again that ancient morass on whose banks they grew long, long ago. He can see their feathery forms tangled in a wealth of green along the ancient valleys. The fossils show us also fishes gliding through the lagoons, and the giant salamanders basking on the muddy flats or crashing through the undergrowth.

The first remains of *Labyrinthodonts* were discovered while a dock was being excavated at Cockatoo Island, and then it was that we got to see some similarity between the Triassic rocks of Australia and those of Europe and America. As is well known, Triassic rocks in the Northern Hemisphere are identified with reptiles, the remains of which abound. No reptilian remains had, however, been discovered up to this date in Australian Triassic rocks. Secondary rocks of

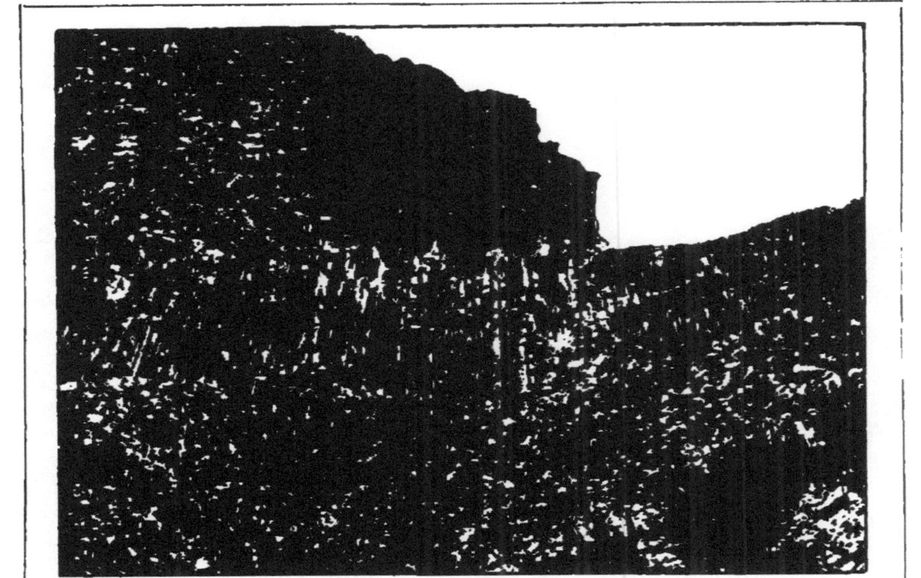

Fig. 32.—Columnar Structure developed in Hawkesbury Sandstone, by contact with intrusive Basalt, Bondi, near Sydney.

Cretaceous age were known in Australia to contain fossil remains of the extraordinary Ichthyosaurus and Plesiosaurus, familiar from the illustration of them so common in text books of geology. The discovery, therefore, of Triassic reptiles in the Hawkesbury-Wianamatta beds was practically a new era in the study of the geology of the district round Sydney.

In 1887 the late Mr. Wilkinson drew attention to the fact that soon after the discovery of the remains of the gigantic labyrinthodon *Mastodonsaurus* in the Hawkesbury Sandstone at Cockatoo Island, other specimens of one of these amphibians were received from Mr. B. Dunstan, who collected them from the Wianamatta Shales near Bowral. He also recognised on some slabs found at Gosford the remains of another of these remarkable "frog-lizards." Professor Stephens undertook to examine the fossil, and in a paper which he read before our Linnean Society, he described it under the new generic name of *Platyceps*. A collector was sent to explore the excavations at Gosford, and succeeded in obtaining not only more Labyrinthodont remains, but a very magnificent collection numbering over 400 specimens of fossil fishes, ganoids and placoids, several of which are of remarkable formation, and appear to be new to science. Splendid impressions both of fishes and *Labyrinthodon* were to be seen on the same piece of rock.

All the world over it has been noted that fossils are not particularly abundant in the New Red Sandstones. But in rocks of this age in the Connecticut

Valley, thousands of impressions are preserved on slabs of sandstone, evidently formed by animals walking over the yet unsolidified sandstone. On some of the slabs, tracks are so abundant that all individual marks are obliterated, and the slabs look not unlike "a muddy road after a flock of sheep had passed." Professor Hitchcock studied these tracks very minutely, and tells us that the discovery indicates more than one hundred species of animals. He reckoned they indicated thirty-one species of birds, seventeen species of lizards, eleven varieties of frogs, a number of bird-lizards, and some creatures resembling marsupials.

One of the birds is described as covering a yard and a half at every stride. It was about twelve feet high, and was quite a quarter of a ton in weight.

Certainly the most remarkable creature of Triassic times is the salamander-like or frog-like reptile named by Professor Owen *Labyrinthodon,* from the labyrinthine appearance of cross-sections of its teeth. This extraordinary creature was first known from its footprints, which resemble rude impressions of the human hand. A frog close on two feet long would in all conscience be uninviting enough, but here we have tracks left by a creature of this sort, and every imprint measures twenty-two inches in length. In weight and bulk they were certainly equal to an elephant.

Even in England *Labyrinthodont* footsteps have been found abundantly near the village of Lynn, and also at the Stourton Quarries, Liverpool. In these localities the footprints occur in Triassic rocks. Later researches have shown that similar animals lived amongst the marshy forests of the Carboniferous age. Not only have magnificent skulls of this creature beeu found in the coal-beds near Glasgow and other places, but impressions of his footsteps have been found, similar to those belonging to the Triassic period. Owen's name of "*Labyrinthodon* is now generally identified with this strange creature, in which science, art, and commerce meet very strangely together. When Owen obtained the first of its teeth, he found in transverse sections of it the labyrinthine structure" (shown in Fig. 37). " Very shortly after that drawing was published it reappeared in Manchester, forming the centre of a printed pocket-handkerchief."

If we add to these reptiles and fish remains a few fresh-water shells, we exhaust the list of known animals of the Australian Triassic age. But it is not unreasonable to suppose that many other forms of life peopled the land and swarmed the seas, of which, so far, no traces have come to light. The discovery of 400 specimens of ganoids and placoids on a few square feet of sandstone at Gosford, points to an abundance of life that will at some time yield a rich harvest to the geologist fortunate enough to unearth these buried treasures. After examining a collection of fossils from Gosford quarries, Professor Stephens wrote: "The collection contains hundreds of specimens of fish, of many genera and families, among which is a possible

Ceratodus, many Belonostomus of all sizes, Cleithrolepis, &c., and many which are at present unknown to me. They are chiefly, if not altogether, ganoids, and many quite new, at least to Australia. Some have been much broken in the quarry, others injured subsequently; but all were otherwise in a wonderful state of preservation. They had evidently been all killed at the same moment, and immediately buried. Some are quite straight and in their natural posture, others convulsed and distorted. One large fish, for example, has the right pectoral fin thrown up on the same plane as the dorsal, with the under side of the head and fore-quarter, and the right side of the rest of the body presented, showing both that the notochord was cartilaginous, and that the fish died suddenly in its struggles. Many others are twisted and bent double; and all seem to corroborate the speculation that they were killed by a sudden influx of ice-cold mud or muddy water into the tepid lagoon where they had been living. There are also with them beautifully-preserved ferns, *Phyllotheca* and the like, which had evidently undergone no decomposition before they were silted up, but had been buried at once in the mud of the torrent which had torn them away. Besides the fish and vegetable remains, there are also two *Labyrinthodont* remains."

The following list shows the more important animals, which we know from their fossils lived while the Triassic rocks hereabouts were being laid down :—

FAUNA.

Tremanotus Maideni.—A Gasteropod Shell, illustrated on page 95.

Estheria Coghlani.
Unionella Bowralensis.
,, Carnei.
Unio Dunstani.
,, Wianamattæ.

Fresh-water bivalves, figures of which are given in a monograph on "The Invertebrate Fauna of the Hawkesbury Wianamatta Series," by Robert Etheridge, junr., Curator of the Australian Museum.

Palæoniscus antipoden.

Cleithrolepis granulatus.—See Figures 26 and 27, page 99.

Myriolepis Clarkei.—See Figure 33, page 135.

Mastodonsaurus. sp.
Platyceps. sp.

See Figures 2, 29, 34, 35, 37, and 39.

Pristisomus latus. See Figure 28, page 105.

Perhaps the most extraordinary discovery of a Labyrinthodont ever made was that brought to light by Sir Charles Lyell and Sir William Dawson when investigating the coal strata of Nova Scotia. A great hollow tree was found fossilised in the Coal Measures. On breaking the specimen, the bones of a little Labyrinthodont were found in the hollow trunk. The interesting bones so fortunately discovered were sent to Sir Richard Owen, who named the creature Dendrerpeton,[1] or the tree-reptile, to perpetuate its wonderful discovery.

1 Greek—*dendron*, tree ; *erpeton*, a reptile.

We have now arrived at that stage when the writer may hope that he has awakened some interest in that strange creature whose remains lie entombed in the rocks of the Hawkesbury series, and portions of which have been actually recovered from these rocks at Biloela, Gosford, and the quarries at St. Peters. It would be hard, indeed, to over-estimate the value of such fragments of the life of a world that is past. And, if it may not be the privilege of everyone to write learned treatises describing these animals, the humblest student may hope to contribute to the advancement of knowledge by collecting every fossil that his observations may help him to discover. Even early in the century the value of the remains of extinct reptiles was duly appreciated. Indeed, a now historic fossil caused no little trouble before it found a resting place in a Paris Museum. It was the jaw of a fossil reptile found in the Mesozoic rocks of St. Peter's Mountain, about a mile south of the city of Maestricht. Dr. Mantell, in his interesting book, *Fossils of the British Museum,* tells its story thus :—

"Some workmen, on blasting the rock in one of the caverns of the interior of the mountains, perceived to their astonishment the jaws of a large animal attached to the roof of the chasm. The discovery was immediately made known to M. Hoffman, who repaired to the spot, and for weeks presided over the arduous task of separating the mass of stone containing these remains from the surrounding rock. His labours

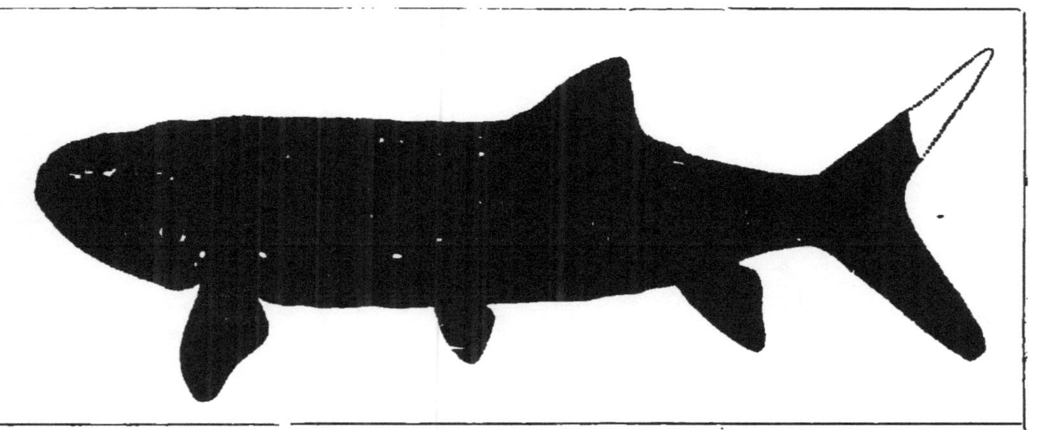

Fig. 33.—*Myriolepis Clarkei.*[1] Egerton (one-sixth nat. size). Fossil fish from Beds of Triassic Age, near Gosford.

1 Woodward's Fossil Fish of the Hawkesbury Series at Gosford, Plate ii.

were rewarded by the successful extrication of the specimen, which he conveyed in triumph to his house. This extraordinary discovery, however, soon became the subject of general conversation, and excited so much interest, that the Canon of the cathedral which stands on the mountain, resolved to claim the fossil in right of being lord of the manor, and succeeded after a long, harassing lawsuit in obtaining this precious relic. It remained for years in his possession, and Hoffman died without regaining his treasure or receiving any compensation. At length the French Revolution broke out, and the armies of the Republic advanced to the gates of Maestricht. The town was bombarded, but at the suggestion of the committee of *savants* who accompanied the French troops to selec their share of the plunder, the artillery were not suffered to play on that part of the city in which the celebrated fossil was known to be preserved. In the meantime the Canon of St. Peter's, shrewdly suspecting the reason why such peculiar favour was shown to his residence, removed the specimen and concealed it in a vault; but when the city was taken, the French authorities compelled him to give up his ill-gotten prize, which was immediately transhipped to the Jardin des Plantes, at Paris, where it still forms one of the most striking objects in that magnificent collection."

The French author who records the history of the fossil remarks : "*La Justice quoique tardive, arrive enfin avec le temps.*" Dr. Mantell adds: "The reader will probably think that although the Reverend Canon was justly despoiled of his ill-gotten treasure, the French Commissioners were but very equivocal representatives of Justice!"

At first sight, the general reader may feel resentful that a simpler and more truly English name should not have been selected for the *Labyrinthodonts.* In this case, however, there is something in a name, for the labyrinth structure of the teeth points to a relationship with some ganoid fishes, which also possessed labyrinth-built teeth. It is also known that certain reptiles possess teeth showing an approach to the same structure. Professor Owen first examined these fossil teeth, and discovered that their internal portion was made up of a series of foldings lined by a continuation of the external cement of the teeth. The name *Labyrinthodont,* then, awkward though it appears, always reminds us that the fossils bearing this name have the same peculiar teeth. Also, that this structure brings them into relationship with the lower fishes on the one hand, and the higher reptiles on the other.

Fishes and reptiles, as is well known, form two clearly-defined classes, perfectly distinct, one from the other. The *Labyrinthodonts,* it has been discovered, form a series of "missing links" between the classes of fishes and reptiles. They are termed, in a general way, *Amphibia,*[1] and *Batrachia,* from the Greek

1 Greek—*Amphi,* both; *bios,* life.

—*Batrachos*, a frog. Joining in their uncouth forms the character of frog and a true reptile, they have been called frog-reptiles, showing at the same time some affinities to fishes. The name *Mastodonsaurus* was given them by Professor Jager, but it must not be taken to indicate any affinity with the true *Mastodon*, which was an extinct elephant of a much later geological age. We have also made use of the term "frog-like reptiles," but, curiously enough, although not by any means an unsuitable name, it is not now used in the sense it was originally intended. The first restoration of the creature was made by Mr. Waterhouse Hawkins, whose models of extinct monsters are so well known in the Crystal Palace Grounds. Although wonderfully successful in other reconstructions, Mr. Hawkins was somewhat unfortunate in clothing with flesh the dried bones of the Labyrinthodon. The fact is, he had not enough bones at his disposal, and so his restoration was based on imperfect materials. Mr. Hawkins' idea of a Labyrinthodon in life is seen in Fig. 39, and as we know now, it gives the creature too much of a frog-like aspect. In later years, more perfect fossils have been discovered. They show us that a tail was well developed, with legs quite as much adapted for walking as for swimming. We can, as already stated, with propriety retain the name frog-lizard, for it has been discovered that some, at least, of the Labyrinthodonts underwent a series of changes similar to the metamorphosis of the common frog.

Dr. Fritsch described some small forms from the Carboniferous of Bohemia, in which traces of the gills of their early life were preserved, showing that they breathed in water as fishes do.

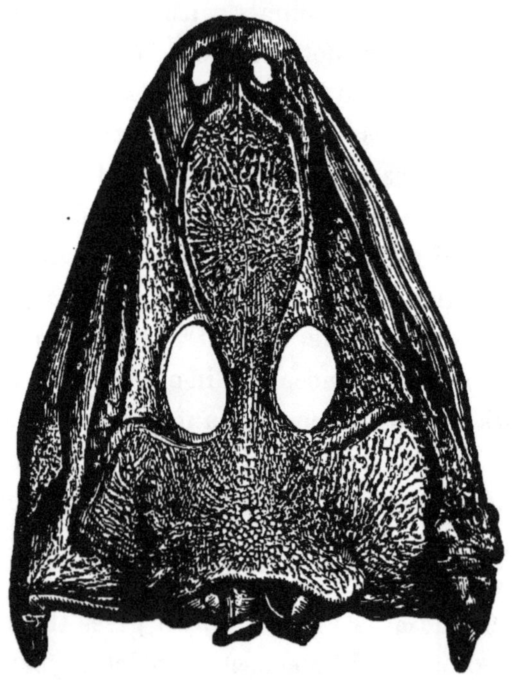

FIG. 34.—Head of Mastodonsaurus. One-seventh the natural size.

While this chapter is being written, the Association for Science, meeting at Sydney, is publishing the fact that its members succeeded in having a whole island reserved on the New Zealand coast for the Tuatara lizard. Now, it may be asked, what possible connection can there be between the *Tuatara* lizard and the extinct Labyrinthodonts that pottered round the ancient swamps, which in Triassic times spread out where Sydney now stands? In Fig. 34 we have reproduced the skull of a *Labyrinthodont.* A little forward from the base of the skull, and behind the eye cavities, a small round hole may be seen, just over the brain cavity. It represents the site of a small third eye. Now, on studying living animals, we find that the little *Tuatara* lizard of New Zealand has a small aperture similarly situated, and overlying the rudiments of an eye. The ancestors of the *Tuatara* lizard no doubt made use of this third eye, and it is extremely probable the Labyrinthodonts made a like use of a third eye. So it comes to pass that the *Tuatara* lizard throws some light upon the use of that aperture in the ancient Labyrinthodont.

As is well known, the vertebræ of the backbones of fishes have hollow articulating surfaces. A single vertebra of a fish will be found cupped-shaped on both surfaces. Indeed, this is one of the characters of the backbone of all fishes. The backbone of Labyrinthodont has similar cupped-shaped vertebræ. So we have here a certain connecting link with fishes. We have said enough now to show the interesting position of the extraordinary creatures we are describing. Quite sufficient to bear out the contention that they are really connecting links between the two well-defined classes of fishes and reptiles. The affinities of

Labyrinthodonts will be best understood for the general reader by the following tabular statement:—

MASTODONSAURUS IS

ALLIED TO FISHES.	ALLIED TO REPTILES.	DIFFERS FROM REPTILES.
By having cup-shaped vertebræ. By breathing with gills in the earlier stages of its growth. The vertebræ are composed of three separate pieces, an arrangement peculiar to some primitive fishes. The infolded teeth connect it with some ganoids.	It was a cold-blooded vertebrate that breathed by lungs, and lived mostly on the land. It had a bony skeleton with well-developed ribs.	By having two condyles, and by breathing by gills when young. The whole of the upper portion of the skull is roofed in by a single bone.

With regard to the imprints resembling the impressions of human hands, and already referred to, it may be inquired if these are really the tracks left by Labyrinthodonts.

As far back as 1834 a German geologist, Dr. Kaup, proposed the name Cheirotherium[1] for the great unknown animal that left the footprints. As Sir R. Owen points out, the impressions of the Cheirotherium resemble the footprints of a modern salamander in having the short outer toe of the hind foot projecting

1 Greek—*Cheir*, hand; *therion*, beast.

at right angles to the line of the middle toe, but yet are not identical with those of any known batrachian or reptile. Still it has been conjectured by the same great authority, as well as by others, that these footprints were the work of the creatures now known as *Labyrinthodonts*, which have left their remains in rocks of the Carboniferous, the Triassic, and the Permian ages. He argued as follows:—

(1) There is proof from the skeleton that the *Labyrinthodon* had hind limbs larger than its fore limbs.

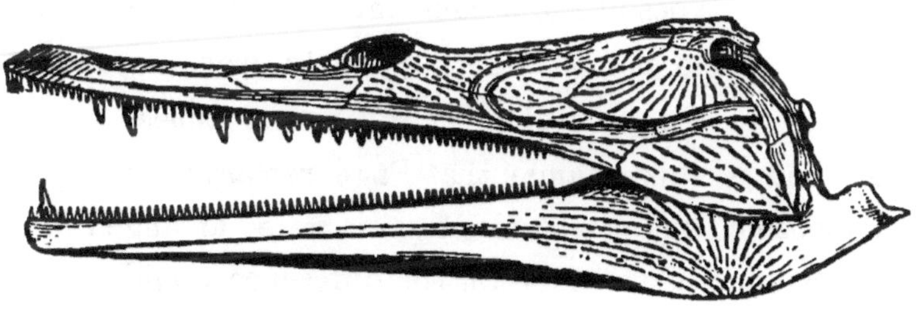

FIG. 35.—Skull of Mastodonsaurus.

(2) That the size of the known species of *Labyrinthodon* corresponds with the size of the footprints of the *Cheirotherium*.

(3) The *Labyrinthodon* occurs in the Triassic strata, in which the Cheirotherium impressions are found.

(4) That no remains of animals likely to have produced such impressions are found in these strata, except the *Labyrinthodon.*

It will be remembered that we are dealing now with the Lower Secondary or Lower Mesozoic rocks, and no picture of the life of this period would be complete without a reference to the extraordinary forms of life that characterise the period as disclosed by an examination of these rocks in Europe and America. We learn from the studies of localities where the Secondary rocks have been minutely examined, that at this time quite new types of life became introduced to this earth. A new cycle begins differing widely from anything known in the preceding or Palæozoic times. So decided is this change that Page remarks: "If the Palæozoic and Mesozoic fossils were arranged on opposite sides of a museum the difference would strike an observer as would that between the brute-man sculptures of Nineveh and the man-god of the Greeks and Romans."

The Palæozoic corals had their septa arranged in fours; corals of later date in sixes. The Palæozoic chambered shells had plain and simple divisions; later shells have a most intricately folded division. Add to this that Palæozoic fishes had unequally lobed tails, while fishes of more recent times have the tail equally lobed or undivided. But, above all, the Mesozoic time is distinguished from all others by the extraordinary development of reptiles. Some of the astonishing characters of these creatures may be guaged from the names given to them by grave and serious scientists. "The huge leader in war," "the huge animal giant," "the terrible lizard," etc., etc. Figures of some of these creatures of other days will be found in the *Century Illustrated Magazine* for November, 1897, pages 12 to 22. Professor Hitchcock, after studying the wonderful abundance of the remains of these creatures, writes: "Who would believe that such a register lay buried in the strata? To open the leaves, to unroll the papyrus, has been an intensely interesting though difficult task, having all the excitement and marvellous developments of romance. And yet the volume is only partly read. Many a new page, I fancy, will yet be opened, and many a new key obtained to the hieroglyphic record. I am thankful that I have been allowed to see so much by prying between the folded leaves. At first, men supposed that the strange and gigantic races which I described were mere creatures of imagination, like the Gorgons and Chimæras of the ancient poets. But now that hundreds of their footprints, as fresh and distinct as of yesterday, impressed upon the mud, arrest the attention of the sceptic on the ample slabs of our cabinets, he might as reasonably doubt his own corporeal existence as that of these enormous and peculiar races."

We have more than once referred to the fact that the age to which the Hawkesbury-Wianamatta series belongs, has been termed the "age of reptiles." Not that abundant life other than reptilian was unrepre-

FIG. 36.—Stratified Triassic Beds exposed in a Railway Cutting, Gosford.

sented, but the reptiles are *par excellence* the distinguishing fossils. It is true that none of the remains of the better known of these enormous reptiles have so far been found associated with our *Labyrinthodonts.* It is more than probable, however, that such remains will yet be discovered, for the *Ichthyosaurus* and the *Plesiosaurus* have been found in the succeeding rocks (Cretaceous) west of the Dividing Range.

We shall now give a short description of the more remarkable Triassic and Jurassic giant reptiles that were contemporaries of, and whose remains are found associated with, our own *labyrinthodont* in more than one quarter of the globe. In our descriptions we will follow, for the most part, the succinct account given by Dr. Dorman Steel.[1]

(1) The **Ichthyosaurus** (fish-lizard) is a striking illustration of a comprehensive type, having the general contour of a dolphin, the snout of a porpoise, the head of a lizard, the jaws and teeth of a crocodile, the vertebræ of a fish, the sternal arch of the water-mole, the paddles of a whale, and the trunk of a quadruped. Its habits were doubtless aquatic, while, like the whale, it breathed atmospheric air, and was thus compelled to come frequently to the surface of the water. Its neck was short and thick, its head large, and its body twenty or thirty feet long. Its jaws had an enormous opening, some having been found with 160 teeth, which could be renewed many times, as above each tooth was always the bony germ of a new one The eyes were often two feet in diameter. Surrounding the pupil of each was a circular series of thin bony plates. The fossil excrements of the *Ichthyosaur* are styled *coprolites*, and when polished are sold as jewellery.

1 "Popular Geology," by J. Dorman Steel, New York 1877.

They reveal distinctly the food and the internal organism of the Mesozoic saurian. In them have been found the scales and bones of smaller animals of their own species. The quarries of Lyme Regis, in Dorsetshire, England, abound in the remains of the *Ichthyosaur*.

(2) The **Plesiosaur** had the head of a lizard, the teeth of a crocodile, a swan-like neck, the trunk of a quadruped, the ribs of a chameleon, and the paddles of a whale. Its tail was shorter than that of the ichthyosaur, being only sufficient to act as a rudder in guiding the body. To compensate this loss and assist propulsion, its paddles were much larger and more powerful. Its appearance presented a striking contrast to that of its more ponderous foe, the *ichthyosaur*, whose attacks it could escape by sinking to the bottom, while its long neck reached to the surface of the water and maintained respiration.

(3) The **Pterodactyle** (wing-fingered), in its apparent monstrosity surpassed even the two reptiles just mentioned. It was so named because the bone of one finger was greatly expanded in order to support an extended membrane for flying. It was a true aërial reptile. Its wings resembled those of bats. Its bones were hollow, like those of birds, but it bore no feathers, and had a mouth full of teeth. Remains have been found indicating a spread of wing of not less than sixteen feet; but, in the usual species of the Liassic, did not exceed ten inches in length. Its ordinary position was upon its hind feet, walking up-

rightly, with folded wings, or perched on trees, or climbing along cliffs with its hooked claws and feet. The smaller ones lived on insects, but the larger probably pounced on struggling reptiles, or, diving into the water, preyed on fish. More than twenty species of the *pterodactyle* have been discovered. Poets have long pictured to us a flying dragon of the oldest time, which played a conspicuous part in pagan mythology. It breathed fire, and disputed with man the possession of the earth. In the Jurassic times we find the realization of this creature of poetic fancy, but it is only an uncouth reptile, utterly unworthy of those fabled conflicts in which gods and heroes shared.

(4) **Dinosaurs** (terrible lizards) were land reptiles of enormous size that roamed elephant-like over the river-plains, or browsed in the forests of Lower Mesozoic times. These included the *megalosaur hylæosaur* and *iguanodon*, etc., huge monsters from forty to seventy feet in length. The *megalosaur* was carnivorous, having teeth curved backward like a pruning-knife, and with a double edge of enamel so as to cut like a sabre equally on each side. The *iguanodon* was herbivorous, twigs having been found fossilized in its stomach, and its teeth often being half-worn to the roots. A party of twenty-one scientific men, at the invitation of Dr. Hawkins, once took dinner within the restored body of this animal. On that occasion Prof. Owen, the celebrated palæontologist, sat in the head for brains! This model contained 650 bushels of artificial

stone, 100 feet of iron hooping, 600 bricks, 20 feet of inch bar iron, 900 plain tiles, and 650 two-inch, half-round drain tiles; while in the legs were four iron columns, nine feet long and four inches in diameter.

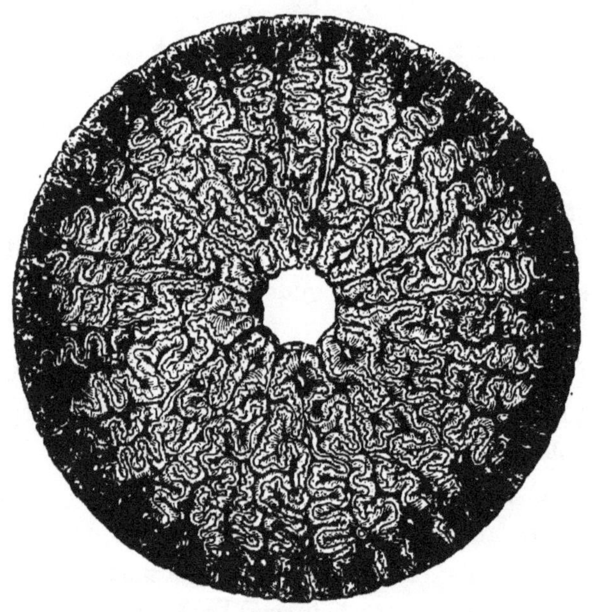

FIG. 37.—Cross Section of a *Labyrinthodont's* Tooth[1] magnified.

There is a restoration of a *megalosaur* in the Crystal Palace at Sydenham, England. This model was also constructed under the direction of Dr. Hawkins. On the back of the animal is a hump somewhat like the withers of a horse. From the few bones discovered at that time, this celebrated anatomist decided that, to

1 Owen's Palæontology, Fig. 67.

make the huge head effective, a mass of muscle and bone on the fore shoulders was essential. This bunch was thought by other geologists to be a mere monstrosity of his own invention. Subsequently, the dorsal vertebræ being found, the conclusion was proved to be correct.

(5) The **Labyrinthodont** has been already sufficiently described.

(6) The **Rhamphorhynchus**, the remains of which have been found in the quarries of Solenhöfen, is a curious intermediate link between birds and reptiles. Its tail, a singular appendage, was long, reptile-like, and dragged upon the ground, while its footprints were bird-like. Stranger still, Marsh has found in the rocks of Kansas, in beds of the next succeeding age, remains of a bird with its mouth full of teeth set in sockets.

It will thus be seen that we have a fairly wide view of the more remarkable forms of life of the Lower Mesozoic. This we owe entirely to the labours of palæontologists whose tireless ardour is building up a new science around us. Professor Winchell describes the character of this age, as well as the importance of the work being done by the men who have drawn aside the heavy curtains of time, and given us the privilege of looking so far into the dim and distant past. He writes:—

"The Triassic Age witnessed also the advent of multitudes of marine saurians of the family of *Ichthyo-*

" Sketches of Creation," p. 175.

saurs, having enormous cavities in their craniums for the lodgment of the eyes. This type of reptiles is restricted to this single age of the world. Here also crawled reptiles resembling gigantic lizards, semi-aquatic or purely terrestrial in their habits, having feet for walking, instead of flat oar-like extremities for swimming."

"These forms all disappeared with the dawn of a new era. Their bones lie buried in the geological cemeteries of Europe. It is almost incredible that information so exact can be drawn from the few scattered fragments which have been brought to light; but such is the unity and persistence of plan which runs through the different classes of the animal kingdom, that a single tooth, whether of a living or an extinct species, will often suffice to enable the expert to disclose all the zoological relationships of the animal to which it belonged, to delineate its form, and size, and habits of life; as the architect from a single capital rescued from a ruined edifice can declare not only the general style of the entire architecture, but can reproduce the size and proportions of the temple whose spirit and method it embodies. Not less sublime than the work of the astronomer, who sits in his own observatory, and, by the use of a few figures, determines the existence and position in space of some far-off, unknown orb, is that of the palæontologist, the astronomer of time-worlds, who, from the tooth of a reptile, or the bony scale of a fish found thirty feet deep in the solid rock, declares the existence, ages ago, of an animal form which human eyes never beheld—a form that passed totally out of being uncounted centuries before the first intelligent creature was placed upon our planet; and by laws as unerring and uniform as those of mathematics, proceeds to give us the length and breadth of the extinct form; to tell us whether it lived upon dry land, in marshes, or in the sea; whether a breather of air or water, and whether subsisting upon vegetable or animal food. It is this unity of the laws of animal life and organisation running through the whole chain of existence, whether past or present, whether extinct or recent, that constitutes the sublime philosophy of palæontological studies, and assures us that one enduring and infinite intelligence has planned and executed every part of creation."

CHAPTER VII—(*Continued*).

THE FOSSIL PLANTS.

THE HAWKESBURY-WIANAMATTA SERIES—THE FOSSIL PLANTS—CHARACTER OF THE TRIASSIC FLORA—FOSSIL PLANTS DESCRIBED—CLASSIFICATION OF FOSSIL PLANTS—THE SANDSTONES AND SHALES BELONG TO THE SAME GEOLOGICAL PERIOD—THE NARRABEEN SHALES; THEIR ORIGIN AND DISTRIBUTION.

RETURNING now to the fossil plants, we find that the rocks supply us with evidence detailed enough to picture to ourselves the trees and plants that clothed this part of the world in Triassic times. The difference between the vegetation of the South of England and Australia is as wide as it well could be. Excepting plants introduced by man, it can be safely said that there is not one tree, and very few species of smaller plants, common to England and Australia. The difference could hardly be greater. It may be safely said that the difference between the flora of to-day and the flora that flourished while our sandstones were being deposited in a shallow sea is just as great. The abundance of plant impressions in the shales, and, indeed, the carbonaceous character of the shales them-

FIG 38.—Permo-Carboniferous Fossils,[1] Newcastle Beds.

1, 2. *Glossopteris linearis*, McCoy. Newcastle, Upper Coal Measures.

3. *Glossopteris Browniana* Bgt. Bowenfels, New South Wales.

3a Part of Fig. 3, enlarged to show the venation.

4. The same with somewhat narrower meshes. Newcastle Upper Coal Measures.

5. *Glossopteris angustifolia* Bgt. Blackman's Swamp, New South Wales. Newcastle Beds.

5a Part of Fig. 5, enlarged to show venation.

---

1 From Feistmantel's Coal and Plant-bearing Beds of Eastern Australia Sydney, 1890.

selves, is proof, if proof were needed, of the abundance of vegetable life. We have a fair knowledge, too, as to its variety, but not a single species that flourished then survives to-day.

The ruling forms of vegetation of Mesozoic rocks are Cryptogams, Lycopods, Equiseta, Conifers, and Cycads. The study, therefore, of Mesozoic plants is more restricted than the study of the almost endless variety of living plants. The real difficulty with the geologist is the finding of plants sufficiently well preserved to determine them. Looking at a slab of Narrabeen Shale, from the cliffs at Pittwater, we find its surface one confused mass of stems, with a few indistinct impressions of ferns, but hardly one in a perfect state of preservation. There are no traces of fruit or flowers; even in Tertiary rocks we seldom have more than leaves preserved. But some eminent botanists, who have given themselves up to the study of fossil plants, distinguish species and genera, with the greatest confidence, from leaves alone. As a rule, botanists require the fruit and flower for the determination of a plant. The present writer collected plants in the interior of this colony for many years, having them named by the late Baron Ferdinand von Mueller. If by any chance I asked the name of a plant of which I only sent leaves and branches, the Baron, by a quaint mingling of idioms, invariably replied, "By their fruits you shall know them." Geologists, however, have to determine plants mostly without flower or fruit. Of course, the leaves of some natural orders are quite distinctive. The *Myrtaceæ* are remarkable for their oil glands, the leaves of *Rutaceæ* are known by their oil dots, the *Proteaceæ* by the fibres of the leaves, and the leaves of *Conifers* and *Cycads* are also characteristic. But palæontologists, such as Heer and Ettingshausen, go further, and distinguish fossil leaf from leaf, in a manner quite incomprehensible to the student. A shepherd can see a different face on every sheep in his flock, while to an ordinary observer there would be no possibility of distinguishing them. So it is when botanists give themselves up to the study of fossil plants: they doubtless become skilled to an extent quite beyond the reach of a beginner.

The fossil plants found immediately around Sydney differ entirely from anything now living in Australia. At the same time, they are not so far removed from living forms as, for example, the plants of the Carboniferous period. The whole history of the earth, as far as plants are concerned, may be divided into three great eras: *the first* and most ancient, characterized by giant lycopods, horsetails and ferns; *the second*, characterized by ferns, lycopods, cycads, conifers, and palms; and *the third*, and more recent, characterized by such plants as we see clothing the earth to-day—dicotyledons for the most part. The Hawkesbury Sandstone, of Triassic age, belongs, of course, to the second of these eras.

Let us picture to ourselves one of these Triassic forests that once clothed the hills and gullies where Sydney and its harbour stand to-day. But, first of all, were there forests? No doubt about it. Every bed of coal represents a succession of ancient forests that grew for ages—how many ages we will say when treating of coal itself. For the present it will suffice to refer to the seams of coal, and to the extensive deposits of carbonaceous shales around Sydney, as evidences of the existence of these ancient forests.

FIG. 39.—*Labyrinthodont* restored.[1] Remains of *Labyrinthodonts* have been found as fossils at Biloela and St. Peters, Sydney.

There remains, however, something to be said as to their character. To begin with, they did not resemble, from a botanical standpoint, any living forests. Great marsh plants, immense ferns—some of them tree-ferns—palms, and horsetails, and lycopods, were the most characteristic forms of plant life. We can well picture to ourselves a dense undergrowth of the stately plant,

1 Since this was drawn, more perfect fossils have been discovered which would modify the figure by the addition of caudal vertebræ.

Macrotæniopteris, illustrated in Fig. 4. One plant which must have been extremely common is shown in Fig. 30. The name (*Thinnfeldia odontopteroides*) is certainly unfortunate, being neither elegant nor appropriate; but it may be considered quite a characteristic fossil, for wherever the Hawkesbury Sandstones occur there this plant is found. It is not quite certain whether it was a fern or a conifer, but of its abundance there can be no possible doubt. Magnificent impressions have been found in the sandstones and shales around Sydney, at Mount Victoria, and as far west as Dubbo. The Dubbo specimens are remarkably fine, and some of them have been figured by Feistmantel in his *Monograph on the Fossil Plants of the Coal-bearing Rocks of Eastern Australia*, although their true locality is not mentioned in that work. Recognisable specimens may be expected almost anywhere, but they are particularly abundant on the thin shales interbedded in the sandstones around Sydney, and in the shales exposed in the cliffs at Narrabeen. Some of its fronds measured three feet in length, and the great abundance of these imprints shows that the plant must have grown plentifully around the old lagoons that are now beds of shale. Writing of *Thinnfeldia*, the late Rev. J. E. Tenison-Woods, says:—

"The genus *Thinnfeldia* is known by its stout, strong, and fleshy leaves. The pinnules are stiff and shining, and of varying shape. The rachis forks frequently, the leaflets are oblong, oval, and united to one another by the base on the rachis. There is a medium rib, but it vanishes towards the apex; the veins emerge at an acute angle, but spread out as they lengthen, forking into venules, all of which reach the margin. This is entirely a Mesozoic genus, and all the European examples belong to the Rhætic or Lias.

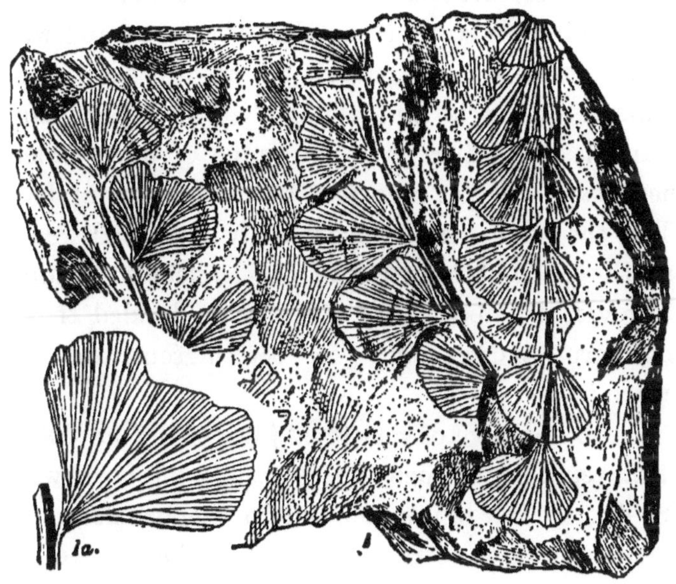

FIG. 40.—(1) *Rhacopteris inæquilatera*,[1] (Gopp). A Carboniferous fossil fern from Stroud. (1*a*) A leaflet enlarged.

Some species have been found in strata of nearly the same age in India. They were evidently strong ferns, with large fronds and thickly-wooded stems. The peculiar character of the leaf is entirely different from any ferns of the present day, so that botanists at first

1 Feistmantel: Coal and Plant-bearing Beds of Eastern Australia and Tasmania, 1890, Plate vii.

were inclined to think that they had to deal with some of the flat-leaved conifers, such as our own *Phyllocladus*, or celery-topped pine, which inhabits New Zealand, Tasmania, and Borneo. It would seem rather difficult to decide whether we are here dealing with a fern or pine, because the venation of the leaves of some conifers is so very like that of a fern; and what makes it still more remarkable in the case of our common species is that, though we meet with large quantities of leaves in every stage of development, there has never yet been seen the least sign of fruit. Then the stipes are so enormously thick and woody, and the mode of insertion of the leaflets so peculiar. However, the best authorities have decided that it is a fern, and as such, for the present, we must regard it."

Another plant of very great interest is *Tæniopteris* a near relation of which, *Macrotæniopteris*, is shown in Fig 4. In the figure referred to the fronds do not resemble those of a fern, any more than the leaves of our common bird-nest fern are suggestive of ferns. *Tæniopteris*, and its other closely-related forms, are ferns with simple fronds of one leaf, having a well-marked mid-rib, and numerous veins emerging from the mid-rib at an oblique angle, but almost immediately becoming horizontal. Some of the veins fork once, rarely twice, and all reach the margin. True *Tæniopteris* is confined to the Secondary rocks in Australia, and is a characteristic Mesozoic plant, so much so that a single specimen of *Tæniopteris* found in association with coal is sufficient to establish the Mesozoic age of the coal. There are coal-bearing beds, for instance, on the Clarence River, but with them are found *Tæniopteris.* On this account geologists do not hesitate to place these coal-beds much higher up in the geological series than our true Australian Coal Measures, as developed at Newcastle (see Fig. 44). Another illustration of the importance of this fossil in geological chronology is seen in its relation to the artesian water-bearing beds of the North-Western district of New South Wales. For many years past the Cretaceous rocks of the colony—a marine formation, by the way—were believed to be the source of artesian water. Recently attention has been drawn to the fact that rocks very much older than Cretaceous were supplying artesian water at Dubbo and Coonamble. More recently the beds that supply artesian water on Salisbury Downs Station were found to underlie Cretaceous rocks, and to contain *Tæniopteris.*[1] This at once shows that these beds, whatever else they are, are *not* Cretaceous. And we are brought face to face with the question as to whether there is any real evidence of artesian water being derived from Cretaceous rocks in New South Wales. *Tæniopteris*, then, is an excellent illustration of the principles to which the study of fossils has been reduced. It may be well, while dealing with this fossil, to say that it is never found in the Newcastle beds, or associated with coal of the same age as Newcastle coal.

1 See abstract of a Report by the Author, *Daily Telegraph*, January 20th, 1891; and also an abstract of a Paper on Artesian Water in New South Wales, *Sydney Morning Herald*, January 12th, 1898, page 4.

The Newcastle series (Palæozoic) are always to be known by the abundance of the fossil fern called *Glossopteris*, and the Ipswich series by a fern called *Tæniopteris*. It will make things a little clearer to anticipate some points of classification, and here note what kinds of ferns are those just named. *Glossopteris* is a simple, entire leaf with a mid-rib, and the small veins united or netted; that is to say, joining so as to form a reticulated mass. *Tæniopteris* is a simple, entire leaf with a mid-rib, and the smaller veins proceed from the mid-rib, at nearly a right angle, towards the margin. These veins seldom divide or fork more than once, and these branches never unite to form a net.

Glossopteris belongs to the family *Dictyopterideæ*, a name which explains itself, since *diktuon* is the Greek for a net, and this family is meant to include all ferns with a netted venation. Some readers may be inclined to ask,—Is this a very natural division? or whether, among living ferns, those with netted veins stand apart as a peculiar family? They do not; in fact, netted veins and simple tongue-shaped fronds, with a mid-rib, are found in almost every family. Botanists are obliged to take what they can get as a means of grouping fossil ferns; and though no fault can be found with this, we must bear in mind that artificial methods of classification bring together very different forms. We give the name of *Glossopteris* to simple fronds with a costa and netted veins; but the same definition would at the present day include more than a dozen different genera, distinguished widely from each other by their fructification, their habits, and the climates they affect.

Glossopteris browniana may be said to be the pride and glory of our Australian coal fossils. It may be found of almost any size. It is beautifully tongue-shaped; hence the name. It appears from Dana's specimens that the leaves grew in clusters, or bunches, and from an Indian species that the fructification was scattered in little round dots, in rows on the leaf. This is nearly the fructification of *Microsorum irioïdes*, or *Polypodium*, which grows on the Queensland coasts.

Glossopteris is best known from *G. browniana*, a very common fossil in all the Newcastle coal-beds. Nine or more species have been described by various authors, and though they depend for their distinction on minor peculiarities of veining and shape, one must not easily reject them, as they may really represent different genera.

Another interesting form is *Cycadopteris*. Cycads are plants or small trees very much like palms; they are rather common in the Mesozoic beds of Europe, but, as is well-known, are quite extinct in that portion of the world, no surviving Cycad being known in Europe. The Cycads are tropical or sub-tropical plants rather common on the East coast of Australia. English Geologists, accustomed to the marvellous development of these plants in Oolitic times, look with great interest on our Cycads, as examples of living fossils.

Phyllotheca is also a common fossil in the shales about Sydney. It is also found in the Newcastle Beds, and, on this account, when found in association with a thin seam of coal at Blacktown, near Sydney, persons were led into the mistake of thinking that the coal seam in question was an outcrop of the true Coal Measures. *Phyllotheca* is connected somehow, or has much in common, with the Equisetaceæ or Horsetails.

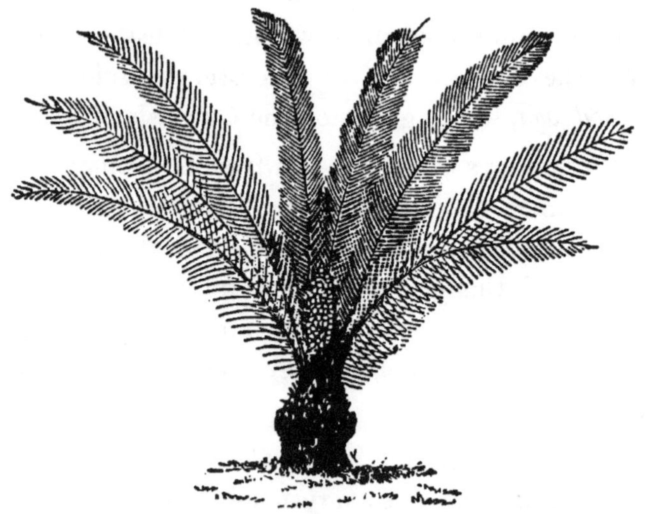

FIG. 41.—*Macrozamia*, a living Cycad; common in the Illawarra coastal district, and known as far west as Dubbo.

Visitors to the Blue Mountains will remember the bundles of so-called moss sold at the railway station; this is commonly known as "Mountain Moss," but is in reality a Lycopod. In former periods of the earth's history Lycopods, with stems forty and fifty feet high, formed vast forests, and we only know their life-history in as far as we can study the living Club Mosses. The name Club Moss suggests some resemblance to true mosses, but they also combine in themselves features usually associated with ferns and conifers.

Sir Frederick McCoy figured a specimen showing the fructification of *Phyllotheca.* The illustration can be found in Volume I., Part 3, of the *Papers and Proceedings of the Royal Society of Van Diemen's Land,* issued in January, 1851. Up to the present time no better examples of the fructification of this plant have been discovered. Impressions of *Phyllotheca* are astonishingly abundant in some of the shales of the Permo-Carboniferous at Newcastle, and in the carbonaceous shales near Narrabeen. We have here an inviting and fertile field of research for the amateur geologist. *Phyllotheca* played an important part in the physical geography and geology of the country around Sydney long ages ago. Forests of it covered the land before any one continent as we know them to-day was finally raised from beneath the sea. Its woody stems formed beds of coal, and its spores gathered into beds now represented by highly inflammable shales. Yet practically nothing is known of the life-history of *Phyllotheca.* There is material more than enough in the shales—Nature's cabinets —along our seaboard to stock the museums of the world. It only awaits the energy of some student to piece together the scattered fragments and read for us the story. The Lycopods are but small plants, and quite insignificant in comparison with what Lycopods have been in former periods of the earth's history. They were all trees at that time —trees with stems 20 to 45 feet high—and very ornamental trees, if we may judge by what is left to us of their trunks and leaves. In those days flowers, properly speaking, had not come into existence; at least, if they existed they have left no traces of their presence. So, most of the bright pageantry of our floral kingdom did not adorn the forests, but in its place were elegant forms, and it may be, for all we know, varieties of colour too. Instead of the rough bark and gnarled, twisted boles of the forest, there were graceful, tapering stems, covered with lozenge-shaped patterns below, and with long, graceful, scale-like leaves above. They were simple forms of vegetable life, according to the way we speak now, though in one sense their ultimate organisation was as intricate as any in the present time. There were not so many special organs, and there was certainly not anything like the variety of the vegetable kingdom of to-day. From the wide distribution of a few species all over the world, we see that plant life was then simple and uniform. It served its purposes, whatever these were, lived its life, and then left us a valuable legacy in the shape of coal.

For the convenience of students anxious to bear in mind the classification of fossil plants, I insert a few descriptions of the leading divisions of fossil plants, from some articles contributed to the *Sydney Mail*, by the late Rev. J. E. Tenison-Woods. He thus defines the principal families of the fossil ferns :—[1]

(1.) *Sphenopteridæ.*—Fronds, entire or subdivided; divisions lobed or wedge-shaped, with a dentate margin; a slender costa often dividing towards the apex or vanishing; veins reaching the margin of the lobes; venules wanting indistinct or only proceeding from the lower veins.

(2.) *Neuropteridæ.*—Fronds, with usually larger and more entire subdivisions than the last; veins extremely numerous and slender, curved, forking frequently, and reaching the margin. They emerge from a costa which always, if present, vanishes in subdivisions, or the veins arise from the rachis.

(3.) *Pecopteridæ.*—Fronds, with usually entire subdivisions, adhering to the rachis by the whole base of the pinnules, which have a conspicuous costa reaching the apex; veins forking; venules forking twice or thrice, but rarely anastomosing. *Thinnfeldia*, as described on page 160, comes under this family.

(4.) *Tæniopteridæ.*—Fronds, simple or pinnate, subdivisions long, entire lanceolate, stalked, or sessile; costa conspicuous, veins emerging obliquely, usually becoming horizontal, simple, or forking once.

(5) *Dictyopterideæ.*—Fronds, simple or pinnate, with or without a costa, but always with a netted venation.

1 These descriptions have been altered somewhat by the present writer.

Besides these divisions, there are fossil ferns which clearly belong to existing families, and are classified with them. It is, however, rarely that we meet with such plant remains, and they must generally be identified by the fructification.

A number of plants other than ferns constantly

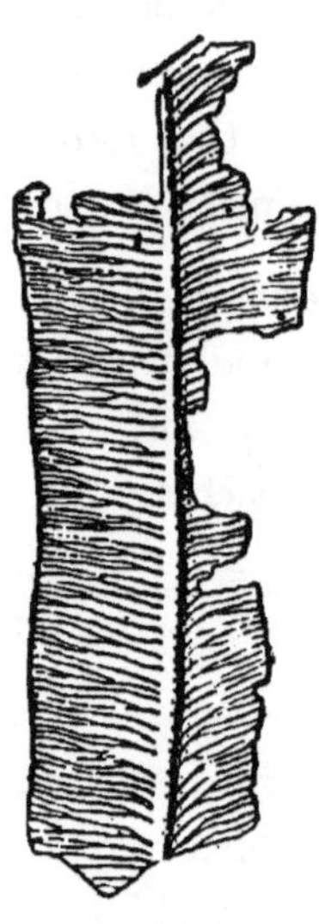

FIG. 42.—*Tæniopteris Daintreii*,[1] McCoy. A Triassic Fern.

associated with our Coal Measures and Triassic rocks may be simply classified as follows :—

Equisetum.—Leaves united in an entire persistent sheath round the stem, which never form themselves into separate leaves ; divisions ribbed or smooth. A specimen is known from the Hawkesbury Sandstone.

Schizoneura.—Leaf sheath very long, and in its

1 Quart. Jour. Geol. Soc. Vol. XXVIII. Plate xxvii.

young stage united, but with age it splits along the line of the grooves between the ribs, and then every division becomes a long, narrow, strap-like leaf, joining a whorl round the transverse partitions. This genus has been noted in the Narrabeen Shales.

Phyllotheca.—Sheath similar to *Equisetum*, but prolonged into long linear leaves, usually like threads of wire, spreading in a whorl.

"*Phyllotheca* is at present little more than a generic name applied to jointed, and more or less costate, stems and branches, the latter springing from above the stem-joints, and bearing linear, verticillate leaves, with a central vein, free distally, but joined into a sheath proximally, and either erect or reflexed. As the name *Phyllotheca* was originally described from Australian material, it follows that the genus must derive its distinctive characters from such, and whatever the fructification eventually proves to be, so will foreign species fall within it, or be relegated to other genera." [1]

Calamites.—Tree-like plants, with jointed cylindrical stems, and long strap-like leaves, longer than the branches. The *Calamites* are somewhat analogous to *Equisetum*, but the verticillate leaves are entirely free or confluent at their base. They had clusters of sporangia similar to Lycopods. This large genus of plants is subdivided into *Calamocladus*, *Calamostachys*, *Huttonia*, *Macrostachya*, and *Bornia*, which being minor distinctions need not occupy us here.

Sphenophyllum.—Leaves in close whorls, wedge-

1 R. Etheridge, Junr. Rec. Geol. Survey of N. S. Wales, Vol. IV., part 4.

shaped entire, but often deeply lobed or toothed, 'on median nerve, and the minor nerves frequently forking.

Annularia.—Leaves in close horizontal whorls, numerous, oval or tongue-shaped, with a medium rib.

Schizoneura is a rather common Indian fossil, of Secondary age, which has never been found with our Permo-carboniferous coals, but was recognised in the Cremorne Bore, in beds of Triassic age.

Most of the other genera mentioned need not occupy us, as they are rare. *Schizoneura* had a sheath also, and a number of longitudinal leaflets with a central vein attached along their margins. See reference to a figure of this plant in the list of fossils at the end of this volume. *Sphenophyllum* has been found in fragments only at Port Stephens, and *Annularia* at Greta Creek. They are both Palæozoic forms, and almost confined to the Coal Measures.

The following is a list of the plants characteristic of the Hawkesbury-Wianamatta Series :—

SOME FOSSIL PLANTS OF THE HAWKESBURY-WIANAMATTA SERIES.

Fillices :

Pecopteris.
Sphenopteris.
Alethopteris Australis—See Figure 43.
Cycadopteris scolopendrina—See Figure 9.
Macrotæniopteris Wianamattæ—See Figure 4.
Thinnfeldia odontopteroides—See Figure 30.
Danæopsis.*

* Danæopsis is figured in *The Fossil Flora of the Gondwana System* by Dr. Ottokar Feistmantel (Mem. Geol. Survey of India). There is a copy in the Free Public Library, Sydney.

Fig. 43.—*Alethopteris Australis*,[1] Morr. A Mesozoic fossil fern, Cape Patterson (Vic.), Ipswich (Qu.), Clarence River and Narrabeen Shales (N.S.W.)

---

1 McCoy's Palæontology of Victoria.

Equisetaceæ:

Phyllotheca Australis.
Equisetum. ‡

Cycadaceæ:

Podozamites lanccolatis.
Otozamites.

Coniferæ:

Jeanpaulia palmata—See Figure 9.
Subsequently referred to as *Salisburia palmata*.*
Schizoneura Australis.
Cleandridium lentriculiformis—See Figure 3.
Ottelia præterita. †
Sheath-wings of *Coleoptera* have been found associated with these plants.

These might be described as the flora of the thickets and swamps. Of the trees of the uplands we know nothing. The carbonaceous character of the shales is evidence that plants flourished in great profusion. We have vast beds of shale, and every layer reveals imprints of numberless specimens. The description given by Winchell would apply in every line to our fossiliferous shales. Each bedding plane is covered with "inimitable representations of the delicate fronds of ferns. We remove a scale of the rock, and behind is still another picture. Remove a second, and from the dark black rock gleams forth another form of grace and beauty. The whole mass of the shaly roof is a portfolio of inimitable sketches. The sharpest

‡ Proc. Linn. Soc. N.S. Wales (2nd Series), Vol. V., plate XVII.
* „ „ „ „ „ Vol. II., p. 137.
† Royal Society, N.S.W., 1879, p. 95.

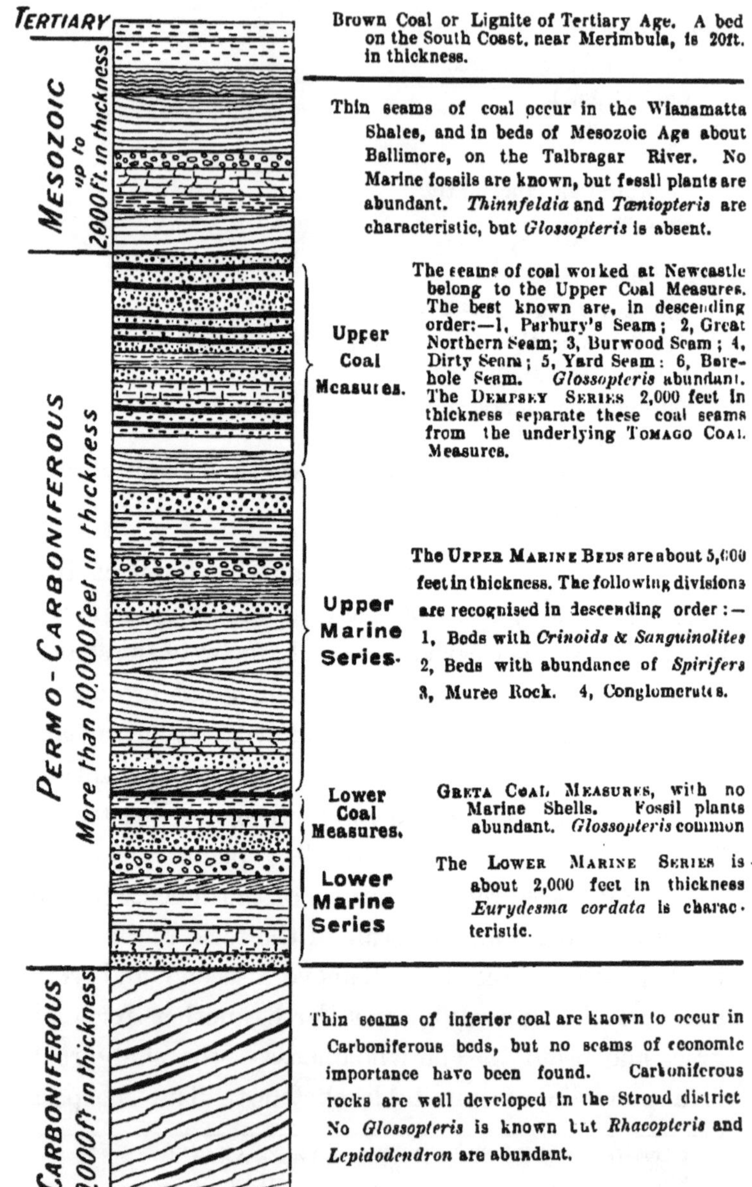

FIG. 44.—Succession of Coal-bearing rocks in New South Wales.

outlines and minutest serratures of the leaves are clearly traced. The very nerves, with their characteristic bifurcations, are accurately depicted on this wonderful lithograph. Petioles, buds, and woody stems, cones and fruits, slender grass-leaves, striated rushes, the fluted stems of gigantic club-mosses, the scarred and pitted trunks of extinct tree-ferns, diversify by turns the crayon sketchings of the dusky ceilings. Prostrate, all! They have stood erect; the soil has held them by their spreading roots, the genial sunlight has warmed them, the vital breeze has fanned their verdant foliage; change, which transforms all things, has swept over them, and graceful fern and giant club-moss, slender reed and arrogant conifer, have lain down together on their couch of sediment, and the old sexton, Time, has piled upon them the accumulated ashes of a hundred succeeding generations of trees, and herbs, and perished populations."

In a work issued as this chapter goes to press[1] many of the fossil plants referred to here are grouped under the general heading *Equisetales.* These are then divided into *Recent* and *Fossil Equisetales*, the latter being thus grouped—

FOSSIL EQUISETALES
- I. EQUISETITES.
- II. PHYLLOTHECA.
- III. SCHIZONEURA.
- IV. CALAMITES.
- V. ARCHÆOCALAMITES.

1 "Fossil Plants." A. C. Seward. Cambridge University Press.

Note.—*Schizoneura*, *Oleandridium*, and *Ottelia* do *not* belong to the family Coniferæ. Through imperfect spacing on page 175, they appear to be classed under that head.

THE NARRABEEN SHALES.

The Narrabeen Shales, which underlie the Hawkesbury Sandstones, are so named from the fact that these beds are well exposed on the coast about Narrabeen, to the north of Manly. These Narrabeen Shales form the lowest beds of the Hawkesbury-Wianamatta series. They are also at the basement of the sediments of Mesozoic age. Between their lowest layers and the coal-bearing rocks below there is a geological break, representing a vast period. Around Sydney, the Narrabeen Shales are seemingly conformable to the underlying Palæozoic rocks. The fossils, however, show that a vast change had come over the face of the earth between the deposition of the Permo-Carboniferous and the overlying Narrabeen Shales. In fact, in most parts of the world, between Primary and Secondary rocks, there is a great change in both marine and terrestrial life, as stated on page 144. Here, close to Sydney, we have rocks in contact, but which are separated in age by a great interval difficult to measure in years. During this "interval"—not, perhaps, synchronous all the world over—nearly all the plants that characterised the coal period have disappeared, and the oldest known mammal appears. With the close of the Palæozoic, marked here by the junction of the Narrabeen Shales and the Permo-Carboniferous, all the corals with septa in groups of four *(Rugosa)* disappear for ever. *Graptolites* and *Trilobites* have long since become extinct, and the greater number of the lamp-shells named Brachiopoda ceased to live, although a few survive to this day with a persistence that is not easy to understand. We find no more *Glossopteris* or *Vertebraria*. But we find, in their place, a large

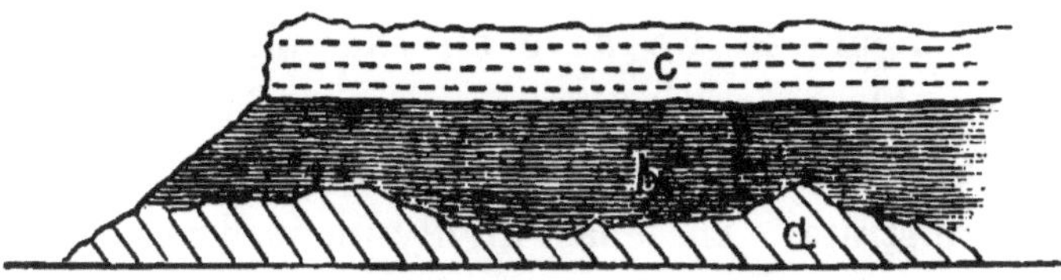

FIG 45.—Sketch Section at Capertee.

c. Hawkesbury Sandstone; b. Permo-carboniferous resting unconformably on Silurian Slate, a.

and robust fern (if fern it be), *Thinnfeldia odontopteroides*, which is common to both Hawkesbury and Wianamatta, and *Ottelia prœterita*, a large water-plant, with fenestrated leaves.

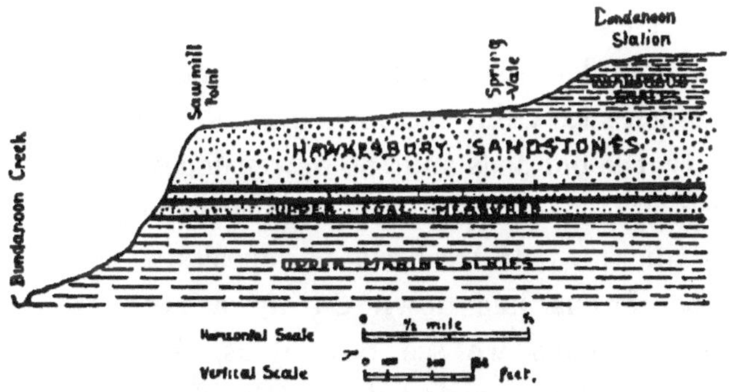

FIG 46.—Sketch Section at Bundanoon.

Professor David drew attention to the fact that an *unconformity* may be observed between the Narrabeen beds and the Permo-Carboniferous coal-measures in the Hunter River district in the neighbourhood of the Pokolbin Hills. As already stated, *unconformities* indicate an interval of time, during which great changes may have taken place, of which the records are "either entirely lost, or have to be sought elsewhere."

In figure 45 we have an example of an unconformable succession, where Permo-Carboniferous beds are shown resting on the upturned edges of Silurian strata. These last highly-inclined rocks were laid down as more or less horizontal beds one above the other. They hardened and compacted probably under pressure, or in part by the solution and re-precipitation of some of their mineral constituents. They were then elevated above sea-level, for they are of marine origin, by a folding or puckering of the earth's crust. The upper portions of the folds were subsequently worn down by denudation. Then they were once more depressed below the sea, and formed a floor on which succeeding marine deposits[1] were laid down. Lastly, the old beds and the newer deposits they now carry were lifted again from beneath the sea, and the vast thickness of fresh-water deposits of the Permo-Carboniferous laid down during a protracted subsidence. Thus we see how it is, that an unconformity such as exists between the Narrabeen Shales and the Permo-Carboniferous means a long lapse of time with no record *here* to tell of the physical changes that were in progress or of the influences affecting the animals or plants that lived.

[1] Marine beds are not shown in this sketch section although such beds are known in the Western districts.

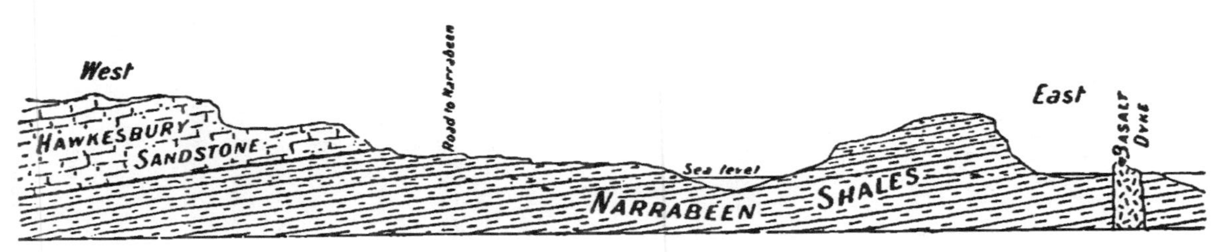

Fig. 47.—Sketch section, showing the relation of the Hawkesbury Sandstone to the Narrabeen Shales, Long Reef, North of Manly. (The beds do not dip at as high an angle as shown.)

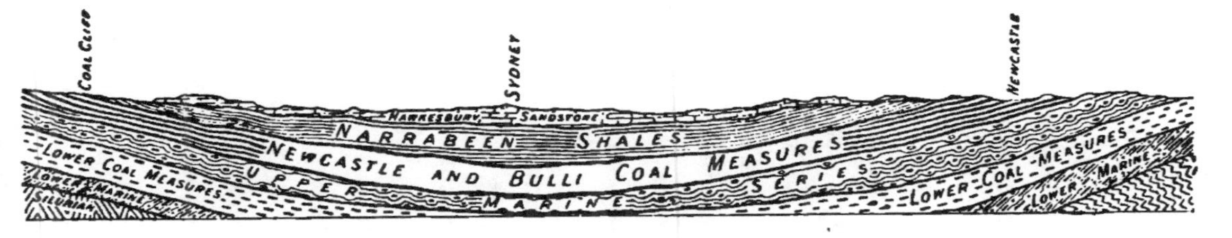

Fig. 48.—Sketch section, showing the relative position of the Hawkesbury Sandstone, Narrabeen Shales and the Permo-Carboniferous under Sydney.

The Narrabeen beds can be studied along the cliffs on the coast, north of Long Reef. Here they are found rising from below the Hawkesbury Sandstone (Fig. 47), and show that chocolate-coloured hue that gives the name *chocolate shales* to these particular beds. The same shales were reached in a boring at Moore Park at a depth of 1000ft. below sea level. At Sutherland they are 520ft. below sea level. "On the side of the hills near the Metropolitan Coal Company's shaft, at Camp Creek, on the Illawarra Railway, 28 miles from Sydney, the chocolate shales crop out at 410ft. above sea level. Thence they may be traced along the face of the coast range as far south as Saddle Back Mountain, near Kiama. Their thickness has not been definitely ascertained, but it is probable that the whole of the strata, including shales, sandstones, and fine conglomerates, 1573ft. thick, lying between the Hawkesbury Sandstones and the top seam of coal passed through in the Sutherland Bore, should be regarded as one series. At Camp Creek these strata have thinned out to about 920ft. in thickness, and at Bulli to about 700ft., gradually diminishing towards the south; whilst to the west, in the Berrima district, they have disappeared, and the Hawkesbury Sandstone rests directly on the coal seam."[1]

In the section shown (Fig. 46) the Hawkesbury Sandstones are seen resting directly on the Permo-

1 C. S. Wilkinson, F.G.S. "Handbook of Australian Association for the Advancement of Science." 1888.

Carboniferous, the intervening Narrabeen Shales being absent. In most of the gorges on the mountains, beyond Mount Victoria, the Narrabeen beds can be easily recognised cropping out in the cliffs, the reddish-brown colour of some of these shales contrasting strongly with lighter coloured sandstones. They can be seen to advantage, also, in the cuttings on the railway, above Eskbank. The Narrabeen beds are not more than 350ft. in thickness on the western flank of the mountains above Lithgow. These shales are, therefore, not unlike a great saucer, the centre and thickest portion of which is under the district around Sydney, and the thin edge of which sweeps round from Coal Cliff to Lithgow, and from there to the coast north of Narrabeen.

ORIGIN OF THE NARRABEEN SHALES.—Glancing at a collection of the fossils that occur so plentifully in the shales, we note an abundance of plant remains, many in a beautiful state of preservation. The only shells known to occur are decidedly not *marine.* There is, then, no evidence of the shales being a marine formation. They were certainly not deposited in the sea. But this much we do know, they were laid down as sediments in water. One of the most impressive of the silent witnesses to this fact is the "ripple-marks" still preserved on some of the slabs. The lapping of the water on the as yet unhardened sands left lines of tiny ridges along the edges of a lake. Dry sand was then blown down, and in this way a mould was cast that has lasted to this day. Plants grew thickly around the water's edge. Their remains form thick carbonaceous materials, and the fact that they are so perfectly preserved shows they were not drifted far, but grew close by where we now find them. We must picture the area now occupied by the Narrabeen Shales as a land-locked lake of considerable extent. Rivers from the surrounding highlands swept into this lake. A dense vegetation fringed the waters, and the hill sides were covered by the straight-stemmed and graceful *Phyllotheca.* The sediments brought down by the rivers and deposited layer above layer we now recognise as the Narrabeen Shales. But it is obvious that a great tract of hill country must have been worn away to furnish material for the accumulation of so vast a mass as we see in these shales. What, it will be asked, was the nature of the country that was used up, so to speak, in the building of the Narrabeen Shales? The hills were formed of Permo-Carboniferous strata, with lavas and volcanic ash deposits—the result of the volcanic outbursts towards the close of the preceding Permo-Carboniferous period. Part of the Narrabeen Shales are, therefore, said to be built up of re-distributed volcanic material. Much, if not all, of the volcanic materials, however, in these beds was, in Professor David's opinion, derived from "contemporaneous volcanic eruptions, which produced layers of greenish-grey ash or tuff."

The peculiar red colour of the chocolate shales can be thus accounted for. Magnetite, a mineral contain-

Fig. 49.—Columnar Basalt, Kiama

ing up to 72 per cent. of iron, is a constituent of basalts, tuffs, and allied igneous rocks. We are familiar with the yellow and red tints of iron rust, or oxide of iron. The magnetite of the original rock is now altered into many varieties of iron oxide, and acts as the colouring constituent of the shales. Iron, in its various forms, has been called Nature's colour-box, and the rich, warm hues of the chocolate shales, the soft yellows of the sandstone, and the rich reds of the ironstone bands are excellent examples of the variety and life given to rocks by iron oxide—Nature's universal dye.

SUMMARY OF THE TRIAS OR TRIAS-JURA.—Between the Palæozoic and Mesozoic rocks there was a great break, during which the "differentiation," as it is called, of the vital functions of animal life became more marked. There was also a progress in "Cephalization," or head development. Other characters appeared, which are so obvious that even a slight acquaintance with geology is sufficient to impress one with the vast advance towards higher types made in the "great interval" between Palæozoic and Mesozoic times.

At the opening of the Mesozoic period the country around Sydney was undergoing depression. The basin now occupied by the Hawkesbury-Wianamatta series was either a great brackish or fresh-water lake or a land-locked sea, into which sediments were carried by rivers that have long since disappeared. The tract of land that supplied the sediments has also disappeared. Plants, many quite new, were abundant, and reptiles and fresh-water shells are known to have existed. Fossil shells allied to the fresh-water mussel are found from the Narrabeen up to the latest beds above the Hawkesbury Sandstone. There were doubtless other forms of animal life, of the existence of which we have no direct proof.

There were few active volcanoes immediately around, and these were probably restricted to the earlier part of the Trias. Much of the scoriæ, ashes and lavas of the preceding period were worn away by such agencies as rain, running water, wind, and the alternating effects of heat and cold. The sediments thus produced were swept into the Triassic lake. The land was undergoing a slow but steady subsidence. Changes were being wrought apace over the country that was being denuded. Through alterations of level in the land, a granitic area to the south-west was brought within the watershed of our great lake. The swollen rivers brought down ever-increasing loads of granitic sand. Gradually the lake became shallow through the accumulation of these sands, and islands appeared here and there, covered with a thick vegetation. Great tracts of shallow water grew into a swamp, rich in plant life. Turbid waters filtering through reed-beds supplied the finely-comminuted material that made our shales. Some beds of shale were formed in depressions in the sandstones, with dry land all around. The dry land referred to, consisted for the most part of unconsolidated sand, and much of this was tossed about and redistributed by the wind over limited areas. Altogether the great Triassic lake at one time might be compared to a vast morass or swamp. Again it showed deeper water, with swift currents and turbid rivers rushing down as torrents laden with sand, to build up the sandstones. Once again we see the morass condition repeated, while the Wianamatta Shales were forming.

Rocks of the same age in Europe yield brine springs, and are the great source of the supply of common salt. The European Trias was also deposited in and around an inland lake or shallow sea, whose waters were charged with salt and gypsum. The conditions were not unlike those around the Dead Sea of the present time. The middle division—the Muschelkalk, a shelly marine limestone—shows that there was a great ingress of sea-water, or perhaps the lake may have become an open sea. Anyhow, the fossils tell us that there was an abundance of marine life. No such episode characterised the Trias in England or Australia.

As to *when* the Hawkesbury-Wianamatta rocks were deposited, there is not much to learn. The series is newer than the Coal Measures, and older than the Cretaceous rocks of the north-west of New South Wales. No better illustration can be given of the vast antiquity of these geologically-speaking modern rocks, than a reference to the stupendous changes that have taken place since their deposition.

Towards the close of the Mesozoic period, and during the Tertiary period, physical, climatic and organic changes of a remarkable character took place, both in the northern and southern hemispheres. Dr. Geikie states that some of the most colossal disturbances of the terrestrial crust of which any record remains took place within the Tertiary period; and adds: "Not only was the floor of the Cretaceous sea upraised into lowlands, with lagoons, estuaries, and lakes, but throughout the heart of the Old World, from the Pyrenees to Japan, the bed of the early Tertiary or nummulitic sea was upheaved into a succession of giant mountains, some portions of that sea-floor now standing at a height of at least 16,500 ft. above the sea."

In other words, the Alpine peaks of Switzerland and a vast tract of England, Ireland and Central Europe were yet beneath the sea when our Triassic rocks were formed. Much, too, of the elevated portions of the earth's surface, from the Pyrenees, across Europe and Asia, to Japan, was slowly formed under marine conditions, and lifted to its present altitude since the deposition of the Triassic Sandstones around Sydney.

Viewed in this light, every vestige of the life that flourished so long ago becomes doubly precious, and the geologist may be pardoned when he treasures in cabinets and museums the records of such antiquity. Hugh Miller gives expression to this idea in his own picturesque way when, writing on the subject, he states:—"The historian or the antiquary may have traversed the fields of ancient or of modern battles, and may have pursued the line of march of triumphant conquerors, whose armies trampled down the most mighty kingdoms of the world. The winds and storms have utterly obliterated the ephemeral impressions in their course. Not a track remains of a single foot or a single hoof of all the countless millions of men and beasts whose progress spread desolation over the earth. But the reptiles that crawled upon the half-finished surface of our infant planet have left memorials of their passage, enduring and indelible. Centuries and thousands of years have rolled away, between the time in which these footsteps were impressed upon the sands of their native Scotland, and the hour when they were again laid bare and exposed to our curious and admiring eyes. Yet we behold them stamped upon the rock, distinct as the track of the passing animal upon the recent snow; as if to show that thousands of years are but as nothing amidst eternity, and, as it were, in mockery of the fleeting perishable course of the mightiest potentates among mankind."

CHAPTER VIII.

THE PERMO-CARBONIFEROUS.

PERMO-CARBONIFEROUS—ORIGIN OF THE TERM—FORMATION OF COAL—BUILDING UP OF THE COAL MEASURES—FRESH-WATER AND MARINE CONDITIONS—VOLCANOES OF THE PERIOD—SUMMARY.

THE series of stratified rocks that underlies the Hawkesbury-Wianamatta, and contains the coal measures, is known as the Permo-Carboniferous. This term was originally proposed by Mr. Robert Etheridge, jun., for a formation "distinguished by a copious marine fauna partaking of a Carboniferous and Permian nature, and a flora from which lycopodaceous plants are almost entirely absent." Anyone familiar with the Carboniferous rocks of Europe will remember that the most characteristic fossil plant is *Lepidodendron.* This is absent in the coal measures of Eastern Australia; and in its place we find plants, and one fern in particular, with quite a Mesozoic aspect. The fern referred to is *Glossopteris* (Fig. 38). This beautiful plant abounds in the coal measures that underlie Sydney, and can be found plentifully at Newcastle or Lithgow. It will, of course, be remembered that the same coal measures that are depressed three thousand feet below sea-level under Sydney come to the surface at Bulli, Newcastle, and Lithgow (Fig. 48 will make this clear). Their outcrop makes a great semi-circle, with Sydney for a centre.

From the standpoint of the general reader, the most impressive fact connected with our coal measures

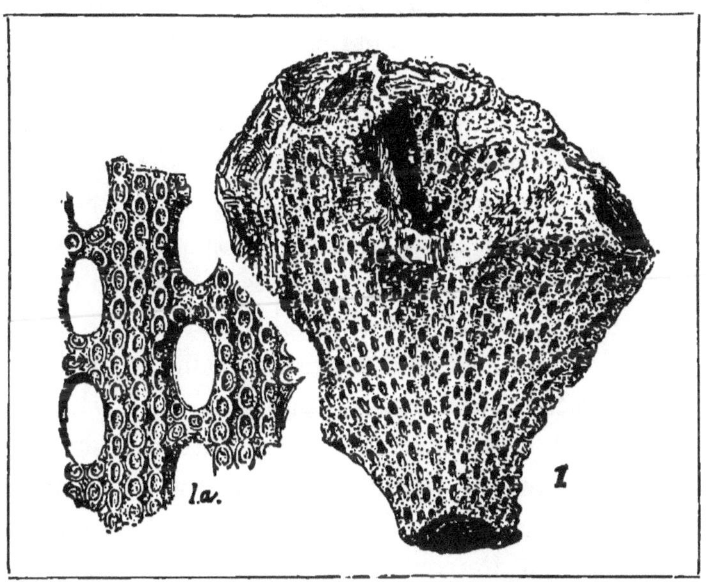

FIG. 50.—*Protoretopora ampla*[1] Lonsdale. A Fossil Polyzoan from Permo-Carboniferous Rocks at Raymond Terrace, and Harper's Hill. 1, Cast of cellular surface, nat. size. 1*a*, Magnified representation of a cast of the cellular surface.

is their occurrence at so great a depth below the surface. Obviously, every coal-seam must have at one time been a mass of living vegetation on the surface. Coal is essentially nothing more or less than somewhat decomposed and very much crushed and compressed

[1] Strzelecki's New South Wales and Van Diemen's Land, Plate ix., as *Fenestella*.

vegetation. That coal once lived in the form of luxuriant plant life is one of the best established conclusions of science. The chemist can help us here. He tells us that the composition of coal is very similar to that of trees and plants. When coal is burnt, an ash is left, not different from the ash left on burning plants. Good coal contains about 80 to 90 per cent. of carbon, while wood contains about 50 per cent. of the same element. Woody matter consists of half its own weight of carbon—the other half of its weight being the gases hydrogen, oxygen, and nitrogen. Carbon is, of course, the more stable of these elements, and the gases are easily driven off. If wood is heated in an open vessel, it burns—that is, its carbon unites with the oxygen of the air, giving out, at the same time, light and heat, and nothing remains but mineral matter, in the shape of ash. But when wood is heated in a closed vessel, out of contact with the air, the unstable gases are driven off, and the wood becomes charcoal or carbon. In a similar way, vegetable matter, when in contact with air, disappears by decomposing—a process not essentially different from burning, decomposition being merely slow combustion. When, however, a vast accumulation of vegetable matter is shut out from the air, and therefore from free oxygen, pressure or chemical action tends to drive off the oxygen and hydrogen constituents, and we have a substance approaching the condition of carbon and coal.

	Wood.	Peat.	Lignite.	Coal.	Anthracite.
Carbon, per cent....	50	CO	66	81	91

The possible derivation of coal from vegetation is thus evident. That it was so formed is equally certain. We see from the coal itself that it is built up in thin layers, and that these layers are rich in impressions of fossil plants. In the coal itself, or in beds associated

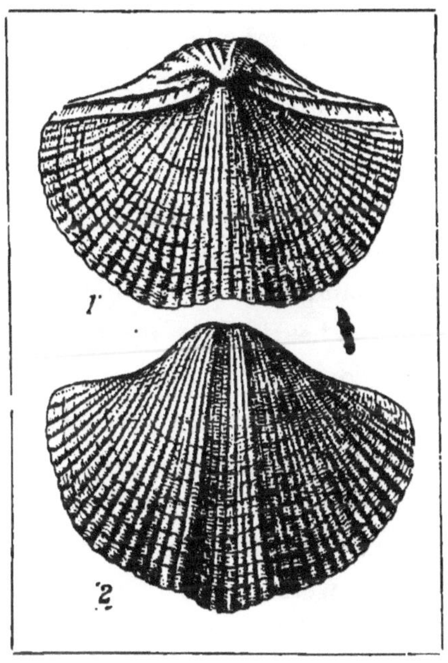

FIG. 51. *Spirifer Tasmaniensis*,[1] Morris. A Permo-Carboniferous spirifer from Raymond Terrace and Nowra.
1, Dorsal aspect. 2, Ventral aspect.

with it, trunks of trees have been found still standing upright, as they grew.

We can see plants growing and forming peat, and trace peat into lignite. Another step and we have coal. Whole tree trunks have been found

1 De Koninck: Atlas of New South Wales, Palæozoic Fossils, Plate ix.

flattened and converted into true coal—and indeed every grade between tree-stems and coal has been met with. Lastly, under every extensive bed of coal an "under-clay" is found, which is really the old soil on which the vegetation grew.

A student will not spend many hours about a coal-mine before he finds some plants, although coal-mines differ much in the relative abundance of the plants preserved as fossils. In a bed of clay-stone at the base of Nobby's, Newcastle, *Glossopteris* can be seen on every slab. The rocks above and below the kerosene shale are usually rich in fossil plants. A coal-mine near Castlecomer, Ireland, had some unique examples that would gladden the heart of the most stoical geologist. On a hard band forming a floor a number of reptiles were displayed in great perfection. The roof immediately above was a tangled mass of *Lepidodendron*, ferns, leaves, and stems. The museums of the world could be stocked from this one gallery of an obscure coal-mine, and the work of plunder could be continued for years to come. The present writer's recollections of that mine is a lasting reminder that the pictures painted by the cunning hand of Hugh Miller are not overdrawn. We do not expect to find such rare examples in every mine, but that they do occur is certain. Buckland's description of a coal-mine is worth quoting:—

"The most elaborate imitations of living foliage upon the painted ceilings of Italian palaces bear no comparison with the beauteous profusion with which the galleries of these instructive coal-mines are overhung. The roof is covered as with a canopy of gorgeous tapestry, enriched with festoons of most graceful foliage flung in wild, irregular profusion over every portion of its surface. The effect is heightened by the contrast of the coal-black colour of these vegetables with the light ground-work of the rock to which they are attached. The spectator feels himself transported, as if by enchantment, into the forests of another world; he beholds trees, of forms and

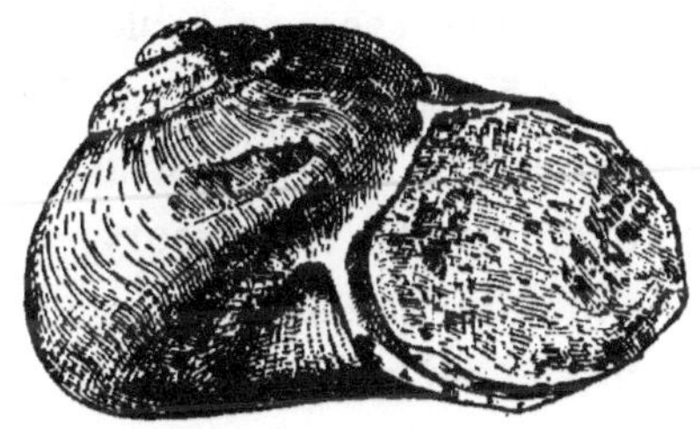

FIG. 52. *Platyschisma oculaa*[1] Morris. A Permo-Carboniferous univalve. Harper's Hill, Newcastle (N.S.W.)

characters now unknown upon the surface of the earth, presented to his senses almost in the beauty and vigour of their primeval life."

If we grant that coal represents the growth through long periods of a luxuriant vegetation—trunks, branches, leaves and seeds or spores—we have to consider under what conditions these great thick masses of organic materials accumulated.

Did the vegetation which forms coal grow just

[1] Strzelecki's Phys. Descript. New South Wales, Plate xviii.

where we find it? Geologists assure us that for the most part the coal plants flourished on old land surfaces now represented by the under-clays. The growing plants, acted on by the sun's energy, separated carbon from the atmosphere, just as living plants do. There is, therefore, much truth in the old measure—

> "'Tis the sun's old heat that cooks our meat,
> 'Tis his bottled-up beam that gives our steam."

When we ask if the plants that formed coal grew just where the coal is formed, we are opening up a question that was at one time much debated. The "drift theory" supposed that the vegetable matter which forms coal grew in forests, and was drifted into lakes, or even into the sea, and in time settled to the bottom Facts are, however, against this theory. Under every bed of coal we find an "under-clay." These "under-clays" represent the old soil on which the vegetation flourished. Trees have been found standing erect in coal-seams, with the roots striking into the "under-clays." The absence of sand and mud shows that the vegetable matter was not drifted. Besides, it is not quite intelligible how *pure* seams of coal of great extent could have been formed by drifted materials. The transition from a peat-bed to a coal-seam is a change in keeping with observed facts. It has been noted, too, that the "under-clays" are deficient in alkalies, these having evidently been extracted by the growing plants. The ashes left, on burning the coal, give up these alkalies once again. When the vegetation that made our coal was growing, the coast-line was far away to the east. A region of unbroken monotony stretched from the granite mountains about Moruya to the sandstone hills of Mount Lambie, and north from there to Stroud—a wild waste of marsh land, where countless generations of plants and trees lived and died, each contributing something to the growing organic *debris* that provides the material for the making of coal.

Even at the present time we may find somewhat similar peat-mosses. A morass as long as England extends along the course of the Prepit, an affluent of the Dnieper. A swamp extends from Norfolk in Virginia into North Carolina. The whole tract, forty miles in length, and twenty-five broad, is covered with water-plants, reeds, and trees. The soil is a mass of grasses, roots, stems, and leaves. Mosses and ferns flourish. The place is appropriately named the Great Dismal Swamp. But all the conditions are there for the beginnings of a bed of coal. If by a gentle subsidence of that part of the earth's crust the Dismal Swamp was lowered, and sediments brought down by rivers from the high lands around, the layer of vegetable matter would be buried below some thousands of feet of newer rocks, and would in time be converted into coal. This is just what happened here in Permo-Carboniferous times. The land was slowly subsiding, and the great Australian morass, with its rich carbonaceous deposits and its waving surface of richest green, was depressed beneath the waters of a great inland lake. Sediments were swept down by broad and noble rivers, fed in their turn by mountain torrents, and gradually stratified beds grew layer by layer above the coal.

The amount of vegetable matter in a single coal-seam six inches thick is greater than the most luxuriant vegetation of the present day would furnish in 1,200 years. Boussingault calculates that luxuriant vegetation at the present day takes from the atmosphere about half a ton of carbon per acre annually, or fifty tons per acre in a century. Fifty tons of stone-coal spread evenly over an acre of surface would make a layer of less than one-third of an inch. But suppose it to be half an inch, then the time required for the accumulation of a seam of coal three feet thick—the thinnest which can be worked to advantage—would be 7,200 years. If the aggregate thickness of all the seams of coal in any basin amounts to sixty feet, the time required for its accumulation would be 144,000 years.[1]

A long time truly for our coal to form, and a vastly longer period until its energies came to be utilized by man. The late Professor Huxley wrote on this aspect of the question :—

"Nature is never in a hurry, and seems to have had always before her eyes the adage, 'Keep a thing long enough, and you will find a use for it.' She has kept her beds of coal many millions of years without being able to find much use for them ; she has sent them down beneath the sea, and the sea-beasts could

1 Winchell's Geological Sketches.

make nothing of them; she has raised them up into dry land, and laid the black veins bare, and still, for ages and ages, there was no living thing on the face of the earth that could see any sort of value in them; and it was only the other day, so to speak, that she turned a new creature out of her workshop, who by degrees acquired sufficient wits to make a fire, and then to discover that the black rock would burn."

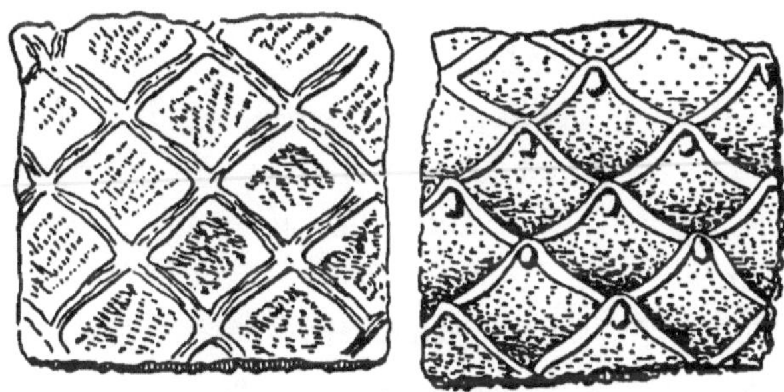

FIG. 53.—*Lepidodendron.*[1] Portion of a fossil plant found in Devonian and Carboniferous Rocks.

The sea played its part, too, in the building up of the Permo-Carboniferous system. If the stratified rocks associated with the coal were deposited for the most part in fresh water, that was not invariably the case. Now and again the sea made inroads on the low country, and brought a rich fauna of sea shells, that remain to prove to us the reality of the change from fresh water to marine conditions. Turning to Fig. 44,

1 Quart. Jour. Geol. Soc., Vol. xxviii., Plate xxvi.

we see that there are two *marine formations* in the Permo-Carboniferous—the Upper and the Lower Marine. The fossils shown on pages 195, 197 and 203, are illustrations of some of these marine forms. They prove conclusively that sediments two thousand feet in thickness were deposited on a subsiding sea-floor. Subsidence still continued, but the succeeding beds of the Greta coal measures were laid down in fresh water. Once again the sea covered these last, and in this sea the Upper Marine series slowly grew. Fossil collectors can, with very little trouble, procure abundance of the marine fossils that characterise the Upper Marine. The best collecting grounds are enumerated in Chapter XIII. The most notable specimens will be *Spirifers,* and the beautiful lace-like films of *Protoretopora* that sometimes encrust them.

The *Spirifers* are often represented by moulds of the interior of the shell, formed by sand or clay which filled them, while the substance of the shell itself has disappeared. There are no *Spirifers* living now. In some periods of the Palæozoic age the sea-floor must have been actually paved with them. They are called *Spirifers,* or spire-bearers, because a part of their processes, somewhat resembling watch-springs, was coiled up within the shell. These were used to support the thread-like organs covered with cilia.

To form anything like an adequate idea of the life that flourished in the Permo-Carboniferous seas, we have only to glance at the fragments preserved in our museums. Corals, crinoids and star-fishes were abundant. Shells strewed the old beaches in apparently endless profusion. *Nautilus* and *Orthoceras* floated their multi-chambered shells on the surface of the sea, and crustaceans and trilobites shoaled amongst the rocks. Fishes existed also, although up to the present very few of their remains have been found in Australia.

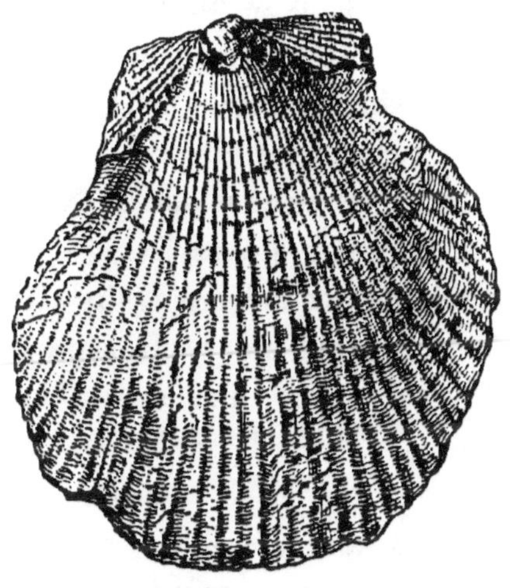

FIG. 54.—*Aviculopecten limaeformis*,[1] Morris. An Upper Palæozoic Fossil found at Norfolk Plains (Tas.), Gympie (Q.), and Wollongong (N.S. Wales).

It must not be forgotten, though, that the many thousand feet of stratified rocks deposited to form the Permo-Carboniferous had to be carried by running water from elsewhere. If we look around, we can see the quarries where the material used to build our city was excavated. Every cubic yard of masonry means a cubic yard less at the quarry. There were hills all

1 Strzelecki's New South Wales and Van Diemen's Land, Plate xiii., Fig. 1.

around the great Permo-Carboniferous depression,—at one time a morass clothed in verdure and again a sea swarming with marine life. It was from these hills that the swollen rivers brought down the sediments.

"There was once a splendid city in Egypt, known as Memphis. A learned Arab of the Middle Ages has told us of its glories. Now all is gone save pyramids and sphinx. But it lives again in another place; its stones once more shelter human beings; for out of its ruins the modern city of Cairo has been built. This use of old building material is one of Nature's devices too. Like the Memphis stones living again with the Arabs, our Palæozoic rocks lived again with new forms of life. This is the old story oft repeated in earth-history. Silurian grits and slates are probably Archæan granites, etc., built up in new ways. From these again some of the Carboniferous and Devonian rocks were derived; and again, the rocks we are about to consider must have been in part derived from Carboniferous and Old Red Sandstone rocks exposed to atmospheric decay. Thus we read the same cycle of change over and over again. The lofty Alpine peak which seems so immovable and indestructible must as surely be borne down to the sea where it was formed as the rain-clouds of heaven must find their way back to earth and sea from whence they came."[1]

"The hills are shadows, and they flow
From form to form, and nothing stands;
They melt like mists, the solid lands,
Like clouds they shape themselves and go."

1 Hutchinson. "The Autobiography of the Earth."

But there was a factor in the building up of Permo-Carboniferous rocks that we have not yet counted upon—volcanoes. Volcanic action contributed a great deal to the sum total of the series we are dealing with. Early in the period, as pointed out by Professor David, there is evidence of active volcanoes. At Seven Hills, near Raymond Terrace, volcanic tuffs are interstratified with coal-seams. This shows that while coal plants were growing in the lagoons showers of volcanic ash settled down and formed thick beds. Lavas flowed down and filled up the depression more than once. Altogether, beds of tuff and lavas fully 1000 feet in thickness were formed in this way.

Later—how long we cannot measure in years—volcanic fires showed themselves at and around Kiama. Towards the close of the Permo-Carboniferous, andesitic lavas were poured out, and vast amounts of volcanic tuffs were deposited. As already stated, these tuffs supplied the building stones, in later times, for the chocolate and purple shales. Three distinct sheets of lava, and a bed of red tuff, still remain to testify to the mighty energies of this old centre of volcanic fires. "The volcano which poured out the lavas and tuffs near Kiama," remarks Professor David, "was probably in its first stages sub-marine, and made its appearance in the shallow Permo-Carboniferous ocean, about thirty miles from the shore line, to the south-west.

SUMMARY OF PERMO-CARBONIFEROUS.

Shortly, then, we can say that the earliest conditions of the Permo-Carboniferous were marine. Near the old shore-line, to the north, an extensive volcano poured out sheets of lava, and darkened the air with volcanic ash. The main coast-line was far out to the east. Gradually marine forms of life disappeared, and fresh or brackish water took the place of the sea. The land continued to subside. Many thousands of feet of coal measures were formed in a vast morass, covered with vegetation, it is true, but monotonous as the Great Dismal Swamp of Carolina. The sea once more made inroads. The land was, however, still subsiding, and the vast beds of vegetation were buried beneath marine clays and sands.

The Upper Marine Series tells us of a sea with fish, swarming with crinoids, crustaceans, and shells. Off the land below Kiama, strange disturbances are in progress. The waters are now and again lifted into billows, and tidal waves sweep the shores. The noise of escaping gases and steam begins to be heard. The wild confusion of the hitherto placid sea tells of heated lavas and the waters of the deep contending for the mastery. At last, the internal fires assert their supremacy, and soon volcanic cones stand above the waves. Clouds of vapour hang low in the air. Electrical discharges produce thunders hardly louder than the roar from the craters below. Lavas are poured out in fiery streams, and tuffs and ash deposits accumulate. But the day comes when the fires are cooled, and now the ejected volcanic material forms a new and fertile soil for a fresh growth of vegetation, which goes to form the coal of the coal measures resting on the Kiama

FIG. 55.—The Three Sisters, Katoomba, showing the effect of subaerial waste.

lavas. Thus the sea has again receded and given place to fresh water. No marine fossils have ever been found in the great thickness of sediments known as the Upper Coal Measures.

North, as far as where Newcastle stands, west to Mt. Lambie and Rylstone, and south to Nowra, there stretches one unbroken and marsh-like plain. *Phyllotheca, Glossopteris* and other ferns, cover the surface in the wildest luxuriance. Our last look into those far-off times shows us the great Permo-Carboniferous morass still subsiding. A richer growth, if anything, clothes its wide expanse. Sluggish and swollen rivers wind their way through the monotonous level, and disappear in the tangled undergrowths, there depositing their loads of sediment to form yet one more layer on the thousands already laid down. Such were the physical features of the country around Sydney at the close of the Permo-Carboniferous period.

"One of the charms of the study of geology is that, while it deals with the plainest matters of fact, it continually calls up to the imagination pictures of past events, of which the general truth is certain, while all the details are left to fancy. That the limestones of the Carboniferous period were formed beneath the waves of a widespread sea is as certain a fact as that they now form the lofty cliffs, at the foot of which the geologist pauses to examine them. The fossils they contain are the remains of animals that once lived and sported in those waves. The shales and sandstones were derived from the waste of the lands on which the ferns and other plants grew; and those plants themselves, now compacted into the rock we call coal, were green with life and toying with the winds. The simple truth is like a fairy tale, the transformation like that in a pantomime; yet, it is a literal fact, while the time that has elapsed during its working out leaves far behind the wildest dreams of the romancer or the poet."[1]

COAL UNDER SYDNEY.

Recent events point to coal and coal supply as the real arbiter of the fate of nations. It is not without interest to us, therefore, that the diamond drill bores put down on the north shore of the harbour proved the extension of the Newcastle coal seams under this city at a depth of about three thousand feet. The completion of these bores by the Government was, from a scientific standpoint, of great value. Economically considered, the results are not so satisfactory. Even if this coal should not, as is most probable, be available in our day, yet its existence adds immensely to our resources, and remains a great national asset for future generations. The generally accepted view of geologists was, for years past, that coal did exist below Sydney. The bores referred to, put down under the direction of Mr. Pittman, Government Geologist, and Mr. Slee, the Chief Inspector of Mines, took the matter from the region of opinion. A vast coal-bearing series under Sydney is now a proven fact.

[1] Jukes. "A School Manual of Geology."

CHAPTER IX.

DEVONIAN.

ORIGIN OF THE NAME—MOUNT LAMBIE—OCCURRENCE OF DEVONIAN—LIFE OF THE PERIOD.

EARLY in the history of geology it was noticed that below the coal-bearing strata of England reddish sandstones occurred. Above the coal measures another red sandstone was known. The lower and older rock received the name OLD RED SANDSTONE, while to the rock above, and newer than the coal beds, the name NEW RED SANDSTONE was given. The Old Red Sandstone, therefore, lies between the Silurian and Carboniferous. In Devonshire a series of limestones and shales are extensively developed between Silurian and Carboniferous formations. These from their position were, it was evident, of the same age as the Old Red Sandstones, and were henceforth known as Devonian.

On the Blue Mountains, rocks newer than Silurian and older than Carboniferous have been recognised at Mount Lambie. Some of these beds can be seen to advantage in a cutting on the railway just beyond Rydal, and can be studied from this point to the summit of Mount Lambie.

West of Mount Victoria, Devonian rocks occur on either side of the Cox River, about two miles south of Hartley. They are intruded by diorites, and are bounded on the north and south by granites, and to the east by the Upper Marine beds of the Permo-Carboniferous.

Devonian Sandstones occur also near Cowra, on the slopes of the Canoblas near Orange, over a large tract of country from Wittagoona to Wilcannia, and

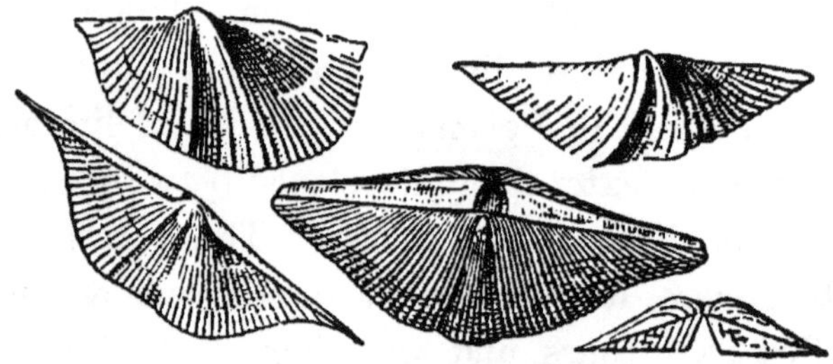

FIG. 56.—*Spirifera disjuncta.*[1] A Devonian fossil found at Mount Lambie. The figures show various forms of this Spirifer.

west of the Darling. It is highly probable that some of these separated areas were once continuous, and that we have now but a few scattered remnants of a once wide-spread formation.

Land plants and marine shells occur in our Devonian rocks. *Lepidodendron* (Fig. 53) has been found associated with the brachiopods *Spirifer disjuncta* and *Rhynchonella pleurodon* (see figures 56 and 57). These last-named fossils are very plentiful

1. Lapperent; Traité de Géologie, p. 707, fig. 227; *b. c. d. e.* Phillips' Fossils of Cornwall, plate xxix.

in some of the sandstones and quartzites, particularly in Ferntree Gully, under Mount Lambie, and in some

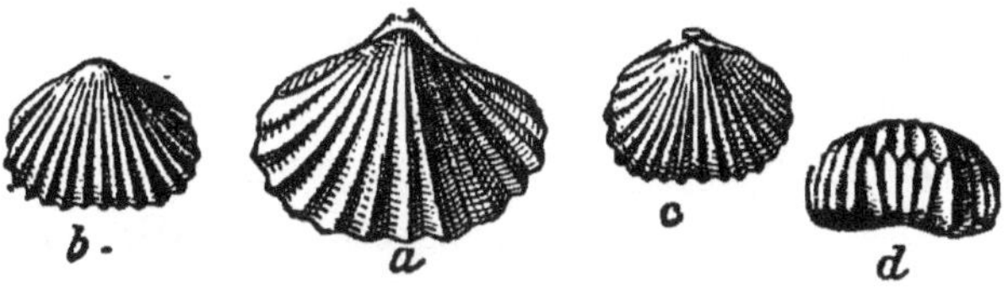

FIG. 57.—*Rhynchonella pleurodon*,[1] Phillips, A Devonian fossil from Mount Lambie.

creeks near Rydal. They can also be noted in water-worn boulders in the Winburndale Creek and other creeks of that neighbourhood.

Our knowledge of the life that flourished during the deposition of Devonian rocks in Australia is not

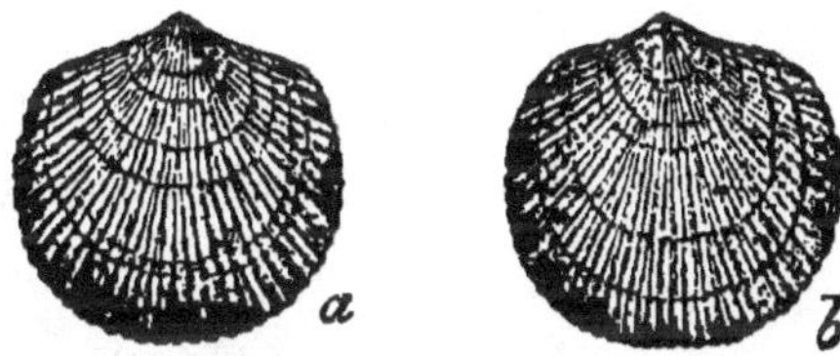

FIG. 58.—*Atrypa reticularis.* A brachiopod common in Australian Silurian and Devonian rocks. *a*, dorsal valve; *b*, ventral valve.

extensive. It is known that corals and marine shells were plentiful. The fact that *Lepidodendron* is found closely associated with *Spirifer disjuncta* and *Rhynchonella pleurodon* shows that these spirifers lived on a coastal area, and near the dry land on which the

1 Phillips' Geology of Yorkshire. Part ii, plate xii; *b. c. d.* De Koninck: Atlas of New South Wales, Palæozoic Fossils, plate ix.

giant lycopod *Lepidodendron* flourished. The last-named plant is one of the oldest representatives of the vegetable kingdom known in Australia. There was dry land, no doubt, in Silurian times, but no trace has yet been discovered of the vegetation with which it was clothed. The oldest land surfaces of which we have evidence in Australia, appeared as dry land in Devonian times.

FIG. 59.—*Murchisonia turris*,[1] de Koninck. A lower Palæozoic fossil shell from near Yass (N.S.W.)

The great thickness of the Devonian sediments is remarkable. At Mount Lambie, near Rydal, on the western line, Mr. Wilkinson measured a section not less than 10,000 feet in thickness. It is evident, therefore, that the area over which such an accumulation of sediments was deposited must have been subsiding for a very long period.

Our present knowledge hardly justifies any attempt to picture the physical geography of Devonian times. As no traces of Devonian beds are found on the eastern slopes of the Blue Mountains, we may assume that the old Devonian sea stretched

1 De Koninck: Atlas of New South Wales Palæozoic Fossils. Plate iv.

from Rydal to beyond the Canoblas, while another expanse of the same waters spread from Cobar, across by Wilcannia, to and beyond the White Cliffs opal field. The sandstones about Eden and Twofold Bay are of a similar age, and, as shown by Mr. Carne, of the Geological Survey, were laid down under marine conditions, *Rhynchonella pleurodon* (Fig. 57) being found at Bellbird Creek, three miles north of Eden.[1]

Devonian rocks of fresh-water origin have also been described by Mr. Carne. They occupy a considerable area in the Nungatta and Yambulla Ranges, towards the head of the Genoa River, and contain the interesting ferns *Archæopteris Howitti* and *Sphenopteris Carnei*, as well as the gymnosperm *Cordaites Australis*. The Devonian rocks on the Blue Mountains are, however, for the most part marine, but not of deep-sea origin. In fact, the abundance of conglomerates and rounded pebbles points unmistakably to shore deposits. The Devonian beds have been invaded, tilted, and altered by intrusions of granite and felsites, some of these last representing what are probably the oldest volcanic flows of New South Wales. The Devonian sediments, hardened and altered to quartzites, have, since their deposition, participated in many great earth movements. They are now often several thousand feet above sea-level, and tilted for the most part from their original horizontal position. They have not, however, been folded and compressed as intensely as the underlying Silurian Slates.

---

1 J. E. Carne, Ann. Rep. Dept. Mines, N.S.W., 1897, p. 163.

CHAPTER X.

SILURIAN.

SILURIAN SLATES TILTED FROM ORIGINAL POSITION—IN CONTRAST WITH PERMO-CARBONIFEROUS — TRUE SLATES AND FLAGSTONES—ORIGIN OF THE SILURIAN—LIMESTONE—SOME LIMESTONES OLD CORAL REEFS—CAVES — CAVE-SHELTERS—LIMESTONE CAVES — STALACTITES—STALAGMITES—THE JENOLAN CAVES.

ONE of the first characters of the Silurian rocks that will be noted is the fact that their stratification layers are, as a rule, highly inclined, making the strata appear to stand on end. This character is fairly persistent over the Silurian areas of the colony; so much so, that we come to look for vertical strata as particularly distinctive of Silurian Slates. It may be remarked, however, that in other countries—notably in parts of North America and Russia—Silurian rocks are very little disturbed, and often rest in their original horizontal position. The nearest locality to Sydney where rocks of Silurian age may be studied is the country around the Jenolan Caves. In the cuttings on the road down Cave Hill, on the way to the caves from Mount Victoria, slates can be seen highly inclined as shown in Fig. 62. This contrasts strongly with the horizontal bedding of the Hawkesbury Sandstone and the Permo-Carboniferous, as seen in Figs. 71 and 23. The angle of inclination which a tilted bed of rock makes with the horizon, is called the *angle of dip*. On page 242 limestone is shown dipping to the west. The illustration herewith pictures some books standing on edge, just as Silurian rocks are often seen to stand. In this instance the rocks or books dip in the opposite direction, and the edges showing on the surface are called "outcrops." The Silurian rocks now standing on edge were once spread out horizontally, layer above

FIG. 60—Illustration showing the meaning of dip, strike and outcrop.

layer. Earth movements on a vast scale folded and compressed them. Denudation, at some subsequent period, removed the upper arches of the folds, and left highly inclined strata so familiar to us. In a small way this has been illustrated experimentally by Sir James Hall. Fig. 61 is a reproduction of his drawing. A number of coloured cloths are laid one above the other, to represent different stratified rocks; a weight is placed above them, and then the whole series is compressed laterally. The layers are thrown into folds, and, as the pressure increases, the folds become more acute. There is ample proof that the Silurian rocks were compressed and folded in a somewhat similar manner. The upper folds were planed off by denuding agencies, leaving the series of inclined rocks shown in the illustration.

The highly inclined and fine-grained Silurian rocks are usually referred to as Silurian "Slates." In one sense the term is not correct, as no true slates are found in this colony. All our Silurian sedimentary

FIG. 61.—Illustration showing how horizontal layers of rock are, by lateral compression, bent in folds.

rocks *split* along the bedding planes. True slates, such as the Bangor roofing slate, *cleave* into thin slabs, but in a direction independent of the bedding planes. Slaty cleavage is induced in rocks by intense pressure. In Fig. 64 we have a series of rocks gently folded at one end of the section and highly inclined at the other end. A slaty cleavage, denoted by fine lines, is developed in the whole series. But it will be noted that, whereas the cleavage and the bedding lines almost coincide towards the right hand of the section, at the other end the cleavage lines are at right angles to the bedding planes. It will thus be seen how the cleavage characteristic of true slate is often quite independent of the planes of stratification or bedding; but cleavage planes may also coincide with the bedding plane. On the Blue Mountains no true cleaved slates are known, the slaty character of the Silurian rocks being due to the original planes of stratification. When the bedding-planes are close, and the bedding well marked, they are known as flagstones.

ORIGIN OF THE SILURIAN SLATES.

The evidence at present available points to the fact of these rocks having been laid down in the waters of a sea. All the forms of Silurian life known as fossils are Marine. We have shells, corals, trilobites, and crinoids, in fine-grained sediments, telling of an open sea far away from shore deposits. The Silurian is notable for its beds of limestone, made up almost entirely of the remains of corals, crinoids, and shells.

LIMESTONE.

Limestone is a general term for all rocks the basis of which is carbonate of lime or calcium carbonate. As this chapter may be read by the beginner, or by visitors to our Caves who may have no special knowledge of geology, it is desirable to explain clearly some every-day terms.

Calcium is ... ... a metal and one of the elements.

Calcium carbonate, a compound forming the greater bulk of all limestones. White crystalline limestone is almost pure calcium carbonate, more commonly called carbonate of lime.

Calcium oxide is ... "quick-lime," and is made by burning limestone.

Calcium hydrate is "slaked lime," and is made by pouring water on "quick-lime."

Shells and Coral ... consist almost entirely of carbonate of lime.

When "lime" is spoken of in every-day language, Calcium oxide of the chemist is referred to.

Limestone is one of the few soluble rocks forming considerable rock masses. The simplest test for limestone is treatment with a few drops of hydrochloric acid, a brisk effervescence telling at once if a rock is limestone or markedly calcareous. Strictly speaking, the test only shows that a soluble carbonate is present. But as limestone is the only commonly occurring rock that is a carbonate, the test is satisfactory. This simple test is made use of even by skilled geologists, as limestone varies much in appearance—pure snow-white and every shade through grey and brown to dead black being known. Some limestones are also brightly coloured. In texture, also, there is a great diversity, many limestones being fine-grained and dull, others being coarsely crystalline. Marble is only a variety of limestone, and usually any limestone hard enough to take a polish is called marble. It may be

Fig. 62.—Highly inclined Silurian Slates, road cutting, Cave Hill, Jenolan Caves.

noted here that many dark-blue limestones, such as those that can be seen at the Jenolan Caves, polish to a rich velvet black. Looked at from their origin, these rocks are equally varied. Some limestones are chemically formed. Most limestones are, however, of organic origin—that is, the materials of which they are made up were separated from the sea-waters by the help of organised living animals.

If we look closely at many samples of limestone, we cannot fail to find traces of shells, corals, crinoids, or other animals. Varieties of this rock are not uncommon, consisting almost entirely of broken shells or the stems of crinoids. A coral reef is a mass of limestone now in course of formation. The coral polyps separate carbonate of lime from the sea, to form the stony frame-work we call coral. The waves break up large quantities into masses; these are tossed together, and the interstices are filled up with finer particles. Nullipores and other plant-like organisms bind the whole together. The Great Barrier Reef is a mass of limestone more than one thousand miles long, formed in this way. The long lines of limestone we find interbedded in Silurian rocks are often nothing more than old coral reefs. The corals are certainly not the species that form reefs to-day, but, in origin, there is no essential difference. Our Australian coral limestones give evidence of a shallow water origin. We have, however, a group of limestones that were undoubtedly formed under conditions that may be termed oceanic. The chalk of Europe is usually taken as a type of oceanic deposit. In the same class must be placed the nummulitic limestone, which spreads through Europe, Asia, and Africa, and the fusulina limestone which extends from Russia to

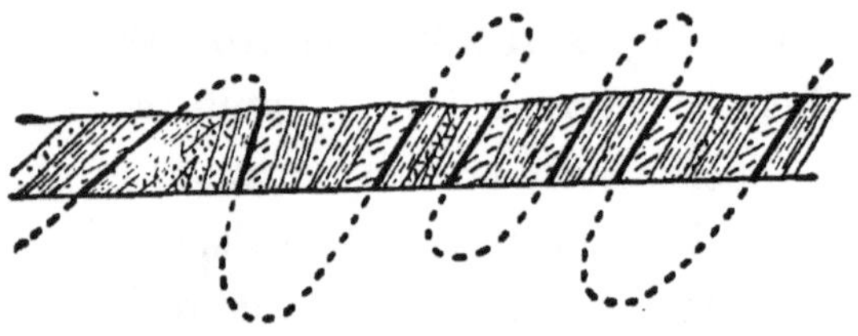

FIG. 63.—Silurian Slates, showing how the same beds are repeated in a section, by folding. The broken lines above show the country removed by denudation.

Japan. It may be stated here that an oceanic limestone is not necessarily deposited in very deep water; the only essential condition seems to be that the rock should accumulate in a region beyond the influence of

FIG. 64.—Figure showing slaty cleavage crossing, and also coinciding with the planes of bedding.

the sediments which are brought down from the land. A shell-bed cemented into stone is another example of an organically formed rock. It will be seen, on turning to page 72, that rocks of aqueous origin are divided

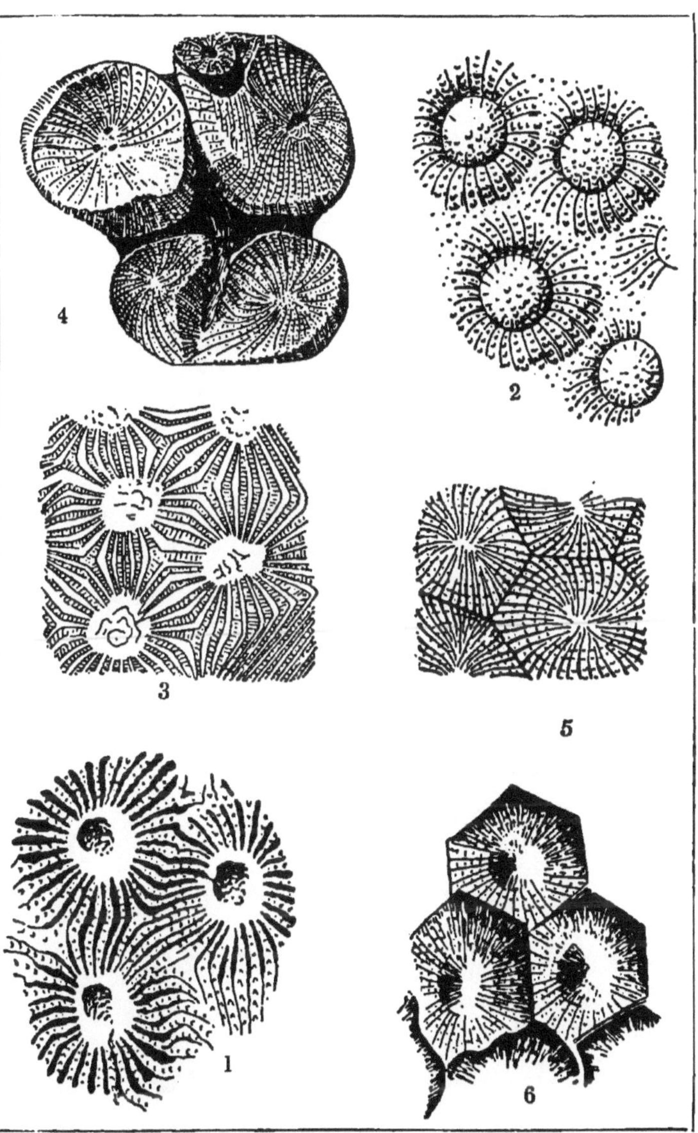

FIG. 65.—SILURIAN CORALS.[1]

1. *Phillipsastræa Currani*, Eth. fil. Limekilns, Bathurst; part of a polished slab. 2. Weathered Surface of same Coral. 3. Microscopic slice of same Coral. 4. *Heliophyllum Yassense*. Eth. fil. A Silurian Coral, Yass, (N.S.W.) 5. and 6. *Cyathophyllum Mitchelli*, Eth. fil. Silurio-Devonian rocks, Cave Flat (N.S.W.)

1. Rec. Geol. Survey, N. S. Wales, Vol. ii, p. 170, 174.

K

into three classes, accordingly as they are—(1) organically, (2) chemically, or (3) mechanically formed. In a certain sense our Silurian limestones belong to all three divisions. They are of *organic* origin inasmuch as every particle at one time or other belonged to a living organism—shell, coral, or crinoid. Much of the carbonate of lime in compact limestones has been chemically precipitated there, and some of the original carbonate has been dissolved out. In this sense limestones are partly of chemical origin. In the building up of coral reefs, their origin is partly *mechanical*, the action of the waves breaking coral from the outer edge of the reef, heaping up the fragments, and filling up the interstices with broken material.

In looking for fossils in ancient limestones, it is well to note that the corals and shells are best seen on weathered or on polished surfaces. It will be observed, too, that many limestones seem devoid of fossils over considerable areas, particularly where the limestone has been altered to a crystalline structure. Carbonate of lime is such a soluble material that limestone rocks may become completely altered in course of ages, merely by percolating waters dissolving and re-precipitating it.

A little observation will not fail to make one note that some limestones are for the most part made up of shells. In this instance the material making the stone once formed an outer covering or defensive shell for living creatures that were inhabitants of the ocean.

But it must not be thought that because shells make up the rock, *all* limestones were therefore formed in the sea. There are also fresh-water limestones, but the character of the shells always settles whether we are dealing with a fresh-water or a marine limestone.

A second class—and this includes our cave limestones—shows, together with fossil shells, the calcareous framework of corals. Now, all corals are marine, and therefore these limestones are of marine origin. Enormous areas in tropical seas are now covered with growing coral, each polyp separating carbonate of lime from the ocean waters. Some belts of Silurian limestone, near Molong, must have resembled these modern coral-reefs, for they are made up almost entirely of masses of the beautiful chain coral known to science as *Halysites Australis.*[1]

A third class of limestones is composed almost exclusively of the remains of crinoids. Many vast beds of limestone are nothing more than masses of the broken stems of these strange and beautiful creatures. Encrinites are also known by the name of sea-lilies or crinoids, from the Greek word *krinon*, meaning a lily. A few of these creatures survive to the present time, but they abounded in forest-like masses in Silurian days. They were known in mediæval times as St. Cuthbert's beads, and are referred to in "Marmion"—

"On a rock by Lindisfarne,
St. Cuthbert sits, and toils to frame
The sea-born beads which bear his name."

1 Etheridge. "Records of the Australian Museum." (See Fig. 70.)

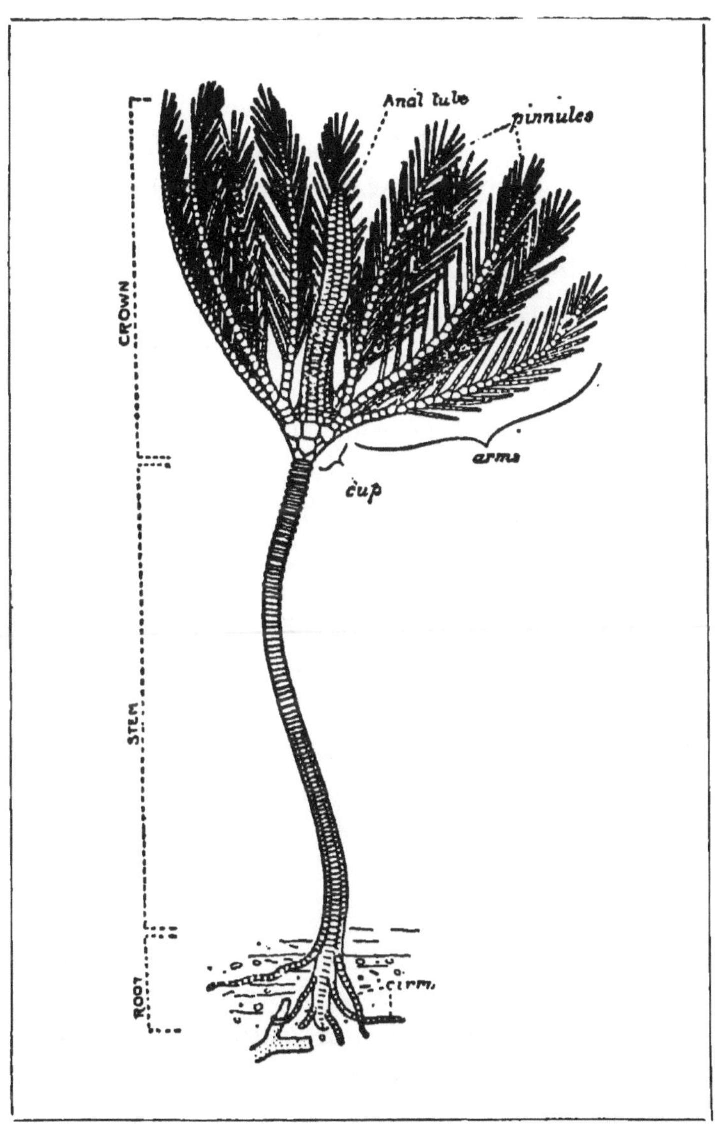

FIG. 66.—Structure of a Crinoid. (After Bather.)

Many extinct crinoids had stems from fifty to seventy feet long, and Buckland calculated that some of them had 150,000 little bones and 300,000 contractile bundles of fibres to move them. The crinoids culminated in Mesozoic times, and then practically died out without giving origin to anything higher.

Turning now to Australian limestones, we can note the types referred to, but it often happens that crinoids, corals, and shells are all preserved on the one slab. But, as the crinoids, as well as the corals, are exclusively marine animals, the marine origin of the limestone is evident.

CAVES IN GENERAL.

Caves are found in almost all kinds of rock. They are more common in limestone and basaltic rocks than others. In the basalts, caves are formed either by violent igneous action, or the flowing away of molten masses, leaving an arch of consolidated or hardened material standing around. Caves are also formed in volcanic rocks, through the removal of softer portions of the mass by denudation or erosion. The well-known Blow-hole at Kiama is an example of this last—a dyke of softer material being carved into by the sea, while the main mass of basalt offers more resistance to the action of the waves.

It may be well to explain here, that the "caves" in the sandstones on the Blue Mountains should be more properly termed rock-shelters. They consist, for the most part, of an overhanging ledge under which the rock crumbled away to a considerable depth. Although the aboriginals made use of these rock-shelters, they could in no sense be called cave-dwellers. We cannot speak of the Australian aboriginal as we do of the ancient Briton in referring to cave-dwellers. Nothing has been found in our cave-shelters to throw much light on the primitive inhabitants of Australia.

We are, however, concerned here with limestone caves; and, in passing, it may be well to say that even in these man has left no geological history. The Australian blackfellow never lived in caves—his aim presumably, in the past, as it is most certainly in the present, being to get away from underground caves as far and as expeditiously as possible. The present writer can vouch for the fact, that a blackfellow develops an astonishing activity and quite unexpected resources in avoiding even the neighbourhood of underground caves.

LIMESTONE CAVES.

Caves and underground caverns open up to the lover of novelty a new world, and they are at the same time hardly less full of interest to the man of science. The natural beauty and ornamentation of limestone caves must have been a fertile source of wonder from the earliest times. There is enough of the weird and uncanny in their dim recesses to have powerfully impressed primitive man. Then, again, legend and story peopled these underground mansions with elfin dwellers, and so added something of awe to the fascination that is ever linked with the mysterious and the unknown.

From a geological standpoint the origin and formation of limestone caves becomes intelligible when we recall the fact that limestone is the most soluble of rocks, and is readily acted on by percolating waters. We note that the sea excavates caverns in sandstones along our coast. This is the result of mechanical action. The force of the waves *tears* masses of loosened rock away, and hurls back the fragments, so as to *grind* and *pound* the cliffs. The action of water on limestone is quite different. Surface waters *dissolve* limestones. The effect is chemical and corrosive, rather than mechanical and erosive. Rivers erode channels in slate rocks, and carry away the eroded materials in suspension. The mud and sand that discolour the waters of a swollen river are merely the ground-up rocks being swept along in suspension. Limestone, on the other hand, is dissolved, and the rivers of the world carry vast quantities of carbonate of lime in invisible loads to the sea. Of course, limestone rocks are eroded and torn away as well, but the hollowing out of caves is due mainly to the dissolving of the limestones. Rivers will carve out a valley or a gorge in the hardest rocks. The finest examples of river action are the famous cañons of Colorado, with, in some places, almost vertical sides three and four thousand feet deep. The valleys on the Blue Mountains are in their own way not less remarkable, as the result of erosion by running water. But in these cases the valley is carved out by mechanical erosion, the stones and sand cutting away the bed of the river,

FIG. 67.—Corals on the Great Barrier Reef of Australia.

or undermining the sides as they are hurried along In the case of the caves, the water chemically dissolves the rock, the removal of which forms the underground passages.

It may be well to state here that pure water is not an active agent in dissolving limestones, but water charged with carbonic acid gas[1] has a powerful effect on these rocks. Now, it will be asked,—Where does the water procure the supply of carbonic acid that renders it so potent a solvent for solid rocks? The reply is: Mostly from the air. But, to make the matter clear, it should be stated that carbonic acid, or (what amounts to the same thing) carbon dioxide is produced—

(1.) By the breathing of all animals; man exhales about one pound of carbon dioxide per day. The production of carbon dioxide in breathing is commonly proved in this way: Some quicklime is shaken up with water, and the clear solution poured off. This is known as lime-water. If the breath is now made to bubble through, by blowing gently through a glass tube or a straw, the clear solution becomes milky, from the formation of carbonate of lime. The carbon is provided from the carbon dioxide exhaled by the lungs. If a saucer of lime-water is left standing, a scum of carbonate of lime soon forms, owing to the presence of carbon dioxide in the air.

(2.) In burning coal, the carbon of the fuel is converted into carbon dioxide, every ton of coal burned producing quite two tons of the gas.

(3.) In all processes of animal and vegetable decay the carbon of the organic matter is oxidised to carbon dioxide.

1 Strictly speaking, carbonic acid is not a correct name for this gas. Acids always contain hydrogen, which this gas does not. Carbon dioxide is a more correct term. Carbon dioxide, however, when dissolved in water, reddens litmus, thus showing one of the special characters of acids.

(4.) Carbon dioxide is given off abundantly in volcanic regions.

There is, therefore, no lack of carbon dioxide, and hence it is that most natural waters contain carbonic acid. All rivers and springs, therefore, that pass through or over limestone rocks, contain carbonate of lime in solution.

"The most clear and sparkling waters often contain a quantity of dissolved limestone, just as the sea contains a quantity of dissolved salts and other matters, and both may be made, by evaporation, to deposit their contents in a solid form. Water trickling through the roofs of limestone caverns, and partially evaporated as it falls, deposits the previously dissolved limestone it contained in the form of stalactites and stalagmites; and brooks and rivers, when broken into spray, in like manner deposit masses of limestone called Travertine or Tiburstone. Encrustations are made in this way, both naturally and artificially, and the substance deposited is precisely the same as that of statuary marble, and is often just as crystalline, and will take as high a polish."[1]

With regard to stalactites, which so quickly arrest attention in limestone caves, Dr. Mantell, in his *Wonders of Geology*, graphically describes the origin and the picturesque appearance of these singular masses of rock :—" One of the most common appearances in limestone caverns is the formation of

1 Jukes. "School Manual of Geology," p. 69.

what are called stalactites, from a Greek word signifying distillation or dropping. Whenever water filters through a limestone rock it dissolves a portion of it; and on reaching any opening such as a cavern, oozes from the sides or roof, and forms a drop, the moisture of which is soon evaporated by the air, and a small circular plate or ring of calcareous matter remains; another drop succeeds in the same place, and adds, from the same cause, a fresh coat of incrustation. In time, these successive additions produce a long, irregular, conical projection from the roof, which is generally hollow, and is continually being increased by the fresh accession of water loaded with calcareous or chalky matter; this is deposited on the outside of the stalactite already formed, and trickling down adds to its length, by subsiding to the point and evaporating as before; precisely in the same manner as, during frosty weather, icicles are formed on the edges of the eaves of a roof. When the supply of water holding lime in solution is too rapid to allow of its evaporation at the bottom of the stalactite, it drops on the floor of the cave, and, drying up, gradually forms, in like manner, a projection rising upwards from the ground, instead of hanging from the roof; this is called, for the sake of distinction, a stalagmite.

"It frequently happens, where these processes are uninterrupted, that a stalactite hanging from the roof, and a stalagmite formed immediately under it, from the superabundant water, increase until they unite, and thus constitute a natural pillar, apparently supporting the roof of the grotto. It is to grotesque forms assumed by stalactites, and these natural columns, that caverns owe the interesting appearances described in such glowing terms by those who witness them for the first time.

"The Grotto of Antiparos, in the Grecian Archipelago, not far from Paros, has long been celebrated. The sides and roof of its principal cavity are covered with immense incrustations of calcareous spar, which form either stalactites depending from above, or irregular pillars rising from the floor. Several perfect columns reaching to the ceiling have been formed, and others are still in progress, by the union of the stalactite from above with the stalagmite below. These, being composed of matter slowly deposited, have assumed the most fantastic shapes; while the pure, white, and glittering spar beautifully catches and reflects the light of the torches of the visitors to this subterranean palace, in a manner which causes all astonishment to cease at the romantic tales told of the place—of its caves of diamonds and of its ruby walls; the simple truth, when deprived of all exaggeration, being sufficient to excite admiration and awe.

"Sometimes a linear fissure in the roof, by the direction it gives to the dropping of the lapidifying water, forms a perfectly transparent curtain or partition. A remarkable instance of this kind occurs in a cavern, in North America, called Wyer's Cave. This cave is situated in a ridge of limestone hills running parallel to the Blue Mountains. A narrow and rugged fissure leads to a large cavern, where the most grotesque figures, formed by the percolation of water through beds of limestone, present themselves; while the eye, glancing onwards, watches the dim and distant glimmers of the lights of the guides—some in the recess below, and others in the galleries above. Passing from these recesses, the passage conducts to a flight of steps that lead into a large cavern of irregular form and of great beauty. Its dimensions are about thirty feet by fifty. Here the incrustation hangs just like a sheet of water that was frozen as it fell; there it rises into a beautiful stalagmitic pillar, and yonder composes an elevated seat, surrounded by sparry pinnacles. Beyond this room is another, more irregular, but more beautiful, for, besides having sparry ornaments in common with the others, the roof overhead is of the most admirable and singular formation. It is entirely covered with stalactites, which are suspended from it like inverted pinnacles, and they are of the finest material, and most beautifully shaped and embossed. In another department an immense sheet of transparent stalagmite, which extends from the floor to the roof, emits, when struck, deep and mellow sounds, like those of a muffled drum.

" Farther on is another vaulted chamber, which is one hundred feet long, thirty-six wide, and twenty-six high. Its walls are filled with grotesque concretions. The effect of the lights placed by the guides at various elevations, and leaving hidden more than they reveal, is extremely fine. At the extremity of another range of apartments, a magnificent hall two hundred and fifty feet long, and thirty-three feet high, suddenly appears. Here is a splendid sheet of rock-work running up the centre of the room, and giving it the aspect of two separate and noble galleries. This partition rises twenty feet above the floor, and leaves the fine span of the arched roof untouched. There is here a beautiful concretion, which has the form and drapery of a gigantic statue, and the whole place is filled with stalagmitical masses of the most varied and grotesque character. The fine perspective of this room, four times the length of an ordinary church, and the amazing vaulted roof spreading overhead, without any support of pillar or column, produce a most striking effect. In another apartment, which has an altitude of fifty feet, there is at one end an elevated recess ornamented with a group of pendent stalactites of unusual size and singular beauty. They are as large as the pipes of a full-sized organ, and range with great regularity. When struck, they emit mellow sounds in various keys, not unlike the tones of musical glasses. The length of this extraordinary group of caverns is not less than one thousand six hundred feet."

JENOLAN CAVES.

Many of the features described by Dr. Mantell are well shown in the Jenolan Caves. We have the vaulted chambers and noble galleries filled with stalactites most varied and grotesque. We have caverns of great beauty, ornamented in a fashion to command

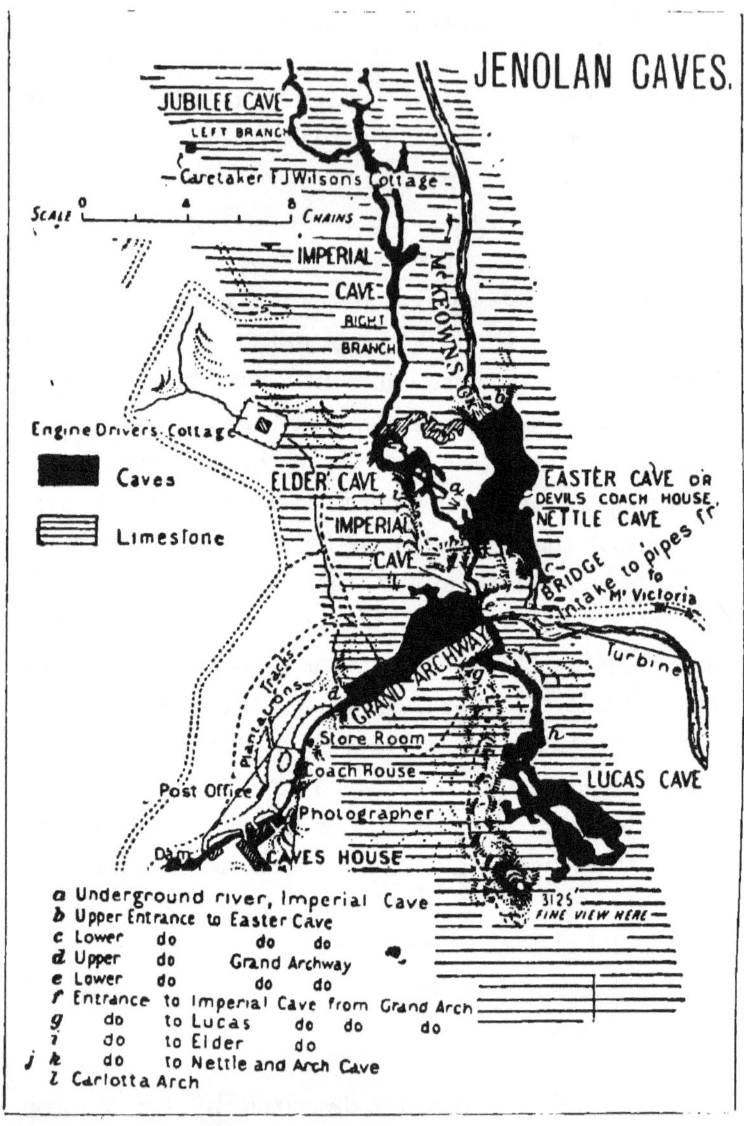

Fig. 68.—Plan of Jenolan Caves, based on the survey of Mr. O. Trickett.

the admiration of every visitor. Just as fancy may prompt the observer, he finds in the handiwork of Nature's own devising the form of a Gothic cathedral, or a Grecian temple with its forest of noble columns. Here and there a suggestion of groined arches in various groupings calls up visions of a fairy palace, some new and startling effects meeting one at every turn. And then the almost magic effect of light and shade lends an enchantment to those subterranean palaces that we may look for in vain elsewhere. Geologically, the existence of the caves depends on the fact that a bar of limestone runs almost directly across a deeply eroded valley—water, the giant sculptor of mountains, having found it easier to make itself a passage by dissolving the limestones, rather than by eroding them to the valley level. Apart from the actual features visible in the caves, a geological student will find much to interest him, not merely around the caves, but all the way from Mount Victoria.

Leaving Mount Victoria (on Hawkesbury Sandstone), the road drops down in a few miles through the Narrabeen Shales and the higher beds of the Permo-Carboniferous, and through the Upper Marine beds, down to the granite at Hartley. Some interesting dykes cut through the granites hereabouts. Many varieties of granite are plentiful on the Cox River close by, red, grey, and blue-black granite being common. Graphic granite, felsite, and diorite are also abundant. Amongst the sedimentary rocks, chert, conglomerate, grit, sandstone, mudstone, clay shale, kerosene shale, and coal, can be noted in the Permo-Carboniferous. Garnet-rock, limestone, and numerous varieties of limonite and hæmatite can be noted in a few square miles of country on the Cox River, a few miles to the south of Hartley. An interesting dark and fine-grained plagioclase rock, in the shape of a dyke, will be found in a creek at the back of the

FIG. 69.—View (looking south) showing a series of bedded Silurian limestones dipping to the west. Molong, New South Wales.

Royal Hotel, Hartley. The dark colour of the dyke makes it noticeable beside the light-coloured granite.

On the hill, just beyond Louther Public School, specimens of a very fine diorite can be collected. When sliced for the microscope, this makes a magnificent rock-section in polarised light. Not far beyond the Half-way House belonging to the Grand Hotel, a few quarries have been opened, near two small churches.

These quarries are in an outlier of Upper Marine Sandstone. It will be noted that the sandstone in the quarries contains water-worn boulders of granite, quartz, and metamorphosed slates. The occurrence of granite boulders is especially interesting, as they prove that the granite is older than the Upper Marine; and evidence is available elsewhere that the same granites are newer than Silurian, and, perhaps, even Devonian rocks. It is for this reason we are able to say that these granites are newer than Silurian and older than the Upper Marine beds of the Permo-Carboniferous.

A few miles beyond the Half-way House referred to, the road follows a cutting around the head of a deep valley. Granite is exposed here, showing concentric and spheroidal weathering, with a distinct disposition to develop a sheeted structure.

Fifteen and a-half miles from the Cox River we leave the granite, and in various places along the road quantities of water-worn pebbles and boulders will be noted. At first sight these would seem to be derived from some vast river deposit. On a closer examination, however, it will be seen that these boulders are all that are left of extensive sheets of Upper Marine Sandstones and conglomerates removed from this region by denudation. In other words, these boulders owe their rounded character to the action of the sea in far-away Permo-Carboniferous times. They were, through long geological ages, embedded in a sandstone matrix which settled round them on the old sea-shore. They were buried beneath many thousands of feet of

Permo-Carboniferous and Triassic sediments, and are now strewn on the surface as silent witnesses of the amount of denudation and wear and tear that this country has suffered.

At various points on the road, walls of sandstone may be seen away in the distance, across the valleys, every wall or cliff showing a slope or talus at its base.

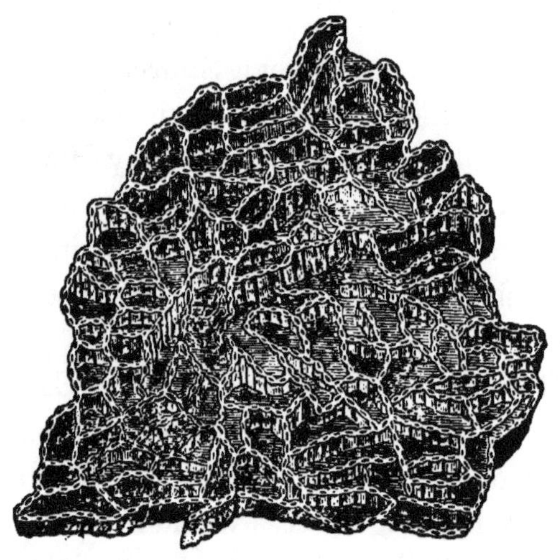

FIG. 70.—*Halysites*, a characteristic Silurian fossil coral, known as "chain coral." Abundant in limestone near Molong, New South Wales.

On the top of Cave Hill we find diorites and porphyries intruding the Silurian sediments. Many examples of these intrusions will be found in the long cutting down to the Caves. Almost vertical slates can also be noted, dipping now in one direction, now in another. A careful examination will show masses of slate floated bodily upwards by the intrusion of quartz and felspar porphyry. The slate rocks will also be seen folded, the core of one anticline being easily noticed near the Grand Archway.

When at the Caves the geological student would do well to observe :—

(1.) A mass of intrusive augite-porphyrite in a cutting made for the erection of the dining-room at Cave House. This interesting rock is altered much in places, through the absorption of overlying rocks while still in a liquid condition. With a little care, specimens may be found showing crystals of augite in a quasi-felsitic base or paste.

(2.) About Inchman's Creek, two-and-a-half miles from Cave House, towards Mount Victoria, fossil corals and crinoids can be found in a matrix that in hand specimens can hardly be distinguished from an igneous rock. This may be taken as a proof that sedimentary rocks, and even limestones, may have been absorbed by the underlying igneous rocks as they worked their way upwards into the solid crust. On the other hand, of course, these sediments may have been depressed into the liquid magma. A more probable view is that while the corals were growing they were buried in a layer of coarse volcanic sand, which rained down into the clear sea-water. Whatever the explanation is, we find casts of marine fossils, such as corals in a matrix which has many of the characters of an igneous rock.

(3.) Fossil corals may be detected in the limestones on

McKeown's Creek, but they do not stand out as we see them oftentimes in limestones. They show merely a dull white outline on the very dark surface of the rock. By following the bed of any stream that enters McKeown's Creek, on one's left going up stream, black radiolarian cherts will be found. It is hardly necessary to say that the radiolaria or radiolarian casts can only be detected on slicing the rock for the microscope. Generally, the radiolarian cherts occur to the west of Cave House.

(4.) White marble limestone can be found about a mile-and-a-half down the Cave River.

(5.) Basalt of Tertiary age is found covering hilltops more than two thousand feet above the Caves. The excavation of all the great valleys around was certainly subsequent to the eruption of this basalt.

It has already been stated that folded and vertical strata may be noted in the cuttings coming down Cave Hill. One fold can be seen on the Cave Hill side of the Grand Archway. This, it will be noticed, is faulted. The second can be observed between here and Inchman's Creek, and portions of another fold are exposed about three-quarters of a mile on the Cave side at Pheasant's Nest Creek.

The belt of limestone in which the Caves occur measures about three hundred yards across, and runs in a general north and south direction, striking a little to the west. Standing on any one of the higher points of the ridge, the limestone can be distinguished even at a distance, as it contrasts markedly with the surrounding Silurian slates. The

Fig. 71.—Hawkesbury Sandstone exposed on the coast to the north of Manly.

whole country is scored and cut into by running water, the rugged hills and precipitous valleys giving rise to some really notable scenery; but in its every aspect the carving of the hills, and in fact the scenery itself, depends upon the geological formations. While one gazes into these ravines and chasms, showing Nature in her wildest moods, it detracts nothing from the beauties and impressiveness of the landscape to look below the surface, and understand the causes that have given birth to those mountains that rise and fall like billows away into the distance. A little thought, and we are back to the far-off time when the grey limestones around were masses of living coral. It is no small triumph for the science of our day to help us to look again into the early days of the earth, and to observe in those ancient sunlit seas the stone-lilies, corals and shells treasuring within them the sole and only forms of life the world knew of. But the fact of life being there, even in its lowliest forms, adds an interest that will ever make these silent rock teachings appeal to the human mind.

Writing on these limestones, the late Mr. Charles Wilkinson, Government Geologist, remarks:—

"And here it is perhaps not out of place to trace some steps in the course of Time that are forcibly presented to us. What a circle in the laws of nature is suggested by this scene! First, the decaying vegetation of some ancient forest is invisibly distilling the gas known as carbonic acid; then a storm of rain falls, clearing the air of the noxious gas, and distributing a thousand streamlets of acid water over the surrounding country, and which, as it drains off, not only wears the rocks it passes over, but dissolves them in minute quantities, especially such as contain much lime, and then, laden with its various compounds, flows off to the distant sea, where reef corals, lying in fringing banks round the coast, are slowly absorbing the lime from the water around them, and building the fragile coatings that protect them during life. Slowly as the land sinks, the coral bank increases in height, for reef corals can only live near the surface of the water; and soon a considerable thickness has been obtained; while below the upper zone of live corals lies a vast charnel-house of dead coral skeletons; then comes a change: suitable temperature, or some other essential condition, fails, killing out all the corals, and through long ages other deposits accumulate over them, gradually crushing and consolidating the coral bank into a firm rock. At last a convulsion of the earth's crust brings it up from the buried depth in which it lies, leaving it tilted on its edge, but still, perhaps, below the surface of the ground; rain, frost, and snow slowly remove what covers it, until it lies exposed again to the sunlight, but so changed that only for the silent but irresistible testimony of the fossil forms of which it is composed, it were hard to believe that this narrow band of hard grey rock was once the huge but fragile coral bank glistening in the bright waters with a thousand hues. And now the process is repeated; the decaying vegetation of the surrounding forest produces the carbonic acid, the rains spread it over the ground, which is now the most favourable for being dissolved, and the consequence is that the acid water saturates itself with the limestone rock, and, whenever the least evaporation takes place, has to deposit some of its dissolved carbonate of lime in one of the many stalactitic forms, before it can flow off to the sea and distribute its remaining contents to fresh coral banks.

"Thus the old coral reef melts away far inland, and the lime that formed the framework of its corals is again utilized for the same purpose. What a simple succession of causes and effects! And yet, before the circle is completed long ages of time have come and gone; and what a fine example of the balance between the waste and reproduction that takes place in nature![1]

1 C. S Wilkinson, "The Jenolan Caves." An article contributed to a Railway Guide of New South Wales. Sydney Government Printer, 1886.

CHAPTER XI.

BASALT, GRANITE AND DIORITE.

IGNEOUS ROCKS—CLASSIFICATION OF IGNEOUS ROCKS—BASALT—BASALTIC DYKES OF SYDNEY—PRISMATIC SANDSTONES—DECOMPOSITION OF BASALT—BASALT AT BONDI—EXAMINATION OF THE BONDI BASALT: MACROSCOPIC, MICROSCOPIC AND CHEMICAL—GRANITE—LA MALADIE DU GRANITE—DIORITE.

IT is abundantly clear to the reader by this time that the Igneous or fire-formed rocks stand in marked contrast to the Aqueous or water-formed rocks. We are no longer dealing with lonely fens, swamps, and marshes, or the peaceful depths of ocean waters. Instead of the splashing of rivulets or the brushing of uncouth reptiles through the tangled undergrowths of ancient valleys, we have the roar and thunder of the volcano. We must picture the hills lighted up with weird fires, and with streams of glowing lava pouring over their smirched shoulders and rolling down to the lowlands. The evidence is complete that basalt is an Igneous rock, and that such basalt-capped hills as Mount Hay and Mount Tomah, and the Bald Hills at Bathurst, are remnants of vast lava streams which flowed from the craters of some long-extinct volcanoes. The dykes intersecting the Hawkesbury Sandstone in so many directions are no less certainly rocks of Igneous origin.

For convenience in their study, Igneous rocks must be classified. Geologists are not, however, agreed as to the best system of classification, although all are agreed on the characters which distinguish them. Igneous rocks are known—

1. By occurring in irregular masses, penetrating stratified rocks, and by sending off tongues and dykes into the sedimentary rocks around them.
2. By their showing characters not unlike furnace slags.
3. By their vesicular structure.
4. By their completely crystalline or partly crystalline structure.
5. By their being identical with rocks now flowing from volcanic vents.
6. By their altering the rocks they are in contact with. Sandstones, for instance, are altered to quartzite, and coal to a natural coke.

Igneous rocks may be grouped according to—

(*a*) Structure.
(*b*) Chemical composition.
(*c*) Origin.

In *structure*, an Igneous rock may be:—Holocrystalline, such as Granite (see Fig. 10); partly crystalline, such as Basalt (see Fig. 6); or glassy, such as Rhyolite.

FIG. 72.—Granite Rocks near Tarana, N. S. Wales, showing the weathering of Granite into boulders of disintegration.[1]

According to *chemical composition*, Igneous rocks are grouped into three classes, depending on the per-

1 Travelling from Sydney by rail, these rocks may be seen from the train, to the left of the railway line, a few miles beyond Tarana.

centage of silica they contain—Acid, Intermediate, and Basic. Ultra-basic rocks are sometimes placed in a separate class.

CLASSIFICATION OF ERUPTIVE ROCKS,

According to their Origin and Composition.

ACIDIC ROCKS,

65 to 80 per cent. of Silica.

Volcanic.	Plutonic.
OBSIDIAN	GRANITE
RHYOLITE	

INTERMEDIATE ROCKS,

55 to 65 per cent. of Silica.

Volcanic.	Plutonic.
TRACHYTE	SYENITE
ANDESITE	DIORITE (mostly)

BASIC ROCKS,

45 to 55 per cent. of Silica.

Volcanic.	Plutonic.
BASALT	DIORITES (some)
DOLERITE	GABBRO
TACHYLITE	

According to *origin*, Igneous rocks are termed *Plutonic* if they consolidated at great depths and under great pressure, in those regions assigned by mythology to Pluto. On the contrary, fire-formed rocks which cooled at or near the surface are known as *Volcanic*. Both Volcanic and Plutonic rocks may be conveniently designated *Eruptive*. It will thus be seen that it is not always necessary to determine exactly whether a rock is Plutonic or Volcanic, some of the more important lessons that may be learned from its history being at once apparent if we can get so far as to conclude that the rock is Eruptive in character.

All the Igneous or Eruptive rocks near Sydney are basalts, and occur in the shape of dykes, or, in a few instances, in the shape of bosses. According to our Table, therefore, they are Basic rocks of Volcanic origin. It may thus be asked: Did our basalts actually flow from a volcano? The basaltic lavas that we are more accustomed to hear about are those that flowed in liquid or often as merely plastic streams from a volcanic vent. The basalts on Mount Hay and Mount Tomah, and also the basalts about Bathurst and Orange, answer exactly this description. The dyke-like walls of basalt that cut through the sandstones and shales about Sydney probably never reached the surface.[1] The liquid magma was forced up from below, and cooled and hardened just where we find it. Although these rocks did not actually flow over the surface of the earth, they correspond to the general characters of rocks that cooled from a molten condition at or near the surface. For the most part, our Sydney basalts occur in the shape of dykes. In most instances the original blue-black basalt is altered, by decomposition, into a soapy cream-coloured clay not

1 Evidence is not wanting that may support an opposite view.

in any way resembling the original rock. It must be always somewhat difficult to convince a beginner that this plastic clay is produced by the decomposition of basalt.

But, a little patience will settle that point. As a matter of fact we can find basalt in every intermediate stage, from the fresh blue-black rock to the pasty clay referred to. We can go farther, and say that even if the clay had disappeared it might still be taken for granted that an Igneous rock once filled the fissures. This, we would conclude, from the fact that the basalt has left its mark, so to speak, on the sandstones, by altering them to a harder rock. In many places around Sydney it is noted that the sandstones are harder than usual, and show a rudely prismatic structure. Stone of this class is much sought after for road-making. Whenever such a hardened sandstone is found it is promptly quarried, and, in the process of excavating, the cause of this hardening is usually discovered, in the shape of a dyke of Igneous rock whose contact altered and hardened the sandstones.

True, as already pointed out, this dyke is often altered almost beyond recognition; the hard rock that once filled the fissures, in a liquid and molten condition, having now succumbed to the inexorable law of change. It will thus be seen why it is that baked and hardened sandstones are accepted as the work, direct or indirect, of intruded basalt. This is quite in keeping with all observed facts. It is also noted that when sandstones are used for the bottoms of furnaces they become hardened, and develop a prismatic structure. A fine example of prismatic sandstone could at one time be seen at a quarry near the outlet of the main sewer, Bondi (Fig. 32). This has long since been quarried away, but some columnar sandstone and masses of basalt can still be seen in the cliffs, although much of the last-named rock is altered to the soapy clay already referred to.

There is another locality where the basalt is to this day hard and undecomposed. This is the Moorefields dyke, Canterbury (Fig. 15). Here we see one of the few basaltic dykes around Sydney in which at some depth the rock is still well preserved, showing very little signs of decomposition. It is mined for road purposes by sinking shafts, at various points, to a depth of 60 to 100 feet, connecting these shafts by drives, and breaking down the rock pretty much in the same way that a quartz reef is worked. The basalt is 10 to 15 feet in width. This interesting example is well worth a visit when stone is being quarried. When work is not being carried on, the shafts are usually full of water.

At Rookwood, just south of the Rookwood-Park, a dyke is worked for road metal, and where the workings are deepest some undecomposed basalt is still procurable. The dyke is, in places, 10 feet in width, with smooth walls of shale on each side. It runs in an easterly and westerly direction. As may be seen by the list given below, unaltered basalt is not at all plentiful, the dykes being usually changed to a soft clay. Thus it is that we value every evidence of the former presence of the fiery masses that intruded the sandstones and shales from unknown depths. Prismatic and hardened sandstones are accepted as almost conclusive evidence of the proximity of basalt, and, in making a record of the occurrence of basalt, we find it almost of equal value to make a record of the presence of prismatised and altered sandstones.

Intrusive masses, mostly in the shape of dykes, of *undecomposed basalt* are known around Sydney at—

1. Prospect Reservoir.
2. Pennant Hills quarry.
3. Dyke running east and west at Rookwood.
4. Moorefields dyke, Canterbury, running in a north-easterly and south-westerly direction.
5. Basaltic dyke at Peakhurst, probably a continuation of the Moorefields dyke.
6. Dyke at Bondi, on the coast, running north and south.
7. Dyke at Long Reef, between Narrabeen and Manly, probably a continuation of the Bondi dyke.
8. Dyke at the head of the small bay between Long Bay and Maroubra Bay.
9. On Humphrey's property, Burwood, a basaltic dyke was quarried some years ago.
10. In a brick-pit, St. Peters.

Good examples of dykes of *decomposed basalt* are known to occur—

1. Near Beecroft Railway Station, crossing the line
2. Crossing the railway line at Petersham.
3. Crossing the line at Belmore Railway Station.

FIG. 73.—Columnar Sandstone, Bondi.

4. At Saunders' quarries, Pyrmont, running east and west.
5. In the quarry at Five Dock tram terminus.
6. In a quarry near Kensington.
7. Cutting through the Greenwich peninsula.
8. At Bondi. (See Map).
9. Small dykes at Long Bay and Maroubra Bay, running into the sea.

10. At Blakehurst, near Hurstville.
11. Near Cremorne, North Shore.
12. At a point, on a tributary of the Lane Cove River, about three miles from Pymble.
13. A decomposed dyke was exposed (while some excavations were being made by the Water and Sewerage authorities) in Riley-street, south side of Albion-street, Surry Hills. The dyke was parallel to the north wall of house No. 292.
14. Another dyke was exposed at the corner of Waterloo and Cooper Streets, Sydney.
15. At the end of the old Rifle Range, Moore Park—dyke runs east and west.[1]

Hardened and prismatic sandstones are known—

1. At Blakehurst, near Hurstville.
2. At La Perouse, in a quarry close to the main road.
3. At Pyrmont, near Saunders' quarries.
4. At Five Dock, in the quarry worked for road-making.
5. On the cliffs, a little to the south of Manly Beach.
6. At Bondi, associated with basalt.
7. About two miles south of Turramurra.
8. In a quarry on the road from Hunter's Hill to Ryde, near the first-named locality.

An illustration showing the relation of hardened and prismatised sandstone to igneous intrusions was

1. See page 339.

afforded at Blakehurst, where a quarry was opened in hardened sandstone, without any visible trace of the Igneous rock. In the course of working the quarry, as was expected, the dyke was found, but altered to a condition seen in the Bondi fissures. Another instance is the occurrence of incipient columnar structure in the sandstone on the North Head, south of Manly. No Igneous rocks are at present known as being exposed here; but it may be noted that the place is right in a line between Bondi and Long Reef, so it is more than probable that the Igneous rock is not far away, and may yet be found in this neighbourhood.

The basalt quarry at Pennant Hills has been described by Mr. C. S. Wilkinson. He states:—"It is an immense excavation, from which road metal is said to have been taken for over fifty years. The rock consists of a dense but jointed basalt, containing small fragments of other rocks, and some huge masses of coaly shale, from which it would appear that this spot is the site of an ancient volcanic point of eruption." Most geologists agree with this view; but it was left to Professor David and his assistants to note the interesting fact that there is chromite and a chrome-bearing mineral associated with the basalt.[1]

Still more interesting is the great mass of intrusive rock at Prospect. The country rock is Hawkesbury Sandstone and shales. "Penetrating these formations are dykes and masses of Igneous rock,

1 In the opinion of the present writer, the chromite occurs in erupted blocks of a much altered serpentine, or a closely related ultra-basic rock.

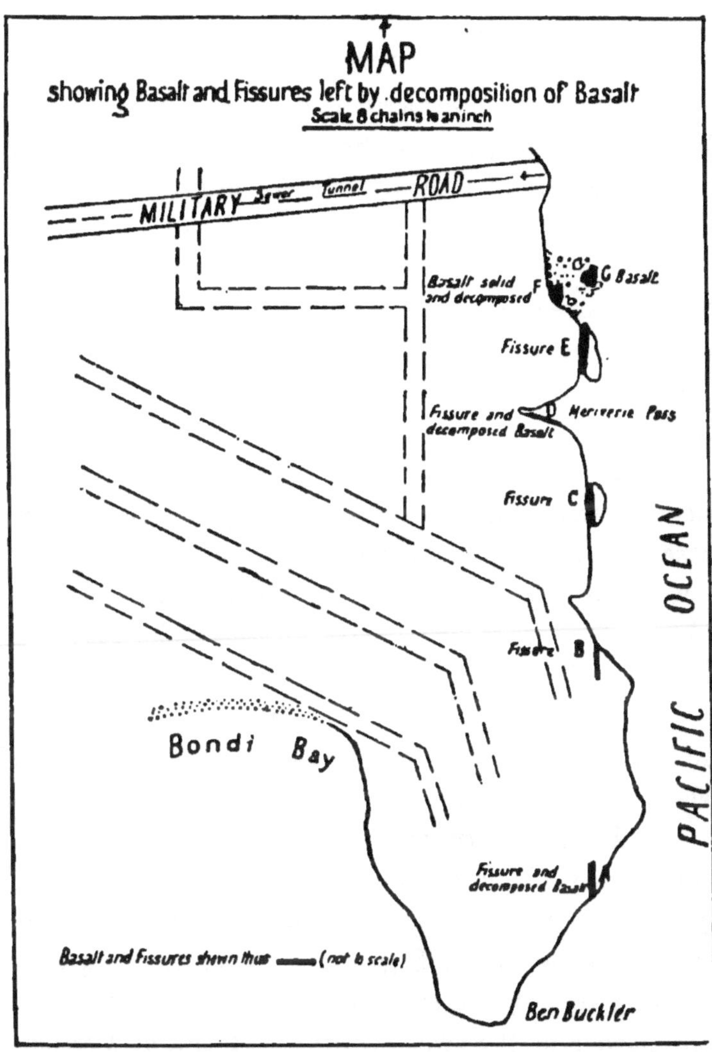

FIG. 74.—Map showing fissures left by the decomposition of previously existing igneous dykes, Bondi.

varying from a dense basalt to a coarse-grained hornblendic greenstone. At Prospect these rocks form a conspicuous and irregularly-shaped hill, which attains an elevation of 430 feet above sea level. From its summit, near Graystanes (the residence of Mr. Wentworth), a very commanding view is obtained of the surrounding country, embracing the City of Sydney, Parramatta, Liverpool, Campbelltown, and the Blue Mountains."

"On the south side of this hill a large quarry has been opened, immediately adjoining the site of the reservoir for the Sydney water supply. This quarry has been abandoned, as road-metal can now be obtained nearer to Parramatta, but the rock on it being less jointed and more uniform in texture than that in any of the other quarries in the district could be hewn in large blocks, and would be suitable for making into slabs for paving-stones."

"For this purpose samples of the stone should be obtained, for I am of opinion that as regards cost of production and durability it might successfully compete with the basalt flag-stones imported from Melbourne, though the stone from Prospect is somewhat the harder of the two. On the west side of Prospect Hill, on the Lawson Estate, and also on the north side of the hill, in a small Reserve, some dense basalt is being quarried yielding good road-metal; it occurs in unlimited quantity."—(Wilkinson.)

At the head of an indentation on the coast, between Long Bay and Maroubra Bay, a dyke enters the sea.

Here the sandstones have been altered into the most perfect examples of quartzite that are known about Sydney. The aboriginals were aware of the nature of this stone, and used it to make skinning-knives. This quartzite is, in places, stained by iron oxides to a rich chocolate brown, and on first sight resembles the iron-stained quartz of some auriferous quartz reefs. Even miners have been misled by this similarity, and worked here for some time sinking and driving. Their efforts were not rewarded with any success. In working they came on to the hard and undecomposed basalt. A considerable quantity of this interesting rock is, at the time of writing, strewn about the old shaft, but will soon disappear before the demands of museums and private collectors.

Between this point and the north head of Maroubra Bay seven dykes may be found, varying in thickness from one to five feet, all running east and west. The rocky headlands to the north and south of Maroubra are thus notable for the number of igneous dykes that intrude the sandstones.

In Gentle's quarry, at St. Peters, a dyke now represented by decomposed basalt can be examined. This dyke is faulted, in two places, by horizontal thrust planes.

When Mr. Wilkinson first drew attention to these basaltic intrusions, the public seemed generally much interested, and to dispel any possible fears he wrote: "Happily these disruptive agencies have ages ago ceased. So that the residents of Petersham, whose houses may happen to be built over these old volcanic vents, need not allow their midnight rest to be disturbed by misgivings as to the security of their peaceful dwellings."

Some years ago basalt used to be quarried on Humphrey's property at Burwood. Fine undecomposed basalt was found, and worked to a depth of one hundred feet, evidently from a dyke, probably a continuation of the Rookwood basalt.

In order to study the intimate structure of basalt, a thin section must be prepared, and mounted upon a glass slip, with Canada balsam. The preparation of these slices is a matter altogether of patience and practice; but it is not nearly so difficult as it first appears. The simplest way to prepare this thin slice is as follows:—

1. Select a sound undecomposed portion of rock; flake off, with a hammer, a chip about the size of a half-penny, and grind down one surface, with emery and water, on an iron plate; these plates are conveniently about 12 x 12 inches. Towards the close of this portion of the operation the emery will have been ground into a very fine paste, so that the face on the rock will be fine and smooth. Should coarse emery remain, the rock will not have that smoothed surface required, and in this case it will be better to finish this part of the operation with some very fine flour-emery and water on a square plate of glass.

FIG. 75.—Hawkesbury Sandstone, showing current bedding, exposed in cliffs to the north of Manly.

2. Finish the surface produced by rubbing on a water-of-ayr honestone.

3. Some Canada balsam is now spread out in a thin layer on a glass plate, and heated or "cooked" until it is of such a consistency that when cold it is sufficiently hard to retain an indentation made by the finger-nail, but yet not so hard as to be brittle. The exact degree can be learned only by experience. When a wooden match is dipped into the balsam and brought away it will carry a thread of balsam after it. If this thread, on cooling, becomes brittle the operation has proceeded far enough. A slip of ordinary double thick window glass (about 2 x 2 inches) is now taken and heated on an iron plate. This iron plate must be supported in table fashion, so that a small lamp may be placed underneath.

4. Take some of the cooked balsam on the glass slip, and, having heated the rock sufficiently to expel all moisture, it is then pressed firmly into the balsam, in such a way as to exclude all air bubbles. The glass slip, with the rock cemented, smooth side down, is now removed and allowed to cool. Grinding operations are now resumed, on the other side of the rock, the square of glass serving as a handle, and, at the same time, acting as a support for the stone when ground down to a film. As the grinding proceeds, the stone will become more transparent as it becomes thinner and thinner, until at last, when pressed on a printed sheet, the print may be read through the stone. Towards the

end of the process it will be necessary to use only flour emery, and to exercise considerable care, as a few extra rubs may destroy the whole preparation.

7. Any superfluous balsam scattered on the slide can be removed by a hot knife, and finally by washing in alcohol. Thus completed, the slide is labelled, and forms the "thin section" of the petrologist.

5. When sufficiently thin, the film must be remounted on an ordinary microscope slide. These slides are usually 3 x 1 inches or 2 x 1 inches. While still on the thick glass on which it was ground, the rock slice must be washed with a brush (a tooth-brush will answer) to get rid of all emery particles. It is next washed in alcohol, to remove any balsam, into which grains of emery may have been forced.

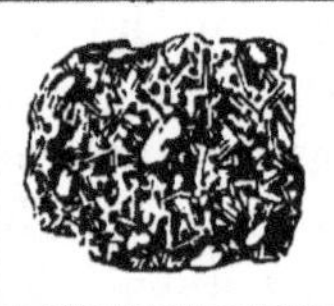

FIG. 76.—A Rock Slice prepared and mounted for the microscope.

6. A clean mounting slip is now laid on the warm iron plate, and a drop of fresh balsam placed in the centre. The thick glass, with its film of stone adhering, is also heated; a drop of old balsam is placed on the rock slice, and a thin cover glass gently laid upon it. The thin cover acts now as a support for the rock slice, and when sufficiently warmed the thin cover and rock slice may be pushed gently from the thick glass on to the new slide. While the balsam is still warm and fluid, the cover glass and thin slice may be moved about to the exact centre of the slide, or placed in any desired position, and then allowed to cool.

There is a distinct advantage in a student preparing his own rock slices. For example, in grinding a slice of basalt from the Bald Hills, Bathurst, long before the slice is thin enough for microscopic exami-

FIG. 77.—Remarkable Weathering of Sandstones, Maroubra Bay, near Sydney.

nation the felspars will have become transparent, showing the beautiful streaming or flow structure so characteristic in this rock. The felspars are seen to have been caught as they floated in the molten magma. In flowing along, the groups part on meeting with an obstruction, meeting again beyond, giving rise to an appearance that may be compared to "logs in a mill-stream, the olivines representing small islands."

In like manner, when a slice of Bondi basalt is prepared in this way, the olivine crystals show the character of the rock before the slide becomes generally transparent.

At Bondi, as shown on the map (Fig. 74), we have fissures left by the decomposition of previously existing dykes, masses of decomposed basalt, and some of the unaltered basalt *in situ*. The main fissure runs north and south, in the direction of the dyke at Long Reef, some ten miles further north. This is at present a line of weakness, and no doubt has been one of the factors in determining the present coast-line.

The Bondi basalt occurs as part of a dyke intrusive in the Hawkesbury Sandstone, on the coast to the east of the city of Sydney. As a land-mark, the ventilating shaft of the Bondi main sewer is easily found. Close by is a quarry of columnar sandstone. From the floor of this quarry a winding path leads down to the base of the cliffs and to sea level. To the right of this path, some fifty feet from the top, undecomposed basalt may be found. Part of the path is cut through the same basalt, decomposed and altered to a grey, soft, and, when wet, pasty rock. A few chains south, a deep and narrow fissure can be seen cutting a mass of sandstone away from the mainland. There is no doubt but that this and similar fissures in the neighbourhood are left by the decomposition of previously existing dykes of basalt.

A second fissure is noted (marked D on map), running in a north-westerly direction, and still retaining some decomposed basalt *in situ*. Further south is a third fissure (C on the map attached). Fig. 13 is a photograph of this fissure, taken from a point at sea level, which may be reached through the Meriveri Pass. The photograph shows basalt filling the lower part of the fissure, but now soft and decomposed. Still further south there are two other fissures—five in all—that unmistakably show they were once filled with basalt. These are shown as A and B on the sketch map. The former retains portions of the decomposed basalt, as an unctuous or soapy-grey and yellowish mass, with amygdules of decomposition products. At this point some very bright green colours seen in the decomposed rock were proved to be due to traces of chromium, which chemical analysis shows the rock to contain.

At the date of writing, undecomposed basalt could be found in two places only in the vicinity of these dykes and fissures—the projecting knob of basalt already referred to, on the path down the cliff, and on a point of rock standing above the sea in calm weather, a few chains from the mainland, and marked G on the sketch map. The small amount of undecomposed basalt remaining is noteworthy, as continued operations at the quarry may hide the little that there is completely from view. But even should the last traces of the basalt proper be lost, the fissures, the decomposed rock filling them in part, and the prismatic sandstone will point unmistakably to the proximity of masses of basalt.

The Bondi basalt dykes have, it is evident, been one of the factors in the shaping of the present coast-line. In my opinion there are two separate intrusions, but not necessarily of different ages. The fissures at A, B, C, and E (see sketch map) are all belonging to a dyke which cut through the sandstones in a northerly and southerly direction. Besides the dyke running north and south, there exists a dyke, as described above by the Rev. W. B. Clarke, coming from the direction of Greenwich, and of which the basalt at D and G may be branches.

The most notable feature of the locality is the columnar sandstone, as shown in Fig. 32. This structure was, no doubt, induced by the proximity of the Igneous rock. Some of the sandstones that were in contact with the molten basalt show very little trace of metamorphism, while in other parts the same sandstones are rendered quartzose in texture and prismatic in structure. No very clear relation can now be made out between the more extreme examples of metamorphism, and any special massing of the Igneous rock. But denudation has so affected the locality that, at this date, it is practically impossible to say whether the basalt may not have almost surrounded the masses that show the columnar structure so perfectly.

It may prove of interest to indicate here some of the lines along which a student may investigate the characters of this basalt.

FIG. 78.—Igneous Dyke cutting up through stratified Permo-carboniferous rocks, Nobbys, Newcastle.

MACROSCOPIC EXAMINATION.

In hand specimens, the Bondi rock is a blue-black dense rock that rings under the hammer. The texture is compact, and, to the unaided eye, a fine glistening structure is the only indication of its varied constituents. A hand-lens will show an occasional porphyritic mineral not more than half a millimetre long. On slicing the rock these prove to be olivines or augites. It decomposes to a light grey crust as seen in the specimens exhibited. This, by the further removal of its more soluble constituents, becomes the soapy stiff rock, in appearance not unlike Fuller's earth, that fills the fissures already referred to. The light grey colour of this decomposed crust is somewhat remarkable, as the rock contains 13% of ferrous and ferric oxide—quite as high a percentage as many basalts that weather to a bright red clay. A polished slab of the rock is etched with more than ordinary rapidity by hydrochloric acid. The polished slab is almost black. When acted on by the acid it shows a light grey ground, with the unattacked minerals standing out as black granules. Its specific gravity is 2·94, a density somewhat above typical basalt.

MAGNETIC PROPERTIES.

The appearance of the etched surface suggested trying the effect of a magnet on the rock. A thin bar of the basalt, five millimetres long, was cut, and I found that a magnet lifted the bar readily. A second bar was cut and mounted as a magnetic needle. Permanent polarity was induced in this by placing it between the poles of an electro-magnet, with the result that the needle of rock became sensitive to opposite poles of a magnet. It is too heavy to respond to the directive influence of the earth's magnetism, but on subjecting the whole apparatus to a gentle vibratory motion, the bar will set north and south.

CHEMICAL COMPOSITION.

The peculiar colour of the weathered basalt immediately around the fresh rock suggested the determination of its solubility in acids; ·5 gram of finely-powdered basalt was digested in dilute hydrochloric acid for two and a half hours, then it was heated with strong acid for one and a half hours, with the result that ·218 gram remained insoluble. This gives 56·4% of the rock as soluble in hydrochloric acid.

A fresh portion of the powder was ground to the finest possible condition in an agate mortar, moistened with water, and just covered with strong hydrochloric acid, in a small watch glass. In six hours the whole mass had gelatinised rigidly at the ordinary temperature of the laboratory, 65—70 F. The mass was just covered with water and let stand for forty-eight hours. The edges of the gelatinised silica then showed, under the microscope, numbers of cubes of sodium chloride—far in excess of what one should expect, even if all the felspars were completely decomposed by the acid. A drop of strong hydrochloric acid was placed on a polished slab of the basalt. In two hours the acid had become rigid and gelatinous, and showed cubes of sodium chloride under the microscope. A portion of the finely-powdered rock was digested for half an hour, with acetic acid, hydrochloric acid added to the filtered solution, and, on evaporating on a glass slide, cubes of sodium chloride were formed in abundance.

In order to guard against the possibility of the sodium chloride being contained in the rock as an impurity, derived from its proximity to the sea, I determined the presence of chlorine in four separate samples of the basalt, in the manner recommended by Messrs. Fouqué and Lévy.[1] A gram of the basalt was powdered and ground in an agate mortar, washed well on a filter with boiling water, and then acted on by nitric acid. The acid was evaporated to dryness to render the silica insoluble, and taken up with water; on the addition of silver nitrate a precipitate of chloride of silver formed immediately.

There can be no question, then, as to the presence of chlorine and some easily soluble soda-bearing mineral in the Bondi basalt.

The soda minerals found in basalt are—soda felspars, nepheline, hauyne and nosean, and analcime as a secondary product.

The soda felspars do not gelatinise with acids, and certainly are not rapidly soluble in weak hydrochloric acid or acetic acid. So we cannot consider the felspars the source of the soda that crystallizes as sodium chloride.

---

1 Minéralogie Micrographique, p. 449.

Nepheline, if present, would certainly answer to the tests just stated, but a microscopic examination of the rock shows that the mineral so readily soluble is isotropic. Certain minute clear six-sided forms can be found under high powers in every slide; but this mineral, too, is isotropic, and, so far as I can observe, no trace of the uniaxial-figure that nepheline would show can be seen.

Hauyne is excluded, as barium chloride gives no reaction in a hydrochloric acid solution of the soluble portion of the rock.

We have then an isotropic and easily soluble soda-bearing mineral in a rock that gives a reaction for chlorine, and contains no sulphuric acid—evidence that points to the presence of sodalite in this rock.

Some of the powdered basalt was gently warmed in weak hydrochloric acid (one part of acid to ten of water) for two hours. The solution was then evaporated to dryness, and repeatedly moistened and almost dried alternately for two days. Well-formed crystals of sodium chloride were then visible. The whole was transferred to a glass slide, and the surplus acid removed by introducing the edge of a filter-paper. The crystals were then dried on the slide, moistened with turpentine, and mounted in balsam. Plate II., Fig. 1, is a micro-photograph[1] of the slide. Fig. 2 shows cubes of NaCl, obtained by etching a square inch of surface of polished basalt. The face of the slab was just covered with a few drops of strong

1 These figures may be seen in Vol. XX., Roy. Soc. New South Wales, 1894.

hydrochloric acid. This was moistened again with acid, as it had gelatinised in three hours. The whole was transferred to a glass slide, and, after standing two days, was photographed. The figure shows the NaCl cubes just as they appeared in the strong acid, × 30 diameters.

ANALYSIS OF BONDI BASALT.

	Fresh undecomposed Basalt.	Decomposed Basalt filling fissures.
Silica	43·50 ...	42·0
Alumina...	14·60 ...	40·2
Ferric oxide	5·40 ...	trace
Ferrous oxide	8·28	
Lime	8·70 ...	nil
Magnesia	6·16 ...	nil
Soda	7·34 ...	4·4
Potash	2·95 ...	1·6
Titanic oxide	·10	
Phosphoric oxide ...	trace	
Chromic oxide	trace ...	trace
Manganese oxide ...	trace	
Chlorine...	·37	
Water	2·50 ...	12·00
	99·90	100·2

Specific gravity, 2·94.

As one would have expected from the preliminary examination of the rock, the notable feature of the analysis is the large percentage of soda. I have already stated my reasons for believing that the rock contains sodalite. An analysis of the decomposed basalt is also given, where it will be noted that iron, lime, and magnesia have been extracted completely by natural weathering.

MICROSCOPIC STRUCTURE.

The general structure of the rock under the microscope may be described as micro-porphyritic, with practically no traces of flow in the disposition of the felspars. The amount of base present is somewhat in excess. Much of the latter is isotropic, or so feebly double refracting as to be undeterminable. The minerals which occur micro-porphyritically in the base are, olivine, augite, plagioclase, with aggregates of magnetite and sodalite. The olivine crystals are abundant on every slide, and only occasionally show alteration into serpentine. The large individuals are idiomorphic, but rarely perfect; they are for he most part broken, and the parts separated. Cubes of magnetite are common as inclusions. The way wedge-shaped masses penetrate the peculiar olivine crystals is really characteristic of all the slices made.

Large olivines are often seen penetrated in this way. The larger olivines show a disposition to develop in lath-shaped forms rather than in forms familiar in basalts. Some of the crystals will occasionally measure one-twelfth of an inch.

The augite in the slides is abundant and characteristic. Idiomorphic crystals can be seen, measuring from the one-twenty-fifth to the one-twelfth of an inch. They show a warm brown border which fades towards the centre of the crystals. A faint pleochroism is noticeable, but not in every augite on a slide.

Plagioclase is not so well defined and distinct as

in ordinary types of our Tertiary basalts, neither is it so abundant. Perfect lath-shaped crystals are not common. There is no difficulty, however, in identifying them, as they are the first to catch the eye and give character to the rock in making a thin slice.

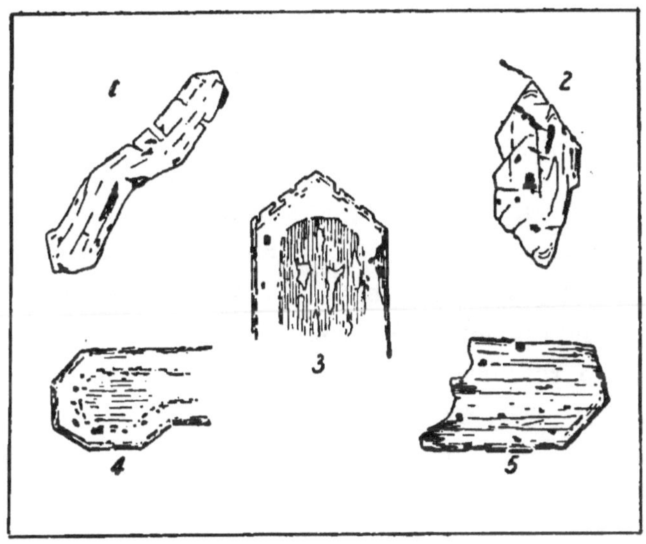

FIG. 79.—Minerals seen in a slice of Basalt from Bondi, magnified 60 diameters.

1.—Olivine Crystal, bent while yet in a plastic condition. 2.—Olivine Crystal, with included grains of magnetite. 3.—Augite, partly attacked by the liquid magma. 4.—Augite Crystal, with a line of magnetite inclusions, showing a stage in the growth of the crystal. 5.—Augite, showing cleavage plates.

The magnetite can be seen on every slide. It is a common inclusion in the olivine and augite, and may be seen forming a fringe or line around the faces of these minerals. A reddish colouration is sometimes seen in the neighbourhood of the magnetite, evidently due to an incipient alteration of the magnetite. As a rule, magnetite is seen in crystals, but also forms irregularly-shaped patches. It was one of the first minerals crystallized out of the magma.

Besides occurring in porphyritic forms, the minerals named are also found as granules embedded in the base. Microliths of apatite can also be found in most of the slices, as an inclusion in other minerals.

CONCLUSION.

The basalt occurring as a dyke at Bondi contains a high percentage of soda. The soda-bearing mineral of the basalt is isotropic and gelatinizes with cold hydrochloric acid. As there is chlorine in the rock and no sulphuric acid, the mineral is most probably sodalite. The hydrochloric acid solution of the rock gives abundant cubes of sodium chloride on slowly evaporating. Based on the chlorine present, we find that there is a surplus of soda, after allowing for sodalite and soda felspars. Probably some soda exists as a constituent of the residual basis.

There are two igneous dykes at Bondi, one including the fissures running north and south, a second along a line coming seawards from the direction of Greenwich. The basalt contains traces of chromium.

A needle of the basalt is susceptible of permanent magnetism, and when swung freely will act as a magnetic needle.[1]

1 From a paper by the author, Roy. Soc. N.S.W., 1894.

The most astonishing feature of these igneous dykes is the great depth from which the molten matter must have been forced. We usually associate the outflow of molten rock with a volcanic orifice or pipe. In the case of these dykes, it is not reasonable to suppose that they were filled with basalt from a pipe or a number of pipes. Everything points to the fact that "the fissures were rent so profoundly in the crust of the earth as to reach down to a reservoir of molten rock which straight away rose in them."

It is not easy to decide the total thickness of the geological formations that the basalt about Sydney welled up through, but approximately we may count on the following:—

STRATA CUT BY THE DYKES NEAR SYDNEY.

	Feet.
Wianamatta Shales ...	300
Hawkesbury Sandstone	1,000
Narrabeen Shales	2,000
Upper Coal Measures ...	2,000
Upper Marine Series	2,500
Lower Marine Series	2,000
Carboniferous	5,000
Older Palæozoic Rocks, Serpentines, and Granites	5,000
	19,800

The dykes have probably risen through nearly four miles of stratified rocks and granite, and the original reservoir of molten matter was no doubt much deeper down in the crust of the earth.

There is very little evidence to decide the age of these intrusions. They were, of course, injected after the consolidation of the sandstones and shales, but whether in the Mesozoic or Tertiary times it is not so easy to decide. It is not unreasonable to assume that these dykes are contemporaneous with the basalts of Mount Hay and Mount Tomah, which are believed to be Tertiary.

The Mesozoic period generally was one of volcanic quiescence in Australia, and contrasted strongly with the Palæozoic period, in which extensive sheets of basalts, diorites, and porphyries were poured out, and also with the Tertiary period, during which originated lavas of a vast extent. We have representatives of these Tertiary lavas on Mount Hay, Mount Tomah, on the Bald Hills, Bathurst, and in the great basalt flows around Orange and Carcoar.

GRANITES.

Granite may be described as a wholly crystalline rock, consisting normally of granules of the minerals —quartz, felspar, and mica. Very often hornblende is also present. These minerals are already described on pages 54 and 55. The question, "What is granite?" is sufficiently answered in the same chapter. The nearest granite to Sydney is that exposed at the base of Mount Victoria, around Hartley Vale, but boulders of granite have been found near Penrith, carried down into the Nepean from the very heart of the mountains. Travelling west by rail, the first granite appears beyond Rydal, towards Locksley. South of Sydney the first granite is met at Moruya. The polished columns in the General Post Office colonnade are good examples of Moruya granite. The felspars are milk-white, and contrast well with the dark mica and almost black hornblende. The rock is remarkable for the abundance of black patches, known as aggregates or inclusions. These patches are, in some instances, merely aggregates of the more basic portions of the rock. In other cases they represent portions of other rocks caught up while the rock was yet in a plastic condition. At Gabo Island we have another granite, but of quite a different character. Here the felspars are a rich flesh colour, giving a warm tone to the rock.

Granites present to the geological student many points of interest. They are all old, very old rocks. They form great basins, in which the sedimentary rocks lie cradled. Granite is in fact the solid foundation on which the upper world rests. When a series of Aqueous rocks are traced downwards, sooner or later granite is reached. If we only sink deep enough anywhere, we must ultimately come to granite or into allied rocks. But what is below granite no man knows.

One feature characteristic of granite country is the great rounded masses of stone that crown the highest points. Boulder-like masses are seen piled one above the other, and often so delicately poised that apparently the least provocation would send them crashing from above. Someone has remarked that mountain-tops are usually in a fearful state of disrepair. Granite peaks are not an exception.

One often hears the question asked, "How did these great boulders get up there?" More than once the writer has been assured that nothing but an earthquake could do it, my informant seemingly forgetting that an earthquake would more probably bring these great rocks down than throw them up to their hardly stable positions. Popularly, earthquakes have taken a firm hold in this direction—a fact worth noting when it is borne in mind that the presence of these delicately-poised boulders is the very best proof that Australia has not for long ages past been subjected to any violent earth movements.

It is interesting, however, to follow the explanation that geologists give as to the origin of granite boulders crowning the summits of mountains. The boulders are simply the harder portions of the granite, which remain when the softer portions of the rock have disintegrated and decomposed. The resulting fine materials are removed by rain and running water. But it will be asked, "Does granite, then, decompose so readily?" No doubt about it. Granite seen in polished slabs may appear "more lasting than brass;" but it is, in truth, liable to disease and decay. In many parts of the world vast areas of granite have been disintegrated, through a predisposition on the part of its felspars to alter into kaolin. The granites of Auvergne in Central France are examples of this seeming mysterious decay, which has been happily called by Dolomieu "*la maladie du granite.*"

But we need not go abroad for examples of this

description. The granites around Bathurst are decomposed *in situ* to a depth of 40 to 100 feet. Before the present water supply for Bathurst was provided, the town depended on wells sunk in this decomposed granite. The wells could usually be put down with a pick and shovel. The explanation is that the felspars of the granite had decomposed, leaving the quartz crystals intact, but with their cementing material removed. If we can picture a noble building of brick, the mortar and binding materials of which have been converted into a non-cohering pasty mass, we have the condition of granite when the felspathic constituents have been decomposed. The Wyalong goldfield is another illustration. Here the granite has decomposed to a depth of quite one hundred feet. No crystal has been disturbed. The quartzes lie just where they were first formed. The mica plates are still where they were born, so to speak. But the felspar! It is there too, so altered, however, by disease as to be scarcely recognizable, even by those benevolent scientists who take a kindly interest in the family of the felspars. The optical properties that the physicist was so proud to develop give no intelligible response to the vibrations of ether. Cleavage faces have lost their lustre, and the strong square shoulders of the orthoclase are rounded and weakly. Thin sections of the mineral show their glassy clearness dimmed. The crystals are cloudy, and transmit light with difficulty, and the light that does struggle through has its undulating battalions travelling helter-skelter as they will, no molecular power remaining to order "halt," "dress," or "forward." The crystals in their debility and decay no longer send the pulsating ether along by companies and columns, or in single file, as was their wont. This is only another way of saying that the decomposed felspar crystals cannot now polarise light, and have lost their doubly refracting properties.

When thin sections of granite are examined with the microscope, under high powers, the quartz crystals are found to contain liquid cavities. Often a gas bubble is seen floating in the imprisoned liquid. These bubbles are supposed to be carbon dioxide—a gas that is particularly active in attacking felspars and converting them into kaolin. This gas was caught up when the granite was formed, and it is thought that the felspars also had their share, but it has long since united with some of the elements of the felspars, thus weakening their constitution. Dolomieu's remark has therefore a great deal of truth in it. Granites do suffer from *la maladie* as he surmised, but it was reserved for the petrologist, with his microscope, to discover that the disease was internal, and it may be added incurable. The sketch shown on page 254 is fairly typical of the boulder-crowned hills that characterize granite country. It may be noted here that these weathered boulders are not to be compared with the perched blocks due to glacial action. The boulders we are dealing with are not transported or carried from a distance, as is the case with ice-borne erratics. The granite boulders are identical in composition with the surrounding rocks.

Boulders of disintegration would be a fairly descriptive term for these rocks.

It has been stated above that the granites form the lowest rocks in the geological series. That is, they underlie all stratified rocks, and if granite does rise into, and form mountains, even then it is the foundation of any sedimentary rocks in that particular locality. Reasons have already been given for believing that the granite is a newer rock than the Silurian slate and Devonian Sandstones. The slates certainly rest on the granite, but the granite is, for all that, the newer of the two.

DIORITE.

Like granite, diorite is a wholly crystalline rock. Its intimate structure is shown in Fig. 7; and the essential minerals that go to make up the rock are felspar (plagioclase) and hornblende. Up to the present no diorite has been found intruded into the Hawkesbury Sandstones, near Sydney. Diorite dykes are common enough outside the sandstone area. It is thought for this reason that the diorites were erupted before the sandstones were formed. Diorite is often called "greenstone," a convenient term enough, provided we reserve it for diorites and allied rocks. There always seems a difficulty with beginners in distinguishing between diorite and basalt, although the distinction is not a matter of difficulty. The following tabulated statement of resemblances and differences may help the reader :—

BASALT.	DIORITE.
Black and blue-black in color.	Greenish black to black in colour.
A basic rock.	An intermediate rock (mostly).
Bulk for bulk, heavier than diorite.	Bulk for bulk lighter than basalt.
In origin Volcanic.	In origin Plutonic.
Basalt, although occurring in dykes, is most commonly found in sheets which have flowed from a volcanic vent.	Diorite, although an Igneous rock, shows no signs of "flow," and did not cool on the surface of the earth.
A hemi-crystalline rock, usually with a paste; often a glassy base.	A holo-crystalline rock, no paste.
Essential Minerals :—Plagioclase felspar + augite + olivine.	Essential Minerals :—Plagioclase felspar + hornblende.
Magnetite mostly present.	Magnetite mostly present.

CHAPTER XII.

ORIGIN OF THE MOUNTAINS.

ORIGIN OF THE BLUE MOUNTAINS—THE MOUNTAINS FROM SILURIAN TO TRIASSIC TIMES—THE SCULPTURING OF THE MOUNTAINS—THE WORK OF RUNNING WATER.

In looking back through the long ages of geological time, the earliest glimpses we get of the area now covered by the dividing chain, west of Sydney, is in Silurian times. We see a wide expanse of ocean, the nearest dry land being probably a pre-Silurian continent, remnants of which are found in the McDonell Ranges, Yorke's Peninsula, and Tasmania. After the deposition of the series of sediments that go to make up our Silurian rocks, vast earth movements caused the stratified rocks to be thrown into great folds, so that beds ten miles long were so compressed as to occupy but one half that length. This folding produced elevated ridges in the earth's crust, with a general north and south trend, and we have here the first indication of a mountain region—a condition that did not, however, long continue. The Silurian sediments are thus the oldest rocks we know of on the Dividing Chain. But it must not be taken for granted that the present mountains were therefore formed in Silurian times. We date the age of a mountain tract from its *latest* appearance from beneath the sea. Looked at in this way, the Mountains are, comparatively speaking, modern, for the area occupied by them was depressed below the sea in Devonian, Permo-Carboniferous and Triassic times. There is no evidence that the Blue Mountains were under water since Triassic times, and we therefore conclude that the range was upheaved subsequent to the Triassic period.

During the deposition of the Devonian sediments we had a comparatively shallow sea, with dry land covered with a vegetation. About this period, molten or semi-plastic granites were slowly eating their way upward, and absorbing at the same time much of the overlying sediments.

In Permo-Carboniferous days the area we are dealing with was also submerged, but under conditions alternately fresh-water and marine. The physical features were not unlike some parts of the earth's surface to-day. The whole area was undergoing prolonged depression. Volcanic phenomena were much in evidence, but none of the present mountain peaks stood above the general level. During the succeeding Trias or Trias-Jura period, no elevatory movements took place. Slow subsidence was still in progress, but a great change was impending, and the first symptoms of mountain building were about to manifest themselves. Through the long preceding periods, the materials were accumulating that go to make the Coal Measures, Sandstones, and Shales. All are now ready; it only needs the mighty power that the earth holds pent up within her, to come into play, and lift the accumulated sediments above the sea.

We have proceeded far enough by this to distinguish three stages in the building of the Blue Mountains—

1. Deposition of the sediments.
2. Lifting up of the sediments.
3. The carving and sculpturing of the uplifted rocks.

In a sense the period of the deposition of the sediments during the Permo-Carboniferous and Triassic, was the age in which the building of the mountains was really done. But it is equally correct to say that, were it not for subsequent upheaval, the Mountains would not exist as such. As to the fact of the sedimentary strata being lifted up, there is no room for doubt—marine beds occurring nearly 3,000 feet above sea-level—the only room for discussion being as to the nature of the upheaval.

The Blue Mountains as such had no existence in Triassic times. At the close of that period a basin extended from Mount Lambie to a point at present far out to sea. The western half of this basin is now elevated, while the eastern half is approximately in its original position. There is reason to believe, however, that the eastern half was also elevated, but is now again at sea-level, through a subsequent depression. There are objections to be answered, and difficulties to

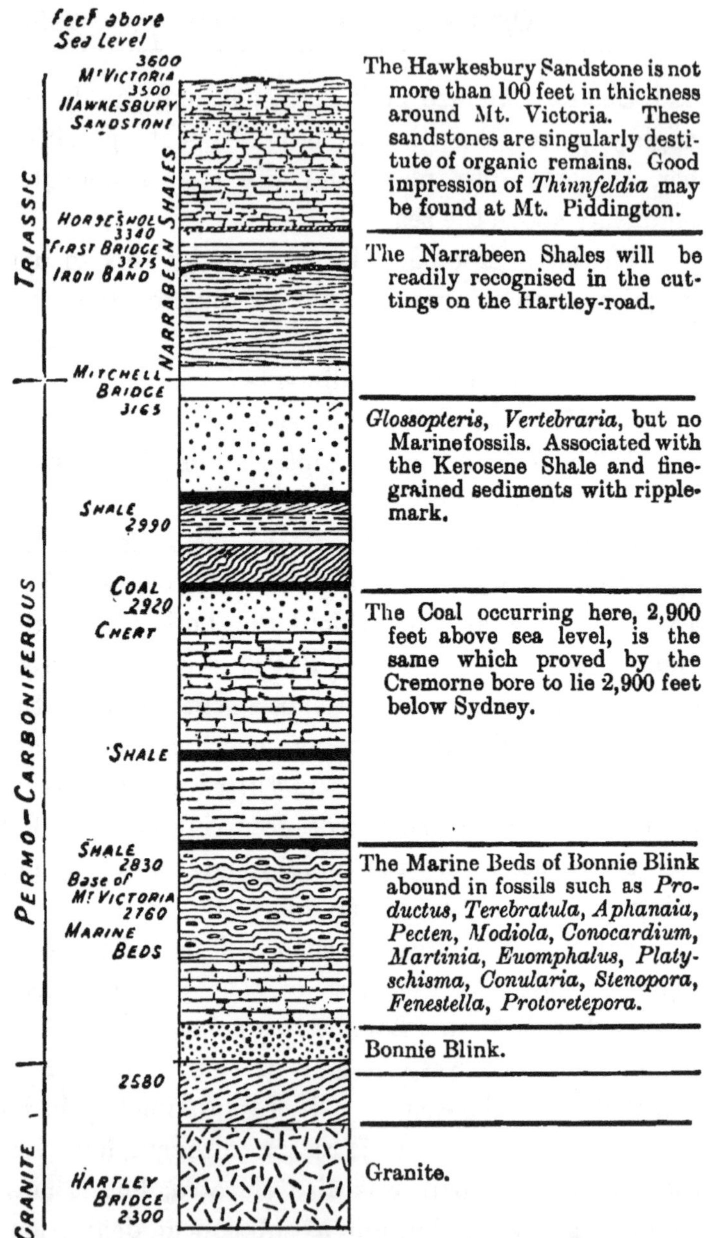

Fig. 80.—Section showing the succession of stratified rocks, from Hartley to the summit of Mt. Victoria, and showing the geological character of the Blue Mountains generally.

be met with, in every attempt to piece together the movements that took place in their actual sequence. To the writer's mind, the following interpretation is most in keeping with observed facts, although there are alternative views which future observation may render more acceptable.

During the earlier Tertiary the whole basin was elevated to the height of about 1,500 feet. We had then a great plateau, watered with rivers of considerable size; there was a heavy rainfall, and the period probably corresponded to the Pluvial period referred to by Mr. Wilkinson. It was during this condition of things that the great valleys of the mountains were carved out by running water. Three or four points of volcanic eruption were in activity. A great volcano poured out its sheets of lava, remnants of which remain on Mounts Hay, King George, Tomah, and Wilson. Volcanic fires were also aglow on the Canoblas—and at the same time, probably, the rending and the fissuring of the strata took place, that allowed the ascent of molten rock to form the dykes around Sydney. Subsequently another earth movement began, something in the nature of a fold; this resulted in the depression of the coastal region allowing the sea to enter the valley of the Hawkesbury and the system of mountain gorges that now form the harbour of Port Jackson. This movement resulted also in a further uplifting of the western points of the region west of Penrith. Thus, while one half of the basin was depressed, the other half was elevated, the axis of the movement running north and south about thirty miles inland from the coast. Evidences of this movement can be found at Lapstone Hill, near Penrith. But authorities are not agreed as to whether a simple fold or a fault exists in that locality. There are no two opinions, however, on the fact that the country on the mountains proper has been uplifted quite 3,000 feet, and that the coastal region has also been uplifted and subsequently depressed.

Mr. Wilkinson was of opinion that the western portion of the basin referred to remains at or nearly at its original elevation. The central part was faulted down, and forms the present coastal region, while the eastern portion is depressed beneath the oceanic depths of the Pacific. "Port Hacking," he wrote, "is over a very deep portion of the coal basin. The eastern portion of this basin has been apparently faulted and thrown down beneath the water of the Pacific Ocean, the precipitous coast, and a line about twenty miles east from it, marking approximately the lines of dislocation. The deep soundings immediately beyond this would seem to favour this view, so that here the bed of the ocean probably consists of the old land surface which once formed a continuation of that upon which the city of Sydney now stands, and which has been faulted to a depth of over 1200 feet. The length of the faulted area is not yet known, but it probably does not extend along the coast beyond, if so far as, the north and south limits of the Colony.

"The abrupt eastern margin of the Blue Mountains, up which the Great Western Railway Zig-zag ascends at Lapstone Hill, near Emu plains, marks the line of a similar though not such an extensive fault, by which all the country between it and the coast was thrown down to its present level—the depression being so great that the ocean wàter flowed into the old river valleys, one of which forms the beautiful harbour of Port Jackson."

THE SCULPTURING OF THE BLUE MOUNTAINS.

The variety and charm of the Blue Mountain scenery depends primarily on the weathering of the rocks and the carving out of the gorges and great valleys. These have been ably described by various authors, and some of their descriptions will help the reader to realise the enormous amount of material removed in the sculpturing of these mountains. An adequate idea of the enormous amount of wear and tear that has taken place is just what one should become familiar with; for, vast as is the work, it must be attributed to the very simplest of natural causes. Dr. Charles Darwin gives us his impressions as follow: "The grand valleys, on the Blue Mountains and other sandstone platforms of this part of Australia, ... which long offered an insuperable obstacle to the attempts of the most enterprising colonist to reach the interior country, form the most striking feature in the geology of New South Wales. They are of grand dimensions, and are bordered by continuous lines of lofty cliffs. It is not easy to conceive a more magnificent spectacle than is presented to a person walking on the summit-plains, when without any notice he arrives at the brink of one of these cliffs,

FIG. 81.—View on the coast near Narrabeen, showing a fold in the Narrabeen Shales, caused by expansion of the underlying and the surface rocks as the result of weathering.

which are so perpendicular that he can strike with a stone (as I have tried) the trees growing at the depth of between 1,000 and 1,500 feet below him; on both hands he sees headland beyond headland of the receding line of cliff, and on the opposite side of the valley, often at the distance of several miles, he beholds another line rising up to the same height with that on which he stands, and formed of the same horizontal strata of pale sandstone. The bottoms of these valleys are moderately level, and the fall of the rivers flowing in them, according to Sir T. Mitchell, is gentle. The main valleys often send into the platform great bay-like arms, which expand at their upper ends; and on the other hand, the platform often sends promontories into the valley, and even leaves in them great, almost insulated, masses. So continuous are the bounding lines of the cliff, that to descend into some of these valleys, it is necessary to go round twenty miles. The first impression from seeing the correspondence of the horizontal strata, on each side of these valleys and great amphitheatre-like depressions, is that they have been in chief part hollowed out, like other valleys, by aqueous erosion; but when one reflects on the enormous amount of stone which on this view must have been removed, in most of the above cases through mere gorges or chasms, one is led to ask whether these spaces may not have subsided."[1]

It will be noted that Darwin suggests that the valleys have been formed by subsidence or a sinking of the strata—a view that is not supported by more recent observers.

Govett's Leap is a "tremendous rent or depression

1 Darwin: "Geological Observations," 2nd edition, p. 151. Lond., 1876.

in the earth, which is said to be the deepest chasm with perpendicular cliffs in the known world. It is almost surrounded with these cliffs, which are believed to be nowhere less than 3,000 feet above the level of the sea. The full sublimity and majestic grandeur of the scene is not realised at a first glance. After contemplating it for a time, the mind becomes filled with awe and wonder as it vainly strives to comprehend

> '——— The vast immeasurable abyss,
> Outrageous as a sea, dark, wasteful, wild.'

The trees in the valley below, although one or two hundred feet high, or perhaps more, are undistinguishable in their individuality. Standing on the abrupt precipitous wall, one cannot help feeling a strong desire to reach the depths of the gorge. But the closer one seeks for a spot at which a descent can be made, the more certain does it appear that such an object is unattainable. It is recorded that Sir Thomas Mitchell (formerly Surveyor-General for the Colony) endeavoured, first by walking and then by crawling between the great fragments of sandstone, to ascend the gorge through which the river Grose joins the Nepean, but in vain. The scenery is full of grandeur, and to add to its beauty there are two streams which are precipitated into the mighty chasm, and although meeting with no impediment but the atmosphere in their descent, they are dissipated into mist long before their waters can reach the bottom; and often when the wind is favourable the spray is wafted upwards and along for a considerable distance."[1]

"Some idea," says Sir Thomas Mitchell, "may be formed of the intricate character of the mountain ravines in the neighbourhood, from the difficulties experienced by the surveyors in endeavouring to obtain access to Mount Hay. Mr. Dixon, in an unsuccessful attempt, penetrated to the Valley of the Grose, until then unvisited by man, and when he at length emerged from the ravines in which he had been bewildered four days, he thanked God (to use his own words, in an official letter) that he had found his way out of them. Even Count Strzelecki tells us, that in the course of his researches he was engulphed in the endless labyrinth of the almost subterranean gullies of Mount Hay, and was unable to extricate himself and his men until after days of incessant fatigue, danger, and starvation."

From a geological standpoint, the following description by Professor David is an excellent summary of the general features of the best known resorts on the Mountains:—

"The plateau of the Blue Mountains proper consists of a deeply-eroded platform of Hawkesbury Sandstone. At the top of the fold at Lapstone Hill the platform attains an altitude of about six hundred feet above the sea, and from here it rises westwards at the rate of about one hundred and sixty feet to the mile, its greatest elevation on the portion traversed

1 Edwin Barton, quoted in Railway Guide. Ed. 1886, p. 57. The chasm described is not by any means the deepest known, and the trees in the valley below are as a rule less than one hundred feet in height.

by the western railway being 3,658 feet at Clarence Siding. The plateau rises in conspicuous peaks at Mount Tomah 3,276 feet, Mount Wilson, Mount King George 3,470 feet, and Mount Hay 3,270 feet. The portion of the plateau which has suffered least from erosion, with the exception of the peaks just enumerated, is the ridge known as the Darling Causeway, which for a distance of about thirty miles forms the line of water-parting between the tributaries of Cox's River and of the Grose River. The course of the western railway line and of the main western road almost exactly follow the trend of this causeway. Westwards the plateau terminates in sheer precipices of sandstone, from two hundred up to nearly one thousand feet in height, of which Hassan's Walls may be taken as a type. The creeks which drain southerly from this water-parting into the Cox, and those which flow northerly to join the Grose, within a few miles of their sources plunge over sandstone precipices, forming waterfalls of which Govett's Leap, Leura Falls, and Wentworth Falls may be taken as types. From the bases of these waterfalls the creeks find their way among masses of densely-wooded talus into more or less wide valleys sloping gently eastwards. Traced a few miles further east, the rivers formed by the junction of these creeks become hemmed in by walls of sandstone, which form almost impassable gorges near the spots where the rivers break through the monoclinal fold at the eastern margin of the plateau."[1]

1 Address to Roy. Soc., N.S.W., 1896.

FIG. 82.—Katoomba Falls, showing the erosion of stratified rocks by running water.

We have now some fair idea of what havoc has been made of the upheaved plateau in its old age. We have traced its checkered history through long cycles of change. Once the bed of an ancient sea, then dry land covered with a rich vegetation, of which not a species has survived, and again depressed beneath the waters. All the time fresh layers were being added to the load, that was from its sheer weight sinking into the earth's crust. Then the pent-up energy left in the globe comes into play, and the sediments are lifted high above the sea, and at once the work of destruction begins. The separate hills were once a solid mass. But Nature sets to work her "agents of denudation," and we have left peaks, crags and cliffs, wrecks of the great plateau that was.

What are these agents of denudation? They are wind, rain, frost, heat and cold, streams and rivers. If we study any one of these vast valleys, it is hard, indeed, to realise that the materials once filling the great gorge at our feet were removed by running water. Even so distinguished an observer as Sir Archibald Geikie confesses that he is taken aback at the amount and extent of the work done by running water. Writing of the region of extinct volcanoes in Auvergne, he tells us :—

"Standing on the plateau of Pradelle, with its remnant of a lava-current, and looking down into the valley of Villar—a deep gorge, excavated by a rivulet through that lava-current, and partially choked up by a later coulee of lava which the stream is now wearing away—I received a kind of new revelation, so utterly above and beyond all my previous conceptions was the impression which the sight of this landscape now conveyed. The ridge of Pradelle is a narrow promontory of granite, extending eastward from the main granitic chain, and cut down on either side, but more especially to the south, by a deep ravine. It is capped with a cake of columnar basalt, which of course was once in a melted state, and, like all lava streams, rolled along the ground, ever seeking its lowest levels. A first glance is enough to convince us that this basaltic cake is a mere fragment, that its eastern and southern edges have been largely cut away, and that it once extended southward across what is now the deep gorge of Villar. Since the eruption of the basalt, therefore, the whole of this gorge has been excavated. But what agent could have worked so mighty a change? We bethink us, perhaps, of the sea, and picture the breakers working their way steadily inland through the softer granite. But this supposition is untenable, for it can be shown on good grounds that, since the volcanic eruption of this district began, the country has never been below the sea. It is with a feeling almost of reluctance that we are compelled to admit, in default of any other possible explanation, that the erosion of the valley has been the work of the stream that seems to run in a mere rut at the foot of the slopes. How truly astonishing must be the working of such an agent, and how immeasurably far into the past does the contemplation of such an operation carry us! . . . Looking round upon the valleys and ravines on every side, each traversed by what seemed such an insignificant stream, I felt as if a new geological agent were for the first time made known to me. Striking as are the proofs of erosion in the country of the Limagne, they fall far short of these in the Haute-Loire. To be actually realized, such a scene must be visited in person. No amount of verbal description, not even the most careful drawings, will convey a full sense of the magnitude of the changes to one who is acquainted with only the rivers of a glaciated country such as Britain. The first impression received from a landscape like that round Le Puy is rather one of utter bewilderment. The upsetting of all one's previous estimates of the power of rain and rivers is sudden and complete. It is not without an effort, and after having analysed the scene feature by feature, that the geologist can take it all in. But when he has done so, his views of the effects of sub-aërial disintegration become permanently altered, and he quits the district with a rooted conviction that there is almost no amount of waste and erosion of the solid framework of the land which may not be brought about in time by the combined influences of springs, frost, rain, and rivers."

If we contrast all the wear and tear and destruction pictured in the foregoing description with the unbroken and solid plateau as it appeared after its elevation above the sea, we may well wonder how and under what conditions all this ruin has been brought about. Darwin, as we have already stated, supposed the valleys were due to subsidence. Other observers thought that ocean currents cut out some of the depressions while the sandstone was actually forming. Popular theories appeal to earthquakes and the paroxysmal effect of internal fires. The geologist, while admitting the *possibility* of such causes to do the work, is satisfied that in running water we have an agent quite equal to the work—only give it time enough. Someone characterised geologists as amiable (!) enthusiasts, who are happy if you give them plenty of what other men least value, namely, past time. For all that, as the science of geology becomes more studied, geologists become more insatiable for time. To repeat the words of Sir Archibald Geikie:—"There is almost no amount of waste and erosion of the solid framework of the land which may not be brought about in time by the combined influence of springs, frost, rain, and rivers."

But, perhaps it will bring the matter more home to us to take a glance at some of the work done by running water in the world around us to-day. Every text-book for students of geology deals with the subject more or less fully. But for the general reader the best epitome of the more striking facts is that made by the Rev. H. N. Hutchinson, in his book "*The Story of the Hills*":—

"The transporting powers of rivers are truly prodigious. Looking at a stream or river after heavy rain, we see its waters heavily laden with mud and sand; but it is difficult to realise from a casual glance the vast amount of material that is thus brought down to lower levels. If we would trace the sediment to its source, we must seek it among the rocks of the mountains far away. Step by step, we may trace it up along the higher courses of the river, then along mountain streams rushing over their rocky beds, tumbling in cascades over broken rocks, or leaping in waterfalls over high projections of rock, until we come to the deep furrows on the sides of mountains, along which loose fragments of rock come tumbling down with the cascades of water that run along these steep channels after heavy rain, leaving at the base of the mountain great fan-shaped heaps of stones.

'Oft both slope and hill are torn,
Where wintry torrents down have borne,
And heaped upon the cumbered land
Its wreck of gravel, rocks and sand.'

"These accumulations are gradually carried away by the larger mountain streams, which, in hurrying them along, cause a vast amount of wear and tear; so that their corners are worn off, and they get further and further reduced in size, becoming mere round pebbles lining the bed of the stream, and finally, by the time they reach the large slow-moving rivers of the plains, are mainly reduced to tiny specks of mud or grains of sand. So, then, the rivers and streams not only transport sediment, but they manufacture it as they go along; and thus they may be considered as great grinding-mills, where large pieces of stone go in at one end, and only fine sand and mud come out at the other.

"A stream moving along at the rate of about half-a-mile (880 yards) an hour, which is a slow rate, can carry along ordinary sandy soil suspended in a cloud-like fashion in the water; when moving at the rate of two-thirds of a mile (about 1,173 yards) an hour, it can roll fine gravel along its bed; but when the rate increases to a yard in a second, or a little more than two miles an hour, it can sweep along angular stones as large as an egg. But streams often flow much faster than this, and so do rivers when swollen by heavy rain.

"A rapid torrent often flows at the rate of eighteen or twenty miles an hour, and then we may hear the stones rattling against each other as they are irresistibly rolled onward; and during very heavy floods, huge masses of rock as large as a house have been known to be moved.

"These are the two principal ways in which streams and rivers act as transporting agents; they carry the finer materials in a suspended state (though partly drifting it along their beds); and they push the coarser materials, such as gravel, bodily along. But there is one other way in which they carry on the important work of transportation, which, being unseen, might easily escape our notice. Every spring is busily employed in bringing up to the surface mineral substances which the water has dissolved out of the underground rocks. This invisible material finds its way, as the springs do, to the rivers, and so, finally, is brought into that great reservoir, the sea. Rain and river-water also dissolve a certain amount of mineral matter from rocks lying on the surface of the earth. Now, the material which is most easily dissolved is carbonate of lime. Hence, if you take a small quantity of spring or river-water, and boil it until the whole is evaporated, you will find that it leaves behind a certain amount of deposit. This, when analysed by the chemist, proves to be chiefly carbonate of lime; but it also contains minute quantities of other minerals, such as common salt, potash, soda, oxide of iron, and silica. All these and other minerals are found to be present in sea-water.

"The waters of some of the great rivers of the world have been carefully examined at different times, in order to form some idea of the amount of solid matter which they contain, both dissolved and suspended; and the results are extremely important and interesting, for they enable us to form definite conclusions with regard to their capacity for transport. This subject has been investigated with great skill by eminent men of science. The problem is a very complicated one; but it is easy to see that if we know roughly the number of gallons of water annually discharged into the sea by a big river, and the average amount of solid matter contained in such a gallon of water, we have the means of calculating, by a simple process of multiplication, the amount of solid matter annually brought down to the sea by that river. But we must also add the amount of sand, gravel, and stones pushed along its bed. This may be roughly estimated and allowed for. These are some of the results :—

"The amount of solid matter discharged every year by that great river, the Mississipi, if piled up on a single square mile of the bed of the sea—say, in the Gulf of Mexico, where that river discharges itself—

FIG. 83.—Diagram (after Dana) showing how the contour of hills depends on the unequal weathering of harder and softer rocks by denudation.

would make a great square-shaped pile, 268 feet high. But the Gulf Stream, sweeping through this gulf, carries the materials many and many a mile away; so that in course of time it gradually sinks, and spreads itself as a fine film or layer over part of the great Atlantic Ocean. The mud brought down by the great river Amazon spreads so far into the Atlantic Ocean as to discolour the water even at a distance of three hundred miles. The Ganges and the Brahmapootra, flowing into the Bay of Bengal, discharge every year into that part of the Indian Ocean 6,368,000,000 cubic feet of solid matter. This material would in one year raise a space of fifteen square miles one foot in height. The weight of mud, etc., that these rivers bring down is sixty times that of the Great Pyramid of Egypt, or about six million tons."

The foregoing facts should prepare even the most unsympathetic to calmly consider the views of geologists. It is surely most reasonable to explain the past by appealing to causes now in operation. It is equally unreasonable to call in the aid of catastrophes and exceptional conditions to explain what may be attributed to causes still in operation around us and with which we are familiar. We must, at the same time, keep in mind this fact, namely, that the causes we see at work at present may have, in the past, differed in intensity or in degree, though not in kind. For instance, it would be quite in keeping with facts to suppose that during the sculpturing of the Blue Mountains, the rainfall might have been much heavier, the rivers larger, and, therefore, the work done much more extensive than would be possible under present conditions. To explain some particular effects, we might even picture to ourselves an exceptional rainfall, and atmospheric and electrical disturbances on a magnificent scale, such as has often been observed when volcanoes are in activity. But, granting all this, the principle is not affected—that the enormous ravines of the Blue Mountains are not the direct work of earthquakes, earth movements or cataclysm, but the result of running water. Our final quotation is from the pen of the late Mr. Charles Wilkinson, whose writings, it is to be regretted, were all too few. He summed up the whole philosophy of modern

FIG. 84.—Narrabeen Shales exposed on the Coast to the north of Narrabeen.

geology in relation to the power of rain and rivers when he wrote :—

"The vastness of the depth and extent of the precipitous gorges and valleys of the Blue Mountains inspire one with feelings of silent awe and wonder, and impress the minds of some persons with the notion we hear so frequently expressed, that such enormous ravines in the mountains must have required violent convulsions in the earth's crust for their formation. But if we examine the rocks on all sides of the valley, we see no breaks nor signs of violent disturbance as suggested. The various beds of rock in horizontal strata may be seen to continue uninterruptedly around the sides of the valley, and the succeeding layers of rock, as we descend one side of the ravine, gradually approach the corresponding layers on the other side, until at the bottom, in the bed of the watercourse, we find that they actually join, which they would not do if the sides of the ravine had been violently torn asunder. We perceive, therefore, that the various out-cropping strata must once have been continuous right across the valley or ravine, and that they have been removed by some agency without disturbance of the underlying beds. What, then, is this agency? Not *volcanic fire*, but *running water*. Look at the sloping surface of any earth-cuttings or embankments that have been exposed to rain action; see the miniature ranges and intervening valleys that the water draining off it has furrowed out. Notice the miniature precipices left where the harder earth material has resisted the action of the running water; also at the bottom of the embankment, where the incline ceases and the water flows gently, how it deposits in miniature alluvial flats the earth it has scooped out and washed down from above. Now, could we look down from a considerable height, and, as it were, take a bird's-eye view of the Blue Mountains, exactly similar features would be presented to us as we observed in the earth embankment. Wherever the soft clay strata of the *Coal Measures* exist, there are sloping surfaces; where the harder *Hawkesbury* rocks appear, there are cliffs, while the easily disintegrated clay-beds have been washed away, even to undermining the over-lying sandstone. The latter has resisted, to a great extent, the denuding agencies, and been left in projecting masses, which, at last, having the supporting soft strata removed, break away and roll in great bosses down the sides of the hill, perhaps as far as into the bed of the stream below, a perpendicular cliff being left where they broke away, from the main mass of rock. It may be objected that the effects of the present streams are not sufficiently powerful to have worked such changes; but then it must be considered that these forces have been operating through an immense period of time; and, moreover, that in the later Tertiary epoch we have geological data indicating that this part of the Continent was subject to a much heavier rainfall. Again, in the earlier Tertiary period a great portion of the Continent was covered by the sea. It was probably during this later epoch that these valleys first began to be marked out as the sea-water receded; and the subsequent draining off from the land of the rainwater gradually scooped out and deepened the drainage channels, till, after a vast lapse of time, they were shaped into the valleys as we now see them." [1]

SYNOPSIS OF THE ORIGIN OF THE MOUNTAINS.

1. The age of a mountain is estimated from the geological period in which it was finally lifted from beneath the sea. This, of course, does not apply to volcanic mountains, but only to mountains of sedimentary material deposited in the sea, or under somewhat similar conditions in fresh water.

2. In Silurian times, a wide stretch of ocean covered the region now occupied by the Blue Mountains.

3. The folding of the Silurian sediments probably produced the first dry land. Between the deposition of the Silurian sediments and the beginning of the Devonian, a long period elapsed, during which the Silurian rocks were lifted from beneath the sea, folded, and then denuded in part. This is expressed by saying that there is an unconformability between.

4. During the Devonian period there was a considerable area of dry land clothed with vegetation. These Devonian rocks were formed, some in fresh water and some under marine conditions. An unconformability also exists between the Devonian and the overlying Carboniferous.

---

1 From an article contributed to the Railway Guide (Edition 1886), by the late Mr. Charles Wilkinson, Government Geologist.

5. In Carboniferous times sedimentary rocks were deposited away to the North of Newcastle and Maitland, and probably much of the Devonian strata was removed by erosion and denudation, to supply the required materials. The Permo-Carboniferous and Carboniferous are also unconformable.

6. The conditions during the Permo-Carboniferous age shows the area from Moruya to Port Stephens and west to Mount Lambie, as a great plain, and in part a morass, well watered and clothed with a rich vegetation. Periodic inundations submerged large areas at a time. A slow, but continuous subsidence was in progress, that permitted the accumulation of the great thickness of the Coal Measures and associated rocks. The sea during two prolonged periods occupied a great part of the whole of the area, giving rise to our *Upper* and *Lower* Marine. About the close of the Permo-Carboniferous great changes, widespread in their effect, took place. This region was not again depressed beneath the sea, and practically all the animals and plants became extinct, giving rise to a totally new fauna and flora.

7. The Mesozoic days witnessed the Hawkesbury-Wianamatta series being laid down, under physical conditions similar to the fresh-water strata of the Permo-Carboniferous. The land was still subsiding.

8. The next step in the building of the mountains was the elevation of the whole region, together with a wide strip of land at present covered by the waters of the Pacific.

9. The sculpturing of the mountains now began, rain and rivers, heat and cold, doing the work. In this way the ravines and gorges were carved out. Volcanoes were also in activity on the mountains.

10. The eastern, or coastal area was subsequently depressed. This made it possible for the sea to fill the gorges referred to. Sydney Harbour, with its many branches and bays, is a system of mountain gorges, into which the sea has flowed. The Hawkesbury "River" is a submerged river valley.

The reader will probably note that mention is made neither of a Glacial Period nor of Pre-Historic Man—two subjects that are, perhaps, the most attractive in the geological record. With regard to a Glacial period, the author is of opinion that no satisfactory evidence has been put forward to show that Australia participated in a Glacial Period in Tertiary or Post-Tertiary times.[1]

No chapter of the geological record is read more eagerly than that in which we first find some traces of man and his works. The added interest of a human element gives every new fact a wider and a higher significance. But for such facts we look in vain throughout Australia. We cannot say what future research may bring to light, but our present knowledge is summed up in a sentence—Man has no Geological History in Australia.

[1] The subject is discussed by the author in a paper entitled "On the Evidence (so-called) of Glacier Action on Mount Kosciusko Plateau." Proc. Linnean Soc. of N.S.W., 1897, part 4, page 790, plates xxxvii-xxxix.

CHAPTER XIII.

PLACES OF GEOLOGICAL INTEREST IN THE VICINITY OF SYDNEY AND THE BLUE MOUNTAINS.

PLACES NEAR SYDNEY—KIAMA—NEWCASTLE AND MAITLAND—THE MOUNTAINS—BATHURST, ORANGE, AND MOLONG.

A GEOLOGICAL student resident in Sydney may visit, without travelling too far, many interesting and instructive localities. Good sections of the Wianamatta Shales may be seen in any of the many brick-pits at St. Peters. Sections of the Hawkesbury Sandstones can be studied almost anywhere along the coast from South Head to Botany. Capital examples of current bedding can be seen wherever the sandstone is exposed, and there is no dearth of exposures, for it has been remarked, with truth, that Sydney stands on a "wilderness of stone-quarries." Almost any of the quarries are worth a visit. But, perhaps, more can be learned at Saunders' Quarries, at the foot of Harris-street, than elsewhere. A magnificent bed 40 feet in thickness is quarried here. The sandstones rest on shales containing fossil plants. A basaltic dyke may be noted, cutting up through the sandstones.

The basalt is now decomposed into a soft, pasty clay. Recognisable specimens of *Thinnfeldia* have been found in the thinly-bedded sandstones.

Recently some portions of the cliff have been cut down at Woollóomooloo Bay, close to the stone steps that lead down from Victoria Street North. The shales removed contain an abundance of *Phyllotheca, Thinnfeldia, Sphenopteris,* and fossil fish.

At Bondi, as has been stated previously, several basaltic dykes, decomposed to a white clay, may be studied. At one point only, on the narrow path leading to the base of the cliff through the old quarry, can undecomposed basalt be procured. The columnar sandstone, well developed here, is being quarried at so rapid a rate for road purposes, that the best examples will soon be things of the past. Columnar sandstone, or traces of columnar sandstone, have also been noted near Pymble, at La Perouse, at the quarry near the tram terminus, Five Dock, Blakehurst, Pyrmont, and on some parts of North Head facing the Pacific Ocean.

A decomposed basaltic dyke is exposed in the cutting at the Belmore Railway Station. About a mile to the south-west, at Moorefields[1], a basaltic dyke is quarried for road purposes. (See Fig. 15.) The locality can be reached in a ten minutes' walk from Belmore Railway Station, and can be found by following the Moorefields Road in a southerly direction from the Moorefields Public School.

1 Not to be confounded with Moorefields, Kogarah.

A dyke, quite twelve feet across, can be seen cutting the exposed sandstones on the high ground at the eastern end of the old rifle range, Moore Park. This, like most of the dykes around Sydney, runs east and west.

The Kensington dyke can be found by taking the Bunnerong Road past Kensington, where a quarry on the left will be noted. In excavating this quarry the dyke was discovered.

The Pyrmont dyke can be traced travelling in an easterly and westerly direction at Saunders' quarries. The three principal quarries are named Paradise, Purgatory, and Hell Hole. It is in the last-named that the igneous dyke occurs.

At Peakhurst a basaltic dyke crops out not far from the Public School. This last is probably a continuation of the Moorefields dyke. A railway cutting exposes a decomposing basaltic dyke at Beecroft (Fig. 11). Mr. Wilkinson drew attention, in 1879, to two igneous dykes laid bare in a railway cutting at Petersham. At Prospect, close to the Reservoir near Parramatta, basalt and dolerite occur in a mass that has been intruded into the Wianamatta Shales.

The dyke at Rookwood may be found by taking the Bankstown Road from the Railway Station towards Potts Hill reservoir. The quarry showing the basaltic dyke will be found close to the road just beyond the southern boundary of the Rookwood Park.

The intrusive mass of basalt forming the Pennant Hills quarry is well worth a visit. The quarry is about two miles from Eastwood Railway Station. There is an excellent road (about three miles) from Parramatta. There is no difficulty in finding the place, it being a well-known locality where basalt has been quarried for road-making for upwards of fifty years. A student may find here good specimens of basalt, chromite-bearing altered serpentine, prehnite, calcite, barite, and quartzite.

Decomposed basalt, probably part of a dyke, can be seen associated with columnar sandstone in the quarry at the tram terminus, Five Dock. Some of the most perfect examples of columnar sandstones known about Sydney were found here. The bed has been used up for road metal, but some good columns are preserved in the Technical Museum.

At Long Reef, between Narrabeen and Manly, the Narrabeen Shales appear, rising from beneath the Hawkesbury Sandstone. A basaltic dyke cuts through the shales near the fore-shore, and, owing to its hardness, it is seen standing like a dwarf wall above the softer shales. Fossil plants are plentiful in these shales. Nearer to Manly, at Freshwater, *Oleandridium* (Fig. 3) was discovered in the Hawkesbury-Wianamatta Series, by Mr. Benj. Dunstan.

The Narrabeen Shales in the Cliffs on the coast, to the north of the entrance of Narrabeen Lagoon, give splendid examples of *Thinnfeldia odontopteroides, Danæopsis,* and *Phyllotheca Australis.* Abundant ripple marks in the sandstones may also be seen.

The fossil fish from Gosford were all unearthed in

a quarry made for railway purposes close to the iron bridge on the Sydney side of the township.

Travelling south from Sydney, the tourist passes from the Hawkesbury Sandstone to the Narrabeen Shales. Near Helensburgh we find the Coal Measures supporting a vegetation very different to that occurring around Sydney. At Clifton the workable coal seams rise from below sea level, and continue to rise till, at Mount Kembla, they reach nearly to the top of the Illawarra Range.

At Kiama, and back to Robertson, extensive basalt flows occur, showing excellent columnar structure in the "blue metal" quarries. (See Fig. 30.)

At Flagstaff Hill, Wollongong, Upper Marine fossils are to be found to the left of the Basin. Large examples of *Cleobis grandis* are not uncommon here.

At Blackhead, two miles south-east from Gerringong Station, abundant Upper Marine fossils occur. *Fenestella, Protoretepora, Stenopora, Spirifers* (very abundant), *Productus, Dielasma, Mœonia, Aviculopecten, Choenomya, Astartila, Pleurophorus, Platyschisma, Mourlonia, Goniatites.*

Taking Nowra as a centre, a number of interesting geological trips can be made in many directions. Both Sedimentary and Eruptive rocks can be studied in the course of these trips.

The Sedimentary rocks include:—

(*a*) Recent deposits.

(*b*) Rocks of the Hawkesbury Series.

(*c*) Permo-Carboniferous.

(1) Bulli Coal Measures.
(2) Upper Marine Series.
  (1) Crinoidal beds.
  (2) Nowra grits.
  (4) Wandrawandian sandstone.
  (4) Conjola beds.
(3) Clyde Coal Measures.

(*d*) Silurian slates.

The Eruptive rocks comprise:—

(*a*) Intrusive dykes of dolerite and gabbro.
(*b*) Volcanic:—
  (1) Bomba lavas.
  (2) Red tuffs.
  (3) Kiama lavas.

Travelling north from Nowra towards Clifton, the hills along the road show splendid sections and outcrops of the Coal Measures, for the most part capped by Hawkesbury Sandstones. Basalt, probably the same age as the Kiama rock, occurs about Dapto and Lake Illawarra. The Bulli Coal Measures outcrop in the Cambewarra Ranges.

At Saddleback Mountain, to the south-west of Kiama, the volcanic rocks are 1,500 feet thick. Professor David is of the opinion that "one of the sources of these lavas has probably been the conical hill which forms an eastern spur of the Saddleback Mountain."

To the north-west of Nowra, on the road to Moss Vale, as we ascend the Cambewarra Ranges, a section showing crinoidal beds, 600 feet in thickness, is exposed, belonging to the Upper Marine Series.

Nowra grits are best studied in a vertical cliff near the Nowra foot suspension bridge. Here they attain a thickness of 50 feet, but are much thicker between the Braidwood Road and the Wandrawandian Bore.

Where the Nowra to Milton Road crosses Wandrawandian Creek, outcrops of Wandrawandian sandstones are well developed.

On the crest of the hill, opposite Mr. J. Arnold's property, near Razorback, on the Southern Road, very fine stems of fossil plants occur, and on the descent towards Picton, near Mr. Apps' house, good specimens of *Thinnfeldia* may be obtained by careful search, some of them identical in character with those figured by Feistmantel.

The stone from the railway cuttings on each side of Glenlee bridge yields a large variety of fragmentary plant remains, among which are representatives of the genera *Sphenopteris, Pecopteris, Alethopteris, Thinnfeldia, Tæniopteris, Macrotæniopteris, Sagenopteris* (?) *Equisetum, Otozamites, Hymenophyllum*, etc. There are also two species of *Estheria*, and the sheath wings of several species of *Coleoptera*. From a cutting on the Narellan-Liverpool Road, about one-and-a-quarter miles from the former place, in some of the ironstone bands elytra of *Coleoptera* are also associated with plant remains. At Pass Creek, near the bridge adjacent to the water-supply tunnel, *Alethopteris* and other plant remains are obtainable. In the railway cuttings in the neighbourhood of Menangle, fragmentary shells occur. At Kenny's Hill, on the Campbelltown-Camden Road, plant remains are abundant. At Mount Hanna near Glenlee, an interesting intrusion of basalt pierces the Wianamatta beds, and a narrow basaltic dyke may be traced for some miles through the Camden Park Estate. Somewhat similar outflows are to be found at Bringelly and near Appin.

At Bundanoon, about two miles to the east of the station, the ravine of the Bundanoon Creek exhibits a good section of the Wianamatta, Hawkesbury, Upper Coal, and Upper Marine Series, in descending order. *Glossopteris, Gangamopteris, Vertebraria* and *Phyllotheca* are abundant in the Coal Measures, and *Spirifer, Productus, Mœonia, Fenestella and Protoretepora* are abundant in the Upper Marine Series.

At Bowral the great mass of intrusive rock commonly called "trachyte" can be studied. It forms a prominent hill close to the town, and is worked extensively for building stone. Teeth of a *Labyrinthodon* and fish-remains have been found in the shales near the railway tunnel, Bowral. The cuttings along the line show dykes intruding the Hawkesbury-Wianamatta rocks. Basalt occurs also near the tunnel, but having no seeming connection with the "trachyte." The last named rock shows fine crystals of the glassy felspar known as sanidine, so that if the term "trachyte" is to be retained, the name sanidine trachyte would be appropriate. Petrologists call the rock either syenite, or sanidine syenite.

"In the railway sections between Penrith and Sydney the shales exhibit folding and faulting on a small scale, due, I think, rather to an expansion of the shales through weathering than to deep-seated disturbances. This is proved by the fact that these folds and faults may be observed to completely disappear downwards as they approach the surface of the underlying Hawkesbury Sandstone; they are, in fact, what may be termed expansion folds and expansion faults. In their upper portions the Wianamatta Shales become arenaceous, and towards Mittagong assume a chocolate or reddish purple colour, which makes them (in hand specimens) almost indistinguishable from the chocolate shales of the Narrabeen Beds. Barytes occurs in these shales as well as in the Hawkesbury Sandstone."[1]

From Sydney to Penrith we have the coastal plain, on which the Wianamatta Shales can be seen almost anywhere. Wells and road-cuttings show good sections of these shales, in which fossil plants are abundant. Ferns, especially, are plentiful. Some wells and shafts at Blacktown have cut through seams of coal ten to twelve inches thick. At Penrith we enter the region that has rendered the Blue Mountains famous. We are on the eastern boundary of the great plateau of Hawkesbury Sandstone, standing from one to three thousand feet above sea level. This plateau is scored by deep and often narrow gorges, cutting down through the sandstone and the

1 David: Anniversary Address. Royal Society, N.S.W. 1896.

underlying Coal Measures almost to sea level. The erosion of these gorges may be studied in many places. At Mulgoa the Nepean leaves the plain, and cuts its way for eight miles through a deep narrow chasm to Penrith, being joined in its course by the Warragamba, the last twenty miles of which lie in a rocky ravine, along which hardly a goat path can be found. The Burragorang and the Cox Rivers (united they form the Warragamba) flow for many miles through valleys more or less wide, and of surpassing beauty and fruitfulness, though shut in by 1800 feet of sandstone cliffs, to be climbed by a coach only at Burragorang, or by the horse pass at Wentworth Falls. From the Oaks, Picton, or Wentworth Falls, an enchanting district of flowing river, placid lake, and sentinel cliffs can be easily reached in one day. Accommodation may be obtained from the settlers. At the foot of the Wentworth Pass there are some limestones that have not yet been investigated and will repay examination. For bolder spirits the rarely trodden gulleys of the Kowmung River afford a fitting task. These valleys generally have a granite floor, and the surrounding cliffs give admirable sections of the Coal Measures, Narrabeen Shales, and Hawkesbury Sandstones.

The upper part of the Cox is easily reached from Katoomba through Nellie's Glen. A visit to the coal and shale mine will be very interesting. A trip can be made along the path from the valley of the waters, under the cliffs to the Wentworth Falls

Perhaps, however, the grandest view on the Mountains, though not the most beautiful, is obtained from Perry's Look Down, five miles from Blackheath on the Hat Hill Road. Here you gaze into the deepest part of the Grose Valley, with Mount King George opposite rising vertically in one sheer ascent of two thousand feet or more, from the gorge below to the basalt-capped crown above.

The Jenolan Caves can be visited from Mount Victoria, and good sections of the Hawkesbury Sandstones, Narrabeen Shales, Upper Coal Measures, and Silurian slates and claystones can be seen *en route.*

1. Within easy distance of Mount Victoria the student may examine :—

1. The lenticular clay shale beds of Mount Piddington, containing *Thinnfeldia.*
2. Well developed sections in the various deep gulleys around, showing Hawkesbury Sandstone, Narrabeen Shale, and several coal seams varying in thickness.
3. Kerosene shale beds at Sugarloaf, Grose Valley, Hartley Vale, with their accompanying fossils, *Glossopteris, Brachyphyllum*, masses of charcoal, etc.
4. Rainprints and ripple marks in sandstone at Fairy Dell.
5. Ferruginous drips coating ferns, etc., at Ross Cave Gulley.
6. Marine fossils at Bonnie Blink, near Little

Hartley, with abundance of *Spirifer*, *Productus*, *Conularia*, and *Fenestella*, etc.

7. Very interesting beds and bands of ironstone are exposed in the railway cuttings at Mount Victoria, and better still near Katoomba. The almost parallel and wavy lines are due to the alteration of ferrous to ferric iron. (See page 116.)

2. A few geological trips from Mount Victoria:—

   1. To Bonnie Blink for Upper Marine beds. Good road for vehicle. Distance 4 miles.
   2. To Cox River. Granite may be seen in great varieties, graphic granite, porphyritic granite, etc., also typical diorites and Devonian beds. Distance 9 miles. The greater part of the road is fit for vehicles.
   3. Hartley Vale, distance 7 miles along a good driving road, Kerosene Shale Mines.
   4. Grose Valley, distance 6 miles, bad driving road, coal seams and kerosene shale.
   5. A walk down to the base of the hill, Hartley Road. The Hawkesbury and Narrabeen beds can be examined, and the Permo-Carboniferous and Granite lower down.
   6. An interesting trip can be made to an igneous intrusion in the valley, near Springwood, or in another direction to the Devonian beds exposed in the railway cutting just beyond Rydal, and from there to the summit of Mount Lambie.

3. The following points may also be noted:—

1. In the gulley at the back of the church Mount Victoria, Hawkesbury Sandstone, Narrabeen Shales, chert bands, coal seams, etc., may be examined.
2. At the waterfall, Mount Wilson, basalt is seen resting on Hawkesbury Sandstone.
3. The kerosene mines show some excellent examples of "faults" with downthrows of from one to twenty feet.

Mr. Rienits, proprietor of "The School," Mount Victoria, has prepared a unique section showing the structure of Mount Victoria, on a scale of 15 feet to the inch. This gentleman has constructed a cabinet, the central compartment of which is made up of a column, representing in their true position the rocks from the granite of Hartley Bridge to the Hawkesbury Sandstone of Mount Piddington. Each bed in this column is represented by a slab of stone taken from the actual bed itself, and shows every lithological variety of shales, sandstones, cherts, conglomerates, etc., that are known to exist in the natural sections exposed in the Blue Mountain ravines. On either side of this column is a series of compartments, those at one side being reserved for the fossils characteristic of each formation, while on the other side are exhibited the minerals, inorganic products, etc., of the various beds. Mr. Rienits, proprietor and head master of "The School," is, with a true scientific spirit, always ready to show this unique and valuable cabinet to visiting geologists.

The cuttings on the great Zig Zig show Hawkesbury Sandstone on the top of the mountain, the chocolate shales lower down, and Permo-Carboniferous claystones below these again. Some of the shales about Lithgow are particularly rich in fossil plants, *Phyllotheca* and *Glossopteris* in particular.

Further west the Coal Measures give place to Devonian sandstones, which can be studied by walking from Rydal Railway Station to the top of Mount Lambie. Fossils—*Spirifer disjuncta* and *Rhynchonella pleurodon*—are abundant in a sandstone at Ferntree Gully. Near Tarana we enter granite country, which continues to Newbridge, beyond Bathurst. A few hundred yards on the Bathurst side of Newbridge platform, a good section of the junction of Silurian slate and granite is exposed in a railway cutting. Nearer to Bathurst a basaltic capping covers the Bald Hills, from Perth to Mount Stewart. Columnar basalt occurs also in some quarries at the racecourse, Orange.

The examples of spheroidal weathering of granite figured on page 254 can be seen in the distance from the railway train just beyond Tarana, to the left of the line as one travels from Sydney.

The following are places of geological interest in these districts:—

1. A good section through Devonian sandstones and claystones in a cutting near Rydal.

2. *Glossopteris*, abundant in the shales at Lithgow.
3. Remarkable weathering of granite immediately around Bathurst. The rock is decomposed *in situ* to a depth of 60 to 100 feet.
4. Basalt, showing a streaming structure of its felspars, capping the Bald Hills.
5. Junction of slate and granite, near Newbridge platform.
6. Contorted slates on the road from George's Plains to Cow Flat, and also in the hills about the old Copper Mines.
7. Diabase, in a quarry near the R. C. Church, Blayney, and on the hills around the Annandale Copper Mine.
8. Gabbro, around the township of Carcoar.
9. Spheroidal weathering of granite, on the hill above Cowra.
10. Fossil corals in the limestone at the limekilns, 18 miles north of Bathurst.
11. Silurian fossils, abundant *Crinoids*, &c., at Cave Creek, near Orange.
12. Fossil corals in limestones, at Molong.
13. At Molong the limestones may be noted dipping west. Six miles to the west of Molong they have an easterly dip.
14. Serpentine, near Lucknow mines, and also at Whitney Green.
15. Basalt, andesite, and slate rocks, Orange—German's Hill Road.

16. Andesite and rhyolite, on the Canoblas, above Ploughman's farm.
17. Tertiary fossil fruit, under basalt, Forest Reefs.
18. The locality where Hargraves discovered gold, at the junction of the Lewis Ponds and Summer Hill Creek, can be reached by a good road from Orange.

The Canoblas are all that now remain of an old volcano. Volcanic rocks, such as basalt and andesite, abound; and trachyte and rhyolite may be seen, as stated, above Ploughman's Farm.

Nowhere can the Silurian slates be studied better than about Orange and Molong. The limestones contain fossils in abundance, in the Molong district in particular.

To study the Permo-Carboniferous rocks, the student must make Newcastle or Maitland his starting point.

The following places are worth a visit:—

1. Near the Church of England, at East Maitland, shales with *Glossopteris*, and also the outcrops of a coal seam can be seen.
2. In the shale overlying the coal at Thornley Colliery, splendid specimens of *Glossopteris*.
3. At Farley Railway Station, marine fossils. The outcrop of the Greta series crosses the railway line a very short distance to the east of Farley Railway Station. Upper Marine fossils can be gathered in the first railway-

cutting that is met when travelling along the line from West Maitland to Farley, and also in the quarries in the Walker paddock, adjoining the R. C. College, West Maitland.

4. About one mile from Farley, on the Cessnock-Road, in the Ravensfield Quarry, Lower Marine fossils.
5. A great anticline has been traced about Harper's Hill, a few miles from Lochinvar. An intrusion of diorite accompanies the anticlinal.
6. At Black Creek, near Branxton, Upper Marine fossils, and the outcrops of coal seams.
7. A raised beach at Largs, about three miles from West Maitland and two miles from East Maitland.
8. An igneous dyke cuts up through the coal series, and is splendidly exposed in the cliff on the seaward side of Nobbys.
9. *Glossopteris* can be found with *Sphenopteris* in loose blocks at base of the cliffs, Nobbys, Newcastle.
10. Upper Marine fossils may be found in a quarry on Mr. J. Kennedy's property on the West Maitland-East Greta Road, and also in a cutting on a road leading from the West Maitland-East Greta Road to Mulbring Creek.
11. Well-preserved Permo-Carboniferous fossils may be found in a cutting on the road passing across Harper's Hill to Allandale Railway

Station, and in a quarry on the south side of Harper's Hill.

12. Raised beach at the riverside below Aberglasslyn House, some four miles from West Maitland.
13. Ravensfield is the best locality in which to find *Conularia.*
14. At the Bow Wow, near Mount Vincent, Upper Marine fossils are found in limestone beds.
15. At "Blair Duguid," some three miles from Allandale Railway Station, eruptive rocks are well developed.

On the Hinton-Seaham Road, *Rhacopteris* beds may be seen, exposed in a quarry.

NOTE.—A dyke of decomposed basalt cuts through Rodd Island, off Leichhardt, and this should be added to the list on page 260. A fine example of a decomposed dyke can be seen on private property at Carroll's Hill, Kogarah. The clay is occasionally used for modelling.

APPENDICES.

APPENDIX A.

The Stones in the Street.

It would be hard to estimate the number of readers who acquired a first taste for geology by reading the Rev. Charles Kingsley's "Town Geology." The book was a successful effort to teach geology to townsfolk, by studying the "stone in the walls, the coal in the fire, the lime in the mortar, and the slates on the roof." Subjects akin to these have been already treated of in the preceding chapters, with reference to the stones used for building and other purposes in Sydney.

1. The sandstone used so extensively in our buildings is quarried from certain massive beds of the Hawkesbury Sandstone. For all-round building purposes it would be hard to surpass this beautiful freestone. It is easily quarried, easily worked, hardens on exposure, and will stand all reasonable wear and tear. In some of our public buildings it is noticeable that the massive blocks forming the first course show a tendency to scale. This the writer attributes to the use of salt water—the one thing that the sandstones are not proof against—in watering the streets. It will be found, also, that it is probably a soluble salt in the stone

that is accountable for the tendency of some of the sandstone to disintegrate and fret, particularly under projecting ledges and mouldings. Hardly anything has been done experimentally to settle the point. Mr. Wilkinson accounted for it as follows :—

"Sydney is built on the Hawkesbury Sandstone, and many fine edifices of the city can testify as to the value of the stone for building purposes. Some of it, however, contains an objectionable quantity of salts. Where this is the case the stone weathers, not on the surfaces exposed to rain, but on the sheltered or under-surfaces of the cornices of buildings. The cause may be easily explained. As the moisture in the stone evaporates on coming to the surface, the salt held in solution crystallizes therefrom, and, by the well-known power which the minute crystals exert when forming, they force asunder the grains of sand, and thus by degrees slowly disintegrate the rock; whereas the upper surface of the stone is exposed to the rains, which continually wash away the salt as it appears, and so prevent its crystallization."

There is hardly a limit to the number of localities where good stone may be found. The very best stone, however, hitherto quarried, comes from the quarries of Mr. Robert Saunders, Pyrmont.

2. The blue metal used for road-making is an andesitic basalt, from a volcanic flow of Permo-Carboniferous age at Kiama. The same stone is also dressed into square blocks for paving. Basalts from Pennant Hills and Prospect are also used.

3. The basements of some of our large buildings are Melbourne "bluestone," a Tertiary basalt with a somewhat vesicular structure, imported from Victoria.

4. The so-called trachyte, from Bowral, is now used extensively by architects. The best example of its application is seen in the Equitable Buildings, near the General Post Office, George-street, where this beautiful stone is used in the rough, dressed, and also polished.

5. Granite is mostly used in the form of turned and polished columns. The Post Office pillars are Moruya granite. Gabo Island granite, of a warm flesh tint, is very often made use of for pavements, and some polished columns of the same material are used in the facade of the Lands Office.

6. Australian marble is not used extensively about Sydney, not from lack of the material however, but rather on account of the great cost of transport and skilled labour. No marbles are known on the coast, so that the carriage of marble from the interior must always remain somewhat prohibitive.

7. Bricks are made from the clays of the Wianamatta Shales, and there is no lack of this material immediately around Sydney. The shales are a bluish-grey colour, the iron present in them being mostly in a ferrous condition. Messrs. Bakewell Bros. courteously informed me that at their pottery works, St. Peters, near Sydney, they manufacture from the Wianamatta Shales such a variety of wares as

the following:—Tesselated and encaustic tiles, Bristol ware, stoneware, buff terra cotta, majolica, general earthenware (including bread crocks, filters, pudding bowls, baking dishes, tea-pots, jugs, stone bottles and sanitary ware in great variety), enamel and common bricks. The supply of shale immediately around Sydney is practically inexhaustible. At Lithgow there are also large pottery works, but there the clays used are of Permo-Carboniferous age.

8. In the suburbs, many of the roads are formed of a sandstone hardened by the proximity of basaltic dykes. The iron-stained varieties of sandstone, containing bands of hæmatite and limonite, are also much in request, as being more durable than the ordinary stone.

9. Where undecomposed basalt is found, it is invariably used for road-making.

10. Specimens of gneiss, with red garnets, can sometimes be seen on our roads. This is brought in as ballast by ships from South America.

APPENDIX B.

SOME ADDITIONAL NOTES FOR STUDENTS.

There are many points concerning the geology of Sydney interesting enough to the student, but too technical to be discussed at length in a popular work. Garnets,[1] for instance, have been recognised sparsely distributed through the sandstones, but no complete explanation has been

[1] Smith, Roy. Soc., N.S.W., 1894, p. 47.

offered as to their occurrence. Small scales of graphite are also commonly noticeable in the sandstones, and no satisfactory explanation has hitherto been given regarding the origin of this graphite. The residue left after washing a quantity of crushed sandstone is often observed to contain very minute green stones, not unlike sapphires. The true character of these has not been decided. Barite is also far from uncommon in the shales, and forms crystals in joints in the sandstones. Some explanation is needed as to the origin of this barite.

At Narrabeen, and also near Rookwood, the sandstones and shales become markedly calcareous. No one has furnished any proof as to whence this calcium carbonate was derived.

It may be useful to indicate a few directions in which even a student might do some acceptable original work :—

1. No map has been yet compiled showing the basaltic dykes around Sydney.
2. More information is needed concerning angular blocks of shale occurring in the Hawkesbury-Wianamatta Series, and which seem to Mr. Wilkinson to be indicative of Glacial Action in some form.
3. Additional knowledge as to the extent and general character of the basalts on the Blue Mountains.
4. The chemical composition and microscopic structures of basalt are subjects hardly touched.
5. In the Hawkesbury Sandstones we find areas of rather coarse and very fine materials, the occurrence of which in juxtaposition needs elucidation.
6. There is room for much research in determining the areas that were denuded to furnish material for

the vast thickness of sediments that are embraced within the limits of the Permo-Carboniferous and the higher beds of the Hawkesbury-Wianamatta. Also, as to the nature of the country denuded.

7. Are the Wianamatta Shales a distinct "formation?"

8. Are Shales, corresponding to the uppermost beds of the Wianamatta Shales, in lithological as well as in palæontological characters, found occurring at various horizons in the Hawkesbury-Wianamatta Series?

9. Has the coastal region around Sydney been under water at any period since Jurassic times?

10. Professor David points out that the fault which was supposed to exist at Lapstone Hill is a monoclinal fold. Information will be acceptable as to the extension north or south of this fold or fault, as the case may be.

11. A more fascinating, if more difficult, subject for research is opened up by the discussion of, from a geological standpoint, the introduction of existing plants and animals to Australia. In fine, any evidence as to man having a geological history in Australia would arrest the attention of the most eminent scientists of the age.

12. The shales about Sydney are often faulted and broken. No very definite information is available as to the extent or the causes of this faulting. Fig. 81 shows some beds of Narrabeen Shale lifted and broken into an anticline, while the underlying strata are undisturbed. The lifting is due

to a mass of ironstone that has expanded through the alteration of its constitution by chemical action. Similar examples are not at all uncommon, but need closer study.

13. Finally, the fossils of the Hawkesbury-Wianamatta Series are rare indeed—so rare that every fragment preserved well enough for identification is of great scientific value. In this direction even a beginner may render a lasting service to tho Republic of Science.

There are lines of cliff about Manly and other places, standing inland, and not now washed by the sea. Does this point to an elevation of the land, or to the accumulation of sand along their bases?

It is probable that the sea recently spread across the low-lying land from the Bay to the Ocean Beach, Manly. The ground between Bondi and the Harbour was, it is possible, also below sea-level in times geologically recent. A study of these localities should throw light on the origin of the present conditions, and decide whether these are due to a change in the level of the land or to the mere accumulation of blown sand.

The Hawkesbury River is a "drowned" river valley, into which the sea-water flowed subsequent to a depression of the land. How is this proved? Could the valley be cut out by the present river, supposing the land to stand at its present level?

The valley of the Nepean affords splendid material for the study of the adjustment of streams to the structure of rocks. Traces of old river systems may also be studied on the Mountains, and the more minute study of this region will doubtless enable us to trace antecedent and super-imposed rivers.

The occurrence of copper in some of the shales in the lower beds of the Hawkesbury-Wianamatta is a subject worthy of further study.

These are merely a few suggestions placed here to show what important questions are open to investigation to anyone who has mastered the first principles of the science.

APPENDIX C.

THE AGE OF THE EARTH.

Geologists rarely take years as units to measure time. With the public generally, it is just the opposite. When speaking of some geological fact, all at once one hears the question: "How long ago?" If people, for instance, become interested on learning that the Pennant Hills quarry is an ancient point of volcanic eruption, we are immediately asked: "How many years ago since all this happened?" Strange as it may appear, the professional geologist seldom endeavours to frame an answer to these questions. In the study of geology one imperceptibly abandons the idea of accepting years as units of geological time. Quite recently, however, a geologist of high professional standing (Mr. J. G. Goodchild) has interested himself in the question. It is not possible here to give even an outline of the data on which he bases his conclusions; but, as they are arrived at evidently with great care and a wide knowledge of the subject, it may be well to give his figures in tabular form:—

1 See note on page 364 in reference to Professor Liversidge's estimate of gold in the Hawkesbury Sandstones.

	Time in Years.
For the Tertiary Period	93,420,000
For the formation of the Chalk, Upper Greensand, Gault, and lower Greensand	31,400,000
Pre-Cretaceous Unconformity in Britain	13,200,000
Time required for the deposition of the Jurassic-Wealden Series	59,400,000
Time represented by the Trias and Permian rocks	87,500,000
Unconformity at the base of the lower New Red in Britain	45,000,000
Duration of the Upper Carboniferous Period in Britain	31,815,000
Time required for the formation of 2,500 feet of Carboniferous Limestone...	62,500,000
Time represented by the Continental Devonian Limestones	125,000,000
Duration of the period represented by the Silurian rocks	56,000,000
Chronological value of the Unconformity at the base of the above	12,000,000
Time required for the accumulation of the upper Ordovician rocks	12,000,000
For the Lower Ordovician rocks	33,000,000
For the Upper and Middle Cambrian rocks ...	36,000,000
For the Lower Cambrian rocks	6,000,000
	704,235,000

The time required for the known geological series, or the time that has elapsed since life is known to have appeared on the earth, is estimated at 704,235,000 years. The age of the earth would, of course, be vastly greater.

FOSSILS OF SYDNEY

AND THE

DISTRICTS AROUND.

FORMATION.	NAME OF FOSSIL.	CLASSIFICATION.
Silurian	*Heliophyllum Yassense*	Coral
	Favosites fibrosa	Coral
	Beyrichia primita	Trilobite
	Cyphaspis Bowningensis	Fish
	Cyathophyllum Mitchelli	Coral
Devonian	*Lepidodendron Australe*	Lycopod
	Murchisonia turris	Gasteropod
	Pteronites Pittmani	Lamellibranch
	Rhynchonella pleurodon	Brachiopod
	Spirifer disjuncta	Brachiopod
Carboniferous	*Phyllotheca Australis*	"Horse-tail"
	Rhacopteris inæquilatera	Fern
	Fenestella ampla	Polyzoan
	Spirifer convoluta	Brachiopod
	Platyschisma ocula	Gasteropod
	Notomya	Lamellibranch
Permo-Carboniferous	*Phyllotheca Australis*	"Horse-tail"
	Glossopteris	Fern
	Vertebraria	Root of Glossopteris
	Productus brachythærus	Brachiopod
	Leaia Mitchelli	Crustacean
	Martiniopsis subradiata	Brachiopod
	Spirifer duodecimcostata	Brachiopod
	Eurydesma Cordata	Lamellibranch
	Aviculopecten limæformis	Lamellibranch
	Sanguinolites	Lamellibranch

Triassic	*Alethopteris Australis*	Fern
	Cycadopteris scolopendrina	Fern
	Equisetum	Plant
	Jeanpaulia palmata	Plant
	Macrotæniopteris	Fern
	Oleandridium lentriculiforme	Plant
	Ottelia præterita	Fern
	Phyllotheca	"Horse-tail"
	Sagenopteris salisburoides	Fern
	Schizoneura Australis	"Horse-tail" (?)
	Sphenopteris	Fern
	Tæniopteris odontopteroides	Fern
	Thinnfeldia odontopteroides	Fern
	Pecopteris	Fern
	Podozamites lanceolatis	Cycad
	Cleithrolepis granulatus	Fish
	Myriolepis Clarkei	Fish
	Palæoniscus	Fish
	Pristisomus latus	Fish
	Labyrinthodont	Amphibian
	Platyceps Wilkinsoni	Labyrinthodont
	Estheria Coghlani	Crustacean
	Tremanotus Maideni	Gasteropod
	Unio Dunstani	Fresh-water bivalve
	Unionella Bowralensis	Fresh-water bivalve
Post Tertiary	*Siphonalia maxima*	Gasteropod
	Thylacinus	Marsupial

REFERENCE LIST

OF

COMMONLY OCCURRING FOSSILS

FOUND IN THE NEIGHBOURHOOD OF SYDNEY AND IN EASILY ACCESSIBLE LOCALITIES BEYOND THE METROPOLITAN DISTRICTS.

PALÆOZOIC.

Genus and Species.	Stratigraphical Sub-division, or Bed.	Reference.

Genus Lepidodendron.

Lepidodendron Australe.	Upper Devonian.	Proc. of Linn. Soc. of N.S.W., vol. VIII. part 1, p. 121, 2nd Series; Rec. Geol. Survey of N.S.W., vol. III., p. 194 and 199.

Loc.: Mt. Lambie, and Carboniferous at Stroud.

Genus Phyllotheca.

Phyllotheca.	Carboniferous, and Permo-Carboniferous	Rec. Geol. Survey of N.S.W., vol. IV., p. 149, plates XVII. and XVIII.

Loc.: Newcastle and Bundanoon. (See also Mesozoic Fossil Plants).

Genus Rhacopteris.

Rhacopteris inæquilatera	Carboniferous.	Feistmantel's Coal and Plant bearing beds of Eastern Australia, 1890, plate VII; Mon. Dept. of Mines, N.S.W.

Loc.: Stroud.

Genus and Species.	Stratigraphical Subdivision.	Reference.

Genus Glossopteris.

G. angustifolia.	Permo-Carboniferous.	Feistmantel's Coal and Plant-bearing beds of Eastern Australia, 1890; Mon. Dept. Mines, N.S.W.

Loc. : Blackman's Swamp; Newcastle Beds.

G. Browniana.	Permo-Carboniferous.	Feistmantel's Coal and Plant-bearing beds of Eastern Australia, 1890; Mon. Dept. Mines, N.S.W.

Loc. : Newcastle; Jerry's Plains; Illawarra District, and Bundanoon.

G. linearis.	Permo-Carboniferous.	Feistmantel's Coal and Plant-bearing beds of Eastern Australia. 1890; Mon. Dept. Mines, N.S.W.

Loc: Wollongong; Arowa; Bowenfels and Newcastle.

Genus Vertebraria.

Vertebraria Australis.	Upper Coal Measures.	Proc. Roy. Soc. of Van Diemen's Land, 1851.

Loc. : Newcastle, and at Bundanoon.

Genus Leaia.

Leaia Mitchelli	Upper Coal Measures.	Proc. Linn. Soc. of N.S.W., vol. VII., part 2, 2nd series.

Loc. : Newcastle District.

Genus Heliophyllum.

Heliophyllum Yassense.	Silurian.	Rec. Geol. Survey of N.S.W., vol. II., p. 170, plate XII.

Loc. : Yass.

Genus and Species.	Stratigraphical Sub-division.	Reference.

Genus **Favosites.**

Favosites fibrosa.	Upper Silurian.	De Koninck's Atlas of N.S.W. Palæozoic Fossils.

Loc. : Limekilns, near Bathurst, and Upper Temora.

Genus **Cyathophyllum.**

Cyathophyllum Mitchelli	Siluro-Devonian	Rec. Geol. Survey of N.S.W., vol. II., p. 174, plate XII.

Loc. : Cave Flat.

Genus **Fenestella.**

Fenestella (Protoretopora) ampla	Carboniferous.	Strzelecki's N.S.W. and Van Diemen's Land.

Loc. : Raymond Terrace ; Harper's Hill ; Bundanoon, and Black Head.

Genus **Beyrichia.**

Beyrichia primita	Bowning Shales (Silurian.)	Proc. Linn. Soc. of N.S.W., 2nd series, vol. v., p. 656.

Loc. : Bowning.

Genus **Cyphaspis.**

Cyphaspis Bowningensis	Silurian.	Proc. Linn. Soc. of N.S.W., vol. VIII., part 2, p. 171, plates VI. and VII. 2nd Series.

Loc. : Bowning.

C. Yassensis	Silurian.	Proc. Linn. Soc. of N.S.W., vol. VIII., part 2, plate IV. 2nd Series.

Loc. : Yass.

Genus and Species.	Stratigraphical Sub-division.	Reference.
	Genus Martiniopsis.	
Martiniopsis subradiata.	Permo-Carboniferous.	Geology and Palæontology of Queensland and New Guinea, by Jack and Etheridge, p. 238.
Loc. : Maitland District; Black Head; Cambewarra Mts; Jervis Bay.		
	Genus Murchisonia.	
Murchisonia turris	Devonian.	De Koninck's Atlas of N.S.W. Palæozoic fossils, plate IV.
Loc. : Near Yass.		
	Genus Pteronites.	
Pteronites Pittmani	Upper Devonian.	Rec. Geol. Survey of N.S.W., vol. IV., p. 28, plate VI.
Loc. : Mt. Lambie.		
	Genus Rhynchonella.	
Rhynchonella pleurodon	Devonian.	De Koninck's Atlas of N.S.W. Palæozoic fossils.
Loc. : Mt. Lambie, and Hartley.		
	Genus Spirifera.	
Spirifera disjuncta.	Devonian.	Trans. Geol. Soc., 1840, vol. V., 2nd series.
Loc. : Mt. Lambie; Bowenfels; Sofala; Capertee; Hartley; and near Cox's River.		
S. convoluta.	Devonian and Carboniferous.	Geology and Palæontology of Queensland and New Guinea, by Jack and Etheridge, p. 229.
Loc. : Black Head, Illawarra, and Korinda.		
S. vespertilio	Devonian and Carboniferous.	Geology and Palæontology of Queensland and New Guinea, by Jack and Etheridge, p. 228.
Loc. : Illawarra; Raymond Terrace.		

Genus and Species.	Stratigraphical Sub-division.	Reference.
S. Tasmaniensis.	Permo-Carboniferous.	De Koninck's Atlas of N.S.W. Palæozoic Fossils.
Loc. : Lewin's Brook ; Raymond Terrace.		
S. duodecimcostata.	Permo-Carboniferous.	Clarke's South'n Goldfields, 1860, p. 287; Rec. Geol. Sur. of N.S.W, vol. IV., p. 34, plate VII.
Loc. : Wollongong ; Muree, and Bombaderra Creek.		

Genus **Aviculopecten.**

Aviculopecten limæformis.	Upper Palæozoic.	Strzelecki's N. S. Wales and Van Diemen's Land, plate XIII.
Loc. : Wollongong and Black Head.		

Genus **Euomphalus.**

Platyschisma ocula.	Permo-Carboniferous.	De Koninck's Atlas of N.S.W. Palæozoic Fossils, plate XXIII.
Loc. : Harper's Hill, near Newcastle, and Black Head.		

Genus **Notomya.**

Notomya.	Permo-Carboniferous.	Proc. Roy. Soc. of Van Diemen's Land, 1851; and Clarke's Southern Goldfields, 1860.
Loc. : Wollongong and Black Head, Illawarra District.		

Genus **Sanguinolites.**

Sanguinolites Etheridgei.	Permo-Carboniferous.	De Koninck's Atlas of N.S.W. Palæozoic Fossils.
Loc. : Wollongong.		

Genus and Species.	Stratigraphical Sub-division.	Reference.
Genus Productus.		
Productus brachythærus.	Permo-Carboniferous.	De Koninck's Atlas of N.S.W. Palæozoic Fossils.
Loc.: Raymond's Terrace.		
Genus Eurydesma.		
Eurydesma cordata.	Permo-Carboniferous.	Strzelecki's N. S. Wales and Van Diemen's Land.
Loc.: Illawarra; and Arthur's Hill.		
MESOZOIC.		
Genus Alethopteris.		
Alethopteris Australis.	Mesozoic.	McCoy's Palæontology of Victoria.
Loc.: Narrabeen Shales; Clarence River, and Ballimore, near Dubbo.		
Genus Cycadopteris.		
Cycadopteris scolopendrina.	Wianamatta Shales (Triassic).	Rec. Geol. Survey of N.S.W., vol I., p. 145, plate XXIII; Proc. Linn. Soc. of N.S.W., 2nd series, vol. 1.
Loc.: Alexandria, near Sydney.		
Genus Equisetum.		
Equisetum.	Hawkesbury Sandstone.	Proc. Linn. Soc. of N.S.W., 2nd series, vol. v., part 3.
Loc.: North Shore, Sydney.		

Genus and Species.	Stratigraphical Sub-division.	Reference.

Genus **Jeanpaulia (Baiera).**

Genus and Species.	Stratigraphical Sub-division.	Reference.
Jeanpaulia palmata (Baiera).	Hawkesbury-Wianamatta Series.	Johnston, Geol. of Tasmania, plate XXVII; Proc. Linn. Soc. of N.S.W., vol. I. (2nd series), plate XVII.

Loc. : St. Peters ; Narrabeen.

Genus **Macrotæniopteris.**

Genus and Species.	Stratigraphical Sub-division.	Reference.
Macrotæniopteris.	Triassic.	Feistmantel's Coal and Plant-bearing Beds of Eastern Australia, 1890 ; Mon. Dept. of Mines.

Loc. : Shales around Sydney ; near Bowral ; Kenny's Hill ; at Mt. Victoria ; and Fairlight, near Manly.

Genus **Oleandridium.**

Genus and Species.	Stratigraphical Sub-division.	Reference.
Oleandridium lentriculiforme.	Triassic.	Rec. Geol. Survey of N.S.W., vol. IV., p. 49.

Loc. : Gosford, and at Freshwater, near Manly.

Genus **Ottelia.**

Genus and Species.	Stratigraphical Sub-division.	Reference.
Ottelia prætcrita.	Hawkesbury Sandstone (Triassic).	Proc. Roy. Soc. N.S.W., 1879, p. 95 (plate).

Loc. : Near Sydney, and in Sandstone near Campbelltown.

Genus **Phyllotheca.**

Genus and Species.	Stratigraphical Sub-division.	Reference.
Phyllotheca.	Hawkesbury Sandstone (Triassic).	Proc. Linn. Soc. of N.S.W., 2nd series, vol. I. Rec. Geol. Survey of N.S.W., vol. IV., p. 33.

Loc. : Shales around Sydney ; Blacktown ; Manly ; Narrabeen ; near Gosford, and in Cremorne Bore, near Sydney.

Genus and Species.	Stratigraphical Subdivision.	Reference.

Genus Sagenopteris.

Sagenopteris salisburoides (?).	Narrabeen Beds (Triassic).	Rec. Geol. Survey of N.S.W., vol. IV., plate VII., figs. 2 & 3.

Loc. : Narrabeen Series.

Genus Schizoneura.

Schizoneura Australis.	Triassic.	Rec. Geol. Survey of N.S.W., vol. III., p. 74, plate XIII., vol. IV., and p. 32, plate VII.

Loc. : Cremorne Bore ; Bulli, above Coal Measures.

Genus Sphenopteris.

Sphenopteris	Triassic.	Strzelecki's N.S.W. and Van Diemen's Land, 1845, p. 246.

Loc. : Newcastle, and Shales, Woolloomooloo Bay.

Genus Tæniopteris.

Tæniopteris odontopteroides.	Hawkesbury—Wianamatta Series, (Triassic).	Quart. Jour. Geol. Soc., vol. XXVII., plate XXVII.

Loc. : Narrabeen, near Sydney ; Talbragar, north of Gulgong ; Trangie, near Dubbo ; Gilgandra, north of Dubbo ; West of the Darling, below Cretaceous rocks.

Genus Thinnfeldia.

Thinnfeldia odontopteroides.	Hawkesbury-Wianamatta Series. (Triassic).	Feistmantel's Coal and Plant-bearing Beds of Eastern Australia, 1890 ; Mon. Dept. of Mines.

Loc. : Mt. Victoria ; Clarke's Hill, near Cobbitty ; Waterloo ; in the Sandstones around Sydney ; Wianamatta Shales ; Narrabeen, and St. Peters.

Genus and Species.	Stratigraphical Sub-division.	Reference.
Genus Pecopteris.		
Pecopteris.	Hawkesbury-Wianamatta Series.	Quart. Jour. Geol. Soc., 1872, vol. XXVIII., p. 355.
Loc. : Clarke's Hill, near Cobbitty.		
Genus Podozamites.		
Podozamites lanceolatis	Triassic.	Feistmantel's Fossil Flora of Eastern Australia, 1890; Mon. Dept. Mines, N.S.W.
Loc. : Woolloomooloo Bay ; South Creek, and Talbragar.		
Genus Cleithrolepis.		
C. granulatus	Triassic.	Proc. Linn. Soc. of N.S.W., 2nd Series, vol. I. Woodward's Fossil Fishes of the Hawkesbury Series at Gosford; Mon. Dept. Mines, N.S.W., 1890.
Loc. : St. Peters ; near Gosford, and Cockatoo Island.		
Genus Myriolepis.		
Myriolepis Clarkei.	Triassic.	Woodward's Fossil Fishes of the Hawkesbury Series at Gosford ; Mon. Dept. Mines, N.S.W., 1890.
Loc. : Near Gosford.		
Genus Palæoniscus.		
Palæoniscus.	Hawkesbury Sandstone (Triassic.)	Proc. Linn. Soc. of N.S.W., 2nd Series, vol. I.
Loc. : Near Gosford, Parsonage Hill (near Parramatta), and St. Peters.		
Genus Pristisomus.		
Pristisomus latus.	Triassic.	Woodward's Fossil Fishes of Hawkesbury Series at Gosford; Mon. Dept. of Mines, N.S.W., 1890.
Loc. : Near Gosford ; Bowral, and St. Peters.		

Genus and Species.	Stratigraphical Sub-division.	Reference.
Genus Labyrinthodont.		
Labyrinthodont.	Triassic.	Proc. Linn. Soc. of N.S.W., 2nd series, vol. I.
Loc.: Biloela; Port Jackson, and St. Peters.		
Genus Platyceps.		
Platyceps Wilkinsoni	Hawkesbury Sandstone (Triassic).	Proc. Linn. Soc. of N.S.W., 2nd series, vol. I.
Loc.: Near Gosford.		
Genus Estheria.		
Estheria Coghlani.	Hawkesbury—Wianamatta Series (Triassic).	Etheridge's Invertebrate Fauna of the Hawkesbury—Wianamatta Series; Mon. Dept. Mines, N.S.W., 1888.
Loc.: Diamond-drill Bore, Moore Park; Shales at Surry Hills, and Dent's Creek, George's River.		
Genus Tremanotus.		
Tremanotus Maideni.	Hawkesbury—Wianamatta Series.	Ann. Rep. Dept. of Mines, for 1886.
Loc.: Biloola, Sydney.		
Genus Unio.		
Unio Dunstani.	Triassic.	Etheridge's Invertebrate Fauna of the Hawkesbury—Wianamatta series; Mon. Dept. Mines, N.S.W., 1888.
Loc.: Bowral, and St. Peters.		
Genus Unionella.		
Unionella Bowralensis	Triassic.	Etheridge's Invertebrate Fauna of the Hawkesbury—Wianamatta Series; Mon. Dept. Mines, N.S.W., 1888.
Loc.: Bowral, and St. Peters.		

Genus and Species.	Stratigraphical Sub-division.	Reference.

CAINOZOIC.

Genus Siphonalia.

Siphonalia maxima.	Post Tertiary.	Rec. Geol. Survey of N.S.W., vol. II., p. 49.

Loc. : Newcastle.

Genus Thylacinus.

Thylacinus.	Post Tertiary.	Rec. Geol. Survey of N.S.W., vol. III., p. 44.

Loc. : Jenolan Caves, and at Bone Cave, Cave Flat.

REFERENCES.

The following papers will give information to those who desire to go deeper into the subject of the Geology of Sydney and the country immediately around :—

Anderson. Petrographical Notes on the Eruptive Rocks connected with the Silver-bearing Lodes at Sunny Corner, near Bathurst. (*Rec. Geol. Survey of N.S.W.*, Vol. I.)

Clarke. Sedimentary Formations of New South Wales. Sydney, 1878.

Clarke. A fossil pine forest on Lake Macquarie (*Ann. Rep. Dept. of Mines, N.S.W.*, 1884.) Plate.

Curran. A Contribution to the Geology and Petrography of Bathurst, N.S.W. (*Proc. Linn. Soc. of N.S.W.*, 2nd Series, Vol. VI. Part 1.)

Curran. On the Structure and Composition of a Basalt from Bondi. (*Jour. Roy. Soc. N.S.W.*, Vol. XXVIII., 1894.)

Darwin. Geological Observations. London, 1876 (2nd Edition.)

David Sketch Sections, showing Relative Positions of the different Coal Measures. (*Ann. Rep. Dept. Mines*, 1890., pages 234 and 254.)

David. The Coal Measures of N. S. Wales and their Associated Eruptive Rocks. (*Jour. Roy. Soc. of N.S.W.*, 1890.) [1]

---

1 The recorded views of the present writer are inadvertently misquoted in this paper, page 266. In his "Notes on the Geology of New South Wales" (Sydney Government Printer, 1887), Mr. Wilkinson writes: "The Rev. J. Milne Curran was the first to point out, in a paper read before the Linnean Society in April, 1885, that the Clarence formation . . . . was stratigraphically older than the Hawkesbury." In the paper referred to by Mr. Wilkinson, the following was the order decided on by the present writer for the coal-bearing beds of New South Wales :—

1.—Hawkesbury Sandstone (series).
2.—Clarence River Series.
3.—Ballimore Series, near Dubbo.
4.—Newcastle Upper Coal Measures.

David. Anniversary Address to the Royal Society of N.S.W. 1896.

David. Preliminary Note on the Occurrence of a Chromite-Bearing Rock in the Basalt at the Pennant Hills Quarry, near Parramatta. (*Jour. Roy. Soc. of N.S.W.*, Vol. XXVII., 1893.)

De Koninck. Atlas of N. S. Wales Palæozoic Fossils.

Dunstan. On the Occurrence of Triassic Plant Remains in a Shale Bed near Manly. (*Jour. Roy. Soc. of N.S.W.*. Vol. XXVII. 1893.)

Etheridge. Geological Observations made in the Valley of the Wollondilly River at its junction with the Nattai River. (*Rec. Aus. Mus.*, Vol. II. No. 4).

Etheridge, David, and Grimshaw. On a Submerged Forest at Shea's Creek. (*Jour. Roy. Soc. of N.S.W.*, 1896.)

Etheridge. The Invertebrate Fauna of the Hawkesbury-Wianamatta Series. (*Monograph issued by the Dept. of Mines, N.S.W.*, 1898.)

Etheridge and David. Discovery of Human Remains in the Sand and Pumice Bed at Long Bay, near Botany. (*Rec. Geo. Survey of N.S.W.*, Vol. I).

Feistmantel. The Plant and Coal-bearing Rocks of Eastern Australia and Tasmania. (*Monograph issued by Dept. of Mines, N.S.W.*, 1890.)

Jukes. Physical Structure of Australia. London, 1850.

Pittman. Geology as an Accessory to Surveying. (*The Surveyor*, Vol. IX., No. 6.)

Pittman & David. The Cremorne Bore. (*Jour. Roy. Soc. of N.S.W.* Vol. XXVII., 1893.)

Smith. On the Occurrence of Barite (Barytes) in the Hawkesbury Sandstone, near Sydney. (*Proc. Linn. Soc. of N.S.W.*, 2nd Ser., Vol. VI., Part 2.)

Stephens. Note on a Labyrinthodont Fossil from Biloela. 1st. Notice (*Proc. Linn. Soc. of N.S.W.*, 2nd Ser., Vol. I., p. 931.) 2nd. Notice (*Proc. Linn. Soc. of N.S.W.*, 2nd Ser., Vol. I., p. 113.)

Stephens. On some additional Labyrinthodont Fossils from the Hawkesbury Sandstone of N. S. Wales. (*Proc. Linn. Soc. of N.S.W.*, Vol. II., 2nd. Ser.)

Stephens. Geology of the Western Coal Fields. (*Proc. Linn. Soc. of N.S.W.*, Vol. VII.)

Taylor. Our Island Continent. London, 1886.

Tenison-Woods. On the Wianamatta Shales. (*Proc. Roy. Soc. of N.S.W.*, 1883.)

Tenison-Woods. The Fossil Flora of the Coal Deposits of Australia. (*Proc. Linn. Soc. of N.S.W.*, Vol. VIII., p. 37.)

Wilkinson. Address to Linnean Society of N. S. Wales, 1884.

Wilkinson. Handbook, Australian Association for the Advancement of Science, Sydney, 1888.

Wilkinson. Geological Formations of Blue Mountains. (*Railway Guide*, 1886.)

Wilkinson. Geological Map of Hartley, Bowenfels, Wallerawang, and Rydal. (*Ann Rep. Dept. of Mines*, 1877.)

Woodward. Fossil Fishes of the Hawkesbury Series at Gosford. (*Monograph issued by the Dept. of Mines, N.S.W.*, 1890.)

Liversidge. Occurrence of Gold in the Hawkesbury Rocks. (*Proc. Roy. Soc., N.S.W.*, 1894, p. 185.)

In the last-named paper, Professor Liversidge, of the University of Sydney, has shown that some of the ferruginous red beds in the Hawkesbury Sandstones contain gold in varying quantities, from three to nine pennyweights per ton. Some deep red samples from the Wianamatta Shales also gave something over three pennyweights to the ton. The ordinary building stone, however, contains, as a rule, no gold.

GLOSSARY.

Acrogens (Gr. *akros*,[1] highest; *gennao*, I produce). Plants which increase in height by additions made to the summit of the stem by the union of the bases of the leaves.

Actinozoa (Gr. *aktis*, gen. *aktinos*, a ray; and *zoön* an animal). That division of the Cœlenterata of which the sea anemones may be taken as the type.

Agnostus (Gr. *a*, not; *gignosko*, I know). A genus of Trilobites.

Alethopteris (Gr. *alēthēs*, true; *pteris*, a fern). A genus of ferns.

Algæ (Lat. *alga*, a marine plant). The order of plants comprising the seaweeds and many fresh-water plants.

Amphibia (Gr. *amphi*, both; *bios*, life.) Animals like the frogs and newts, which have gills when young, but can always breathe when adult.

Angiosperms (Gr. *angeion*, a vessel; *sperma*, a seed). Plants which have their seeds enclosed in a seed-vessel.

Annularia (Lat. *annulus*, a ring). A genus of Palæozoic plants, with leaves in whorls.

Aqueous (Lat. *aqua*, water). Formed in or by water.

---

1 The Greek *k*=English *c*, and the Greek *u*=English *y*.

Arenaceous (Lat. *arena*, sand). Sandy, or composed of grains of sand.

Argillaceous (Lat. *argilla*, clay). Clayey.

Articulata (Lat. *articulus*, a little joint). A division of the animal kingdom, comprising Insects and Crustaceans, characterised by the possession of jointed bodies or jointed limbs. The term Arthropoda (Gr. *arthron*, a joint; *pous*, gen. *podos*, a foot,) is now more usually employed.

Asteroid (Gr. *astēr*, a star; and *eidos*, form). Star-shaped, or possessing radiating lobes or rays like a star-fish.

Asterophyllites (Gr. *astēr*, a star; *phullon*, a leaf). A genus of Palæozoic plants, with leaves in whorls.

Athyris (Gr. *a*, without; *thuris*, a door). A genus of Brachiopods.

Atrypa (Gr. *a*, without; *trupa*, a hole). A genus of Brachiopods.

Augite. (Gr. *augē*, brightness), a mineral; a silicate of magnesia, lime and iron; usually green or dark green in colour.

Avicula (Lat., *aviculus*, a little bird). The genus of Bivalve Molluscs comprising the Pearl-oysters.

Azoic (Gr. *a*, without; *zoe*, life). Destitute of traces of living beings.

Barytes (Gr. *barus*, heavy). Barium Sulphate.

Basalt. A rock of igneous origin, dark in colour and compact in structure, composed chiefly of a felspar, augite, olivine, and some magnetite.

Batrachia (Gr. *batrachos*, a frog). Often loosely applied to any of the Amphibia, but sometimes restricted to the order embracing frogs and toads.

Bivalve (Lat. *bis*, twice; *valvæ*, folding-doors). Composed of two plates or valves; applied to the shell of the Lamellibranchiata and Brachiopoda, and to the carapace of certain Crustacea.

Brachiopoda (Gr. *brachion*, an arm; *pous*, a foot). A class of the Molluscoida, often called "Lamp-shells," characterised by possessing two fleshy arms, continued from the sides of the mouth. The Terebratula of Sydney Harbour is an example.

Branchia (Gr. *branchion*, the gill of a fish). The respiratory organs, called gills, adapted to breathe the air dissolved in water.

Breccia (It. *breccia*, a crumb). Angular, irregular, not water-worn fragments.

Bronteus (Gr. *brontē*, thunder—an epithet of Jupiter the Thunderer). A genus of Trilobites.

Calamites (Lat. *calamus*, a reed). Extinct plants with reed-like stems, believed to be gigantic representatives of the Equisetaceæ.

Calcareous (Lat. *calx*, lime). Composed of carbonate of lime.

Calymene (Gr. *kalummene*, concealed). A genus of Trilobites.

Caudal (Lat. *cauda*, the tail). Belonging to the tail.

Cainozoic (Gr. *kainos*, recent; *zoe*, life). The Tertiary period in Geology, comprising those formations in which the organic remains approximate more or less closely to the existing fauna and flora.

Centrum (Gr. *kentron*, the point round which a circle is described by a pair of compasses). The central portion or "body" of a vertebra.

Cephalic (Gr. *kephalē*, head). Belonging to the head.

Cephalopoda (Gr. *kephalē*; and *podes*, feet). A class of the Mollusca, comprising the Cuttle-fishes and their allies, in which there is a series of arms ranged round the head.

Ceratodus (Gr. *keras*, a horn; *odous*, a tooth). A genus of Dipnous fishes.

Cheirotherium (Gr. *cheir*, a hand; *thērion*, a beast). The generic name applied originally to the hand-shaped foot-prints of Labyrinthodonts.

Chert. Differing from flint in being a rather less pure form of silica and having a flatter fracture.

Clastic (Gr. *klastos*, broken). Fragmentary, non-crystalline.

Coleoptera (Gr. *koleos*, a sheath; *pteron*, wing). The order of Insects (Beetles) in which the anterior pair of wings are hardened, and serve as protective cases for the posterior pair of membranous wings.

Condyle (Gr. *kondulos*, a knuckle). The surface by which one bone articulates with another. Applied especially to the articular surface or surfaces by which the skull articulates with the vertebral column.

Conglomerate. Cemented and hardened gravel.

Coniferæ (Lat. *conus*, a cone; *fero*, I bear). The order of the Firs, Pines, and their allies, in which the fruit is generally a "cone."

Contorted (Lat. *contorqueo*, I twist together). Applied to rocks deformed by pressure.

Coprolites (Gr. *kopros*, dung; *lithos*, a stone). Properly applied to the fossilised excrements of animals; but often employed to designate phosphatic concretions which are not of this nature.

Cretaceous (Lat. *creta*, chalk). The group of rocks which in Europe contains white chalk as one of its most conspicuous members. Chalk is not known to occur in Australian cretaceous rocks.

Crustacea (Lat. *crusta*, a crust). A class of Articulate animals, comprising Crabs, Lobsters, &c., characterised by the possession of a hard shell or crust, which they cast periodically.

Cryptogams (Gr. *kruptos*, concealed; *gamos*, marriage). A division of plants, in which the organs of reproduction are obscure. They have no true flowers.

Ctenoid (Gr. *kteis*, gen. *ktenos*, a comb; *eidos*, form). Applied to those scales of fishes, the hinder margins of which are fringed with spines or comb-like projections.

Cycloid (Gr. *kuklos*, a circle: *eidos*, form). Applied to those scales of fishes which have a regularly circular or elliptical outline with an even margin.

Deinosauria (Gr. *deinos*, terrible; *saura*, a lizard). An extinct order of reptiles.

Denudation (Lat. *denudo*, I lay bare). Wearing down of rocks.

Diatomaceæ (Gr. *diatemno*, I sever.) An order of minute plants which form siliceous envelopes.

Diorite. A rock of igneous origin, and made up of two minerals, namely, a triclinic felspar and hornblende, felted together without a "paste." Accessory minerals are often present, such as quartz or mica. Quartz diorite and quartz-mica-diorite are varieties of typical diorite.

Diprotodon (Gr. *dis*, twice; *protos*, first; *odous*, gen. *odontos*, a tooth). A genus of extinct marsupials, of gigantic size, that flourished in Australia in Pliocene times

Dolerite (Gr. *doleros*, deceptive). A coarse-grained variety of Basalt.

Dolomite (named after M. Dolomieu). Magnesian Limestone.

Dorsal (Lat. *dorsum*, the back). Connected with or placed upon the back.

Dyke. An injected mass of rock.

Echinodermata (Gr. *echinos*, the hedgehog; and *derma*, skin). A class of animals comprising the Sea-urchins, Star-fishes, and others, most of which have spiny skins.

Elasmobranchii (Gr. *elasma*, a plate; *branchion*, a gill). An order of fishes, including the Sharks and Rays.

Eocene (Gr. *eos*, dawn; *kainos*, recent). The lowest division of the Tertiary rocks, in which species of existing shells are, to a small extent, represented.

Equisetaceæ (Lat. *equus*, a horse; *seta*, bristle). A group of Cryptogamous plants, commonly known as "Horse-tails."

Favosites (Lat. *favus*, a honeycomb). A genus of Palæozoic Tabulate Corals.

Felspar. A group of minerals differing somewhat in form and composition. All are silicates of alumnia; some contain potash, others soda, others lime or lime and soda.

Felstone. A rock of igneous origin, compact in structure, often chemically identical with granite, but not showing the holo-crystalline structure of granite.

Fenestellidæ (Lat. *fenestella*, a little window). The "Lace-corals," a group of Palæozoic Polyzoans.

Flora (Lat. *Flora*, the goddess of flowers). The general assemblage of the plants of any region or district.

Foliation (Lat. *folium*, a leaf). Splitting into layers.

Gabbro. A rock, not unlike coarse-grained basalt, and usually containing a special variety of augite, which has a "platy" structure.

Ganoid (Gr. *ganos*, splendour, brightness). Applied to those scales or plates which are composed of an inferior layer of true bones, covered by a superior layer of polished enamel.

Garnet. A very varied group of minerals, the commonest being wine-red; they are all silicates of alumnia, and among other possible constituents are iron, magnesia, lime, and manganese. Some red garnets are valued as gems.

Gasteropoda (Gr. *gaster*, stomach; *pous*, a foot). The class of Mollusca comprising the ordinary Univalves, in which locomotion is usually effected by a muscular expansion of the under surface of the body (the "foot").

Gneiss. A rock composed of the same minerals as granite, but exhibiting a certain bedded or leaf-like arrangement of its constituent minerals, called foliation.

Granite. A rock of igneous origin, composed of crystalline constituents, the principal being quartz, felspar, and mica.

Graphite (Gr. *grapho*, I write). Mineral carbon. (The familiar "blacklead" is graphite).

Graptolitidæ (Gr. *grapho*, I write; *lithos*, a stone). An extinct sub-class of the Hydrozoa.

Gymnosperms (Gr. *gumnos*, naked; *sperma*, a seed). The Conifers and Cycads, in which the seed is not protected within a seed-vessel.

Hæmatite (Gr. *haima*, blood). Sesqui-oxide of iron; has a red streak.

Heterocercal (Gr. *heteros*, diverse; *kerkos*, a tail). Applied to the tail of Fishes when it is unsymmetrical, or composed of two unequal lobes.

Hornblende. A mineral which is silicate of magnesia, lime and iron; usually green or dark in colour; chemically identical with, but mineralogically distinct from augite.

Ichthyosauria (Gr. *ichthus*, a fish; *saura*, a lizard). An extinct order of Reptiles.

Iguanodon (*Iguana*, a living lizard; Gr. *odous*, a tooth). A genus of Deinosaurian Reptiles.

Invertebrata (Lat. *in*, without; *vertebra*, a bone of the back) Animals without a spinal column or backbone.

Labyrinthodontia (Gr. *laburinthos*, a labyrinth; *odous*, a tooth). An extinct order of Amphibia, so called from the complex microscopic structure of the teeth.

Lepidodendron (Gr. *lepis*, gen. *lepidos*, a scale; *dendron*, a tree). A genus of extinct plants, so named from the scale-like scars upon the stem, left by the falling off of the leaves.

Lepidostrobus (Gr. *lepis*, a scale; *strobilos*, a fir-cone). A genus founded on the cones of Lepidodendron.

Limestone. Ordinary calcium carbonate.

Magnetite. Magnetic iron ore. (Fe_3O_4).

Marble. A rock formed, properly speaking, wholly, or almost wholly, of crystalline carbonate of lime, differing from ordinary limestone in being crystalline with a texture often resembling loaf-sugar. Popularly, the word is often extended to include any limestone which will take a polish.

Marsupialia (Lat. *marsupium*, a pouch). An order of Mammals in which the females have with few exceptions an abdominal pouch in which the young are carried.

Mastodon (Gr. *mastos*, a nipple; *odous*, a tooth). An extinct genus of elephantine mammals.

Mesozoic (Gr. *mesos*, middle; *zoe*, life). The Secondary or middle period in Geology.

Mica. A group of minerals of "platy" habit, with a metallic lustre; some light, some dark in colour.

Microlestes (Gr. *mikros*, little; *lestes*, a thief). An extinct genus of Triassic mammals.

Miocene (Gr. *meion*, less; *kainos*, new). The middle Tertiary period, in which recent or living species of mollusca were *less* in number than species now extinct.

Mollusca (Lat. *mollis*, soft). The sub-kingdom which includes the shell-fish proper, the Polyzoa, the Tunicata, and the lamp-shells; so called from the generally soft nature of their bodies.

Neuroptera (Gr. *neuron*, a nerve; *pteron*, a wing). An order of Insects characterised by four membranous wings with numerous reticulated nervures (*e.g.*, Dragon-flies).

Oligocene (Gr. *oligos*, few; *kainos*, new). A name used by many Continental geologists as synonymous with the Lower Miocene.

Olivine. A mineral; a magnesium and iron silicate.

Palæaster (Gr. *palaios*, ancient; *astēr*, a star). An extinct genus of Star-fishes.

Palæontology (Gr. *palaios*, ancient; *onta*, living things, *logos*, discourse). The science of fossil remains or of extinct organized beings.

Palæozoic (Gr. *palaios*, ancient; *zoē*, life). Applied to the oldest of the great geological epochs.

Pecopteris (Gr. *peko*, I comb; *pteris*, a fern). An extinct genus of fern.

Pecten (Lat. a comb). The genus of bivalve molluscs comprising the Scallops.

Pentamerus (Gr. *pente*, five; *meros*, a part or division). An extinct genus of Brachiopods, with septa dividing the shell into five chambers.

Phacops (Gr. *phakos*, a lentil; *ops*, the eye). A genus of Trilobites.

Phanerogams (Gr. *phaneros*, visible; *gamos*, marriage). Plants which have the organs of reproduction conspicuous, and which bear true flowers.

Phyllotheca. (Gr. *phullon*, a leaf; *thēkē*, a box). Species of Horsetail. For description see Text—pages 167 and 171.

Placoid (Gr. *plax*, a plate; *eidos*, form). Applied to the irregular bony plates, grains, or spines, which are found in the skin of various fishes (Elasmobranchii).

Plagioclase (Gr. *plagios*, slanting; *klastos*, broken). A felspar with the planes of cleavage not at right angles to each other.

Pleistocene (Gr. *pleistos*, most; *kainos*, new). Often used as synonymous with "Post-Pliocene."

Pliocene (Gr. *pleion*, more; *kainos*, new). The later Tertiary period, in which recent or living species of mollusca were more numerous than the forms now extinct.

Polype (Gr. *polus*, many; *pous*, a foot). Restricted to the single individual of a simple Actinozoon, such as a sea anemone, or to the separate zooids of a compounded Actinozoon. Often applied indiscriminately to any of the Cœlenterata, or even to the Polyzoa.

Polyzoa (Gr. *polus*, many; and *zoön*, an animal). A division of the Molluscoida comprising compound animals, such as the Sea-mat, sometimes called Bryozoa.

Producta (Lat. *productus*, drawn out or extended). An extinct genus of Brachiopods in which the shell is "eared," or has its lateral angles drawn out.

Pumice. A volcanic rock full of cavities formed by steam, commonly more nearly related to trachyte than to basalt.

Pyrites (Gr. *pur*, fire). Sulphides of iron and copper.

Quartz. The crystalline form of silica (oxide of silicon).

Reptilia (Lat. *repo*, I crawl). The classes of the Vertebrata comprising the tortoises, snakes, lizards, crocodiles, &c.

Rhynchonella (Gr. *rhunchos*, the nose or beak). A genus of Brachiopods.

Sand dunes. Sand-drifts usually formed along the coast.

Sauria (Gr. *saura*, a lizard). Any lizard-like reptile is often spoken of as a "Saurian," but the term is sometimes restricted to the Crocodiles alone, or to the Crocodiles and Lacertilians.

Schist. (Gr. *schizo*, I cleave). A crystalline foliated rock. When the name of a mineral is prefixed, this indicates that the mineral is abundant in the schist.

Schizoneura. A fossil plant, see Text—page 172.

Septa. Partitions.

Sigillariods (Lat. *sigillum*, a little seal). A group of extinct plants, of which Sigillaria is the type, so called from the seal-like markings on the bark.

Sphenopteris (Gr. *sphēn*, a wedge; *pteris*, a fern). An extinct genus of fern.

Spirifera (Lat. *spira*, a spire or coil; *fero*, I carry). An extinct genus of Brachiopods, with large spiral supports for the "arms."

Spongida (Gr. *spongos*, a sponge). The division of Protozoa commonly known as sponges.

Stalactites (Gr. *stalasso*, I drop). Icicle-like masses and deposits of calcium carbonate hanging from the roofs of caverns in limestone.

Stalagmite (Gr. *stalagma*, a drop). A mass of calcium carbonate rising from cavern floor.

Stigmaria (Gr. *stigma*, a mark made with a pointed instrument). A genus founded on the roots of various species of Sigillaria.

Syringopora (Gr. *surinx*, gen. *suringos*, a pipe; *poros*, a pore). A genus of Tabulate Corals.

Terebratula (Lat. *terebratus*, bored or pierced). A genus of Brachiopoda, so called in allusion to the perforated beak of the ventral valve.

Thylacoleo (Gr. *thulakos*, a pouch ; *leon*, a lion). An extinct genus of marsupials.

Trachyte (Gr. *trachus*, rough). An igneous rock, breaking with a rough surface, and composed chiefly of glassy felspar.

Travertine. A rock composed of carbonate of lime precipitated from water, practically indentical with tufa.

Trigonia (Gr. *treis*, three ; *gonia*, angle). A genus of bivalve molluscs.

Trilobita (Gr. *treis*, three ; *lobos*, a lobe). An extinct order of Crustaceans.

Tuff. A term used in this work to indicate the less coarse and more distinctly bedded kinds of volcanic ash.

Tufa. A precipitate of carbonate of lime from water.

Univalve (Lat. *unus*, one ; *valvæ*, folding-doors). A shell composed of a single piece or valve.

Ventral (Lat. *venter*, the stomach). Relating to the inferior surface of the body.

Vertebra (Lat. *vertebra*, a bone of the back, from *vetere*, to turn.) One of the bony segments of the vertebral column or backbone.

Vertebraria. A peculiar genus of fossil plants hitherto known with certainty only from India and Australia. Probably roots of Glossopteris. Common in the Permo-Carboniferous beds, Newcastle.

Vertebrata. The division of the animal kingdom roughly characterised by the possession of a backbone.

Students about to begin the study of Geology are often at a loss where to look for specimens. When possible, every student should make his own collection. But, whether specimens are collected or purchased, the study of Geology, without actually handling the more common rocks and minerals, is waste of time. Twenty-four specimens, named and numbered, may be had from the publishers, Messrs. Angus and Robertson, in two small boxes, price 15s. Mr. D. Murfin, lapidary, 256 Pitt-street (top floor). prepares thin sections of rocks for the microscope, and deals in minerals, rocks, and the apparatus generally required for the study. His rock slices are quite equal to those prepared at home. A mounted rock slice costs from one shilling to one shilling and sixpence to cut.

INDEX.

Webedale, Shoosmith, and Co., Printers, 117 Clarence-street, Sydney.

BY THE SAME AUTHOR.

Contribution to the Microscopic Structure of some Australian Rocks. With three plates. 8vo., sewn, 3s.; post free, 3s. 2d. (Royal Society Prize Essay, 1892.) Reprint from Roy. Soc. N. S. Wales.

Contribution to the Geology and Petrography of Bathurst, New South Wales. With four plates. 8vo., sewn, 3s.; post free, 3s. 2d. Reprint from Linnean Society.

Gems and Precious Stones of New South Wales. With eight plates. 8vo., sewn, 3s.; post free, 3s. 2d. (Royal Society Prize Essay, 1896.)

Notes and Tables for Chemical Students. 202 pages. Demy 8vo., cloth gilt, 4s. 6d.; postage, 7d.

Silver Ores, and How to Test Them. Foolscap 8vo., 120 pages. [*Out of print.*

Useful Minerals: How to tell them. With 30 illustrations. 3s. 6d.; post free, 3s. 8d. [*In preparation.*

Elementary Geology for Australian Students, with about 200 illustrations, mostly of Australian subjects. [*In preparation.*

ANGUS & ROBERTSON,

PUBLISHERS, SYDNEY.

March, 1900.

PUBLICATIONS AND ANNOUNCEMENTS

OF

Messrs. Angus & Robertson,

89 CASTLEREAGH STREET, SYDNEY.

THE SNOWY RIVER SERIES.

THE MAN FROM SNOWY RIVER & OTHER VERSES.

BY A. B. PATERSON.

Eighteenth Thousand. With photogravure portrait and vignette title. Crown 8vo, cloth, gilt top, 5s.; post free, 5s. 6d.

The Times: "At his best he compares not unfavourably with the author of 'Barrack Room Ballads.'"

Spectator: "These lines have the true lyrical cry in them. Eloquent and ardent verses."

Athenæum: "Swinging, rattling ballads of ready humour, ready pathos, and crowding adventure. . . . Stirring and entertaining ballads about great rides, in which the lines gallop like the very hoofs of the horses."

MR. A. PATCHETT MARTIN, in **Literature** (London): "In my opinion it is the absolutely un-English, thoroughly Australian style and character of these new bush bards which has given them such immediate popularity, such wide vogue, among all classes of the rising native generation."

Melbourne Argus: "They have caught the tone and the spirit of Australian bush life to perfection."

The Scotsman: "It has the saving grace of humour, a deal of real laughter, and a dash of real tears."

WHEN THE WORLD WAS WIDE & OTHER VERSES

BY HENRY LAWSON, Author of "While the Billy Boils."

Ninth Thousand. With photogravure portrait and vignette title. Crown 8vo, cloth, gilt top, 5s.; post free, 5s. 6d.

MR. R. LE GALLIENNE, in **The Idler**: "A striking volume of ballad poetry. A volume to console one for the tantalising postponement of Mr. Kipling's promised volume of sea ballads."

Weekly Chronicle, Newcastle (Eng.): "Swinging, rhythmic verse."

Sydney Morning Herald: "The verses have natural vigour, the writer has a rough, true faculty of characterisation, and the book is racy of the soil from cover to cover."

Melbourne Age: "'In the Days when the World was Wide and Other Verses,' by Henry Lawson, is poetry, and some of it poetry of a very high order."

Otago Witness: "It were well to have such books upon our shelves . . . they are true History."

New Zealand Herald: "There is a heart-stirring ring about the verses."

Bulletin: "How graphic he is, how natural, how true, how strong."

AT DAWN AND DUSK: POEMS.

By Victor J. Daley.

Third Thousand. With photogravure portrait. Crown 8vo, cloth gilt, gilt top, 5s.; post free, 5s. 5d.

Sydney Morning Herald: "There is undeniable music in these poems, and there is lavish yet fastidious and artistic colouring. Verses that are touched with the true spirit of the old romances. Mr. Daley's book marks a distinct advance for Australian verse in ideality, in grace and polish, in the study of the rarer forms of verse, and in true faculty of poetic feeling and expression."

The Australasian: "It is unmistakable poetry . . . Mr. Daley has a gift of delicate construction—there is barely a crude idea or a thought roughly moulded in the book."

Queenslander: "The book, we repeat, is worthy of a place in our literature. Victor J. Daley is one of the singers Australia will remember."

Sydney Daily Telegraph: "In 'Lethe' Mr. Daley touches a distinctly major conception, the stern and solemn splendour of his treatment of which will assuredly be recognised by the critics, who are kingmakers in the realms of poetry. Complete and perfectly-worded thought abounds plentifully."

RHYMES FROM THE MINES AND OTHER LINES.

By Edward Dyson, Author of "A Golden Shanty."

Second Thousand. With photogravure portrait and vignette title. Crown 8vo, cloth, gilt top, 5s.; post free, 5s. 5d.

The Academy: "Here from within we have the Australian miner complete: the young miner, the old miner, the miner in luck, and the miner out of it, the miner in love, and the miner in peril. Mr. Dyson knows it all. What we prize in Mr. Dyson, as in Mr. Lawson, is the presentation of some observed oddity of human nature."

Sydney Morning Herald: "Mr. Dyson has done good work in this book."

The Queenslander: "His work has a ring that will always make it popular in Australia."

Melbourne Punch: "The mines have wanted a man to sing their stories, and the hour and the man have arrived. The hour is now, and the man is Edward Dyson."

Daily Telegraph: "Shows the trained intelligence of an observant-eye, a musical ear, and a mind and taste in sympathy with his subject."

WHERE THE DEAD MEN LIE AND OTHER POEMS.

By Barcroft Henry Boake.

Third Thousand. With photogravure portrait and 32 illustrations by Mahony, Lambert, and Fischer. Crown 8vo, cloth, gilt top, 5s.; post free, 5s. 5d.

J. Brunton Stephens, in **The Bulletin**: "The contents of the volume amply justify their reproduction in collected form. The impression of native power is confirmed by reading the poems in bulk. Boake's work is often praised for its local colour; but it has something better than that. It has atmosphere—Australian atmosphere, that makes you feel the air of the place—breathe the breath of the life."

Sydney Morning Herald: "There is no question, can be none, of the intimate faithfulness of every touch that gives us landscape, atmosphere."

Sydney Daily Telegraph: "An essential publication, full of human interest. It is among the most excellently-printed and illustrated books issued in Australia."

The Australasian: "There is enough merit in these remains to show that Boake was, to say the least, a writer of premise, and to make us regret that his life was cut short in so sad and untimely a manner."

FOR THE TERM OF HIS NATURAL LIFE.

By Marcus Clarke.

With a Memoir of the Author by A. B. Paterson. Crown 8vo, cloth gilt, gilt top, 5s.; post free, 5s. 6d. Uniform with "The Man from Snowy River."

Illustrated with a portrait of Marcus Clarke and 15 full-page plates, viz.:—Relics of Convict Discipline (Leg-irons, Handcuffs, Guns, Cat o' Nine Tails)—Hell's Gates, Macquarie Harbour—The Grummet Rock, with Convicts Rafting Pine Logs—Hobart Town in 1829—Plan of Port Arthur during Convict Occupation—Court House, Hobart Town, with Convict Carrying-Gang—Gaol, Hobart Town, with Chain-Gang—Isle of the Dead—Corridor of Underground Cells at Coal Mines—The Suicide's Rock, Point Puer—Convict Railway, Port Arthur—Eaglehawk Neck—The Devil's Blow-Hole—The Settlement at Norfolk Island during Convict Occupation—Ruins of Rufus Dawes' Cell, Norfolk Island.

The Queenslander: "The book's value is enhanced by an introductory memoir of the author from the pen of A. B. Paterson, and it has also many illustrations of various places where incidents narrated in the book took place."

The Australasian: "This edition can be recommended to all who desire to possess one of the few works of original genius produced in Australia."

Maitland Mercury: "There can never be a time when Australians will cease to care to read Clarke's enthralling narrative, and the form in which this edition submits it ought to become a very favourite one."

Melbourne Argus: "The memoir written by Mr. A. B. Paterson is kindly and appreciative, and, on the whole, is a very just estimate of the man and of the writer."

Otago Witness: "An edition which is absolutely excellent in every respect."

WHILE THE BILLY BOILS: Australian Stories.

By Henry Lawson.

Author of "In the Days when the World was Wide."

Twelfth Thousand. With eight plates and vignette title by F. P. Mahony. Crown 8vo, cloth, 3s. 6d.; paper cover, 2s. 6d. (postage, 6d.)

Also in two parts (each complete in itself), in picture covers, at 1s.; post free, 1s. 3d. each (Commonwealth Series).

The Academy: "A book of honest, direct, sympathetic, humorous writing about Australia from within is worth a library of travellers' tales. Mr. Lawson shows us what living in the bush really means. The result is a real book—a book in a hundred. His language is terse, supple, and richly idiomatic."

Mr. A. Patchett Martin, in Literature (London): "A book which Mrs. Campbell Praed, the Australian novelist, assured me made her feel that all she had written of bush life was pale and ineffective."

The Spectator: "In these days when short, dramatic stories are eagerly looked for, it is strange that one we would venture to call the greatest Australian writer should be practically unknown in England. Short stories, but biting into the very heart of the bushman's life, ruthless in truth, extraordinarily dramatic, and pathetically uneven. . . . ."

The Times: "A collection of short and vigorous studies and stories of Australian life and character. A little in Bret Harte's manner, crossed, perhaps, with that of Guy de Maupassant."

TEENS. A Story of Australian Schoolgirls.

By Louise Mack.

Third Thousand. With 14 full-page illustrations by F. P. Mahony. Cloth gilt, 3s. 6d.; post free, 4s.

N.S.W. Educational Gazette: "The tone of the book is admirable. It bears the stamp of success on its every page."

Sydney Morning Herald: "Ought to be welcome to all who feel the responsibility of choosing the reading books of the young . . . its gaiety impulsiveness, and youthfulness will charm them."

Sydney Daily Telegraph: "Nothing could be more natural, more sympathetic."

The Australasian: "'Teens' is a pleasantly-written story, very suitable for a present or a school prize."

Bulletin: "It is written so well that it could not be written better."

Review of Reviews: "The book is pleasantly written, pure in tone and ought to delight many girls."

GIRLS TOGETHER. A Sequel to "Teens."

By Louise Mack.

Second Thousand. Illustrated by G. W. Lambert. Cloth gilt, 3s. 6d. post free, 4s.

Sydney Morning Herald: "They are Sydney girls, the like of whom, fortunately, are to be found in many a home. . . 'Girls Together' should be in the library of every girl who likes a pleasant story of real life. . . Older people will read it for its bright touches of human nature."

Sydney Daily Telegraph: "The youthful readers of 'Teens,' by Miss Louise Mack, will welcome with delight her 'Girls Together.' . . . The book should prove a popular Christmas gift."

Sydney Mail: "Pleasant and cleanly reading for girls which they will appreciate. . . The incidents are homely and everyday; there is no straining after unusual effect."

Brisbane Queenslander: "A story told in a dainty style that makes it attractive to all. It is fresh, bright, and cheery, and well worth a place on any Australian bookshelf."

THE SPIRIT OF THE BUSH FIRE AND OTHER AUSTRALIAN FAIRY TALES.

By J. M. Whitfeld.

Second Thousand. With 32 illustrations by G. W. Lambert. Cloth gilt, 3s. 6d.; post free, 4s.

Sydney Morning Herald: "It is frankly written for the young folks. . . The youngster will find a delight in Miss Whitfeld's marvellous company."

Daily Telegraph: "We venture to predict that 'The Spirit of the Bush Fire' will be the success of the Christmas season among our small people. Miss Whitfeld's fairies are native to the soil."

South Australian Register: "A number of fascinating creations of the imagination . . . will last and be popular."

New Zealand Mail: "A ready and graceful pen. We can answer for it that oldsters as well as youngsters will find delight in her clever little tales. There is not one of them which does not display considerable power of originality in idea and treatment."

THE MUTINEER: A Romance of Pitcairn Island.

By Louis Becke and Walter Jeffery.

New Edition. Crown 8vo, cloth, 3s. 6d.; paper cover, 2s. 6d. (postage, 6d.)

The Scotsman: "The charm of the description of Tahitian scenery, the interest of the savage mythology and customs, the fine simplicity and trustfulness of the native character as contrasted with the jealousies and disagreements of the mutineers, all combine to make an impressive story. The story is so true that it will prove especially welcome."

Saturday Review: "So skilfully is fact woven up with fiction that most readers will feel inclined to accept the narrative as a truthful record of actual events. The authors of this volume have produced a story of enduring interest."

A SHORT HISTORY OF AUSTRALASIA.

By Arthur W. Jose.

Author of "The Growth of the Empire."

With 6 maps and 64 portraits and illustrations. Crown 8vo, cloth gilt, 3s. 6d.; post free, 3s. 11d.

N.S.W. Educational Gazette: "Everything that a schoolboy need know respecting the history and progress of the colonies will be found in this volume, told in clear, compact, and pithy language; indeed, the reader of more mature years who has mastered its contents will find that he has laid down for himself a very sure foundation."

Daily Telegraph: "There was ample room for a cleverly-condensed clear, and yet thoroughly live account of these colonies, such as Mr. Jose now presents us with."

The Australasian: "It is a useful summary of the eventful history of Australia, Tasmania, and New Zealand, from the voyages of De Quiros and Torres down to the virtual accomplishment of federation."

New Zealand Herald: "The history is concise and clear, and gives a mass of information in a small compass."

West Australian: "A valuable feature about this little work is its accuracy. This, with the author, has evidently been a condition precedent, and in pursuance of it he has had recourse to original sources for his information, and to specially authentic and contemporary documents."

THE GROWTH OF THE EMPIRE.

A Handbook to the History of Greater Britain. (Covering the period set for the N.S.W. Public Service Examinations.)

By Arthur W. Jose (formerly Scholar of Balliol College, Oxford).

Second Edition. With 14 Maps. Cloth gilt, 5s.; post free, 5s. 6d.

Morning Post (London): "This book is published in Sydney, but it deserves to be circulated throughout the United Kingdom. . . Possesses considerable literary merits, and is eminently readable. The picture of the fashion in which British enterprise made its way from settlement to settlement has never been drawn more vividly than in these pages. . . Mr. Jose's style is crisp and pleasant, now and then even rising to eloquence on his grand theme. His book deserves wide popularity, and it has the rare merit of being so written as to be attractive alike to the young student and to the mature man of letters."

Literature (London): "He has studied thoroughly, and writes vigorously . . . . Admirably done. . . . We commend it to Britons the world over."

Saturday Review: "He writes Imperially; he also often writes sympathetically. . . . . We cannot close Mr. Jose's creditable account of our misdoings without a glow of national pride."

HISTORY OF AUSTRALIAN BUSHRANGING.

By CHARLES WHITE, author of "Convict Life in New South Wales and Van Diemen's Land" and "The Story of the Blacks."

To be completed in four parts, picture covers, profusely illustrated. 1s. each; post free, 1s. 3d. (Commonwealth Series.)

Part I.—The Early Days, containing Historical Sketch, Lives of Michael Howe, Brady, Britton, Cash, Kavanagh, Jones, Donohue, Underwood, Webber, Sullivan, Dignum, McKewin, The Jew-Boy, "Scotchey," Witton, Williams, Flanagan, Day, &c., Illustrations of Sarah Island (Macquarie Harbour, Tasmania), Frenchman's Cap, Port Arthur, Eagle Hawk Neck, Hobart Town, The Bushranger's Cave (Blue Mountains), *Fac-similes* of Tickets of Leave and other official papers, and portraits of bushrangers and others mentioned in the book. (*Now Ready.*)

Parts II., III. and **IV.** in preparation.

THE GEOLOGY OF SYDNEY AND THE BLUE MOUNTAINS; A POPULAR INTRODUCTION TO THE STUDY OF AUSTRALIAN GEOLOGY.

BY REV. J. MILNE CURRAN, Lecturer in Chemistry and Geology, Technical College, Sydney.

Second Edition. With a Glossary of Scientific Terms, a Reference List of commonly-occurring Fossils, 2 coloured maps, and 83 illustrations. Crown 8vo, cloth gilt, 6s.; post free, 6s. 6d.

Melbourne Argus: "The book is written in a popular style, and it deals with a subject of general and perpetual interest. As a handbook for schools in which it is desired to interest the advanced classes in the study of nature, the volume has great value."

Sydney Morning Herald: "Mr. Curran is the most admirable guide that any geological student can require for the interpretation of the hieroglyphics of Nature."

South Australian Register: "Mr. Curran has extracted a charming narrative of the earth's history out of the prosaic stone. Though he has selected Sydney rocks for his text, his discourse is interestingly Australian."

The Australasian: "Mr. Curran lets us see at once that his purpose is to deal with the geological history of Australia, and not to pad his treatise out with matter common to text-books in general. When he introduces what appear to be hard words, he does not close the remarks that they are associated with without fully explaining them."

Sydney Daily Telegraph: "Information on the geology of Sydney and the mountains hitherto buried in Blue-book reports and scientific papers. The style, simple, clear, and enticing, leaves nothing to be desired."

QUALITATIVE ANALYSIS: NOTES AND TABLES FOR USE OF STUDENTS.

BY REV. J. MILNE CURRAN, Lecturer in Chemistry and Geology, Technical College, Sydney.

With illustrations, 202 pages, Demy 8vo, cloth gilt, 4s. 6d.; post free, 5s. 1d.

*** This volume of Notes and Tables has been prepared for the use of Students in the Chemistry and Mineralogy Classes in the Technical College, Sydney. It is printed by the Government Printer of N.S.W., and the price (4s. 6d.) is a nominal one.

A COURSE OF INSTRUCTION IN ARCHITECTURAL AND TRADES DRAWING, Elementary Series.

By Cyril Blacket, Lecturer on Architecture and Building Construction, Technical College, Sydney.

24 Hand-coloured Plates (size, 19 by 13 inches), mounted on strong mill-board and accompanied by printed explanations. In strong deal box. Price, £12 12s.

*** This series is now in use in the Drawing Classes of the Technical Colleges throughout New South Wales.

DIET LISTS FOR AUSTRALIAN MEDICAL PRACTITIONERS.

By J. W. Springthorpe, M.D., and George Lane Mullins, M.D.

Cloth, 3s. 6d.; post free, 3s. 9d.

Containing 160 Detachable Diet Lists, 12 kinds assorted, or—1. Albuminuria—2. Anæmia and Debility—3. Biliousness—4. Constipation—5. Convalescence—6. Diabetes—7. Diarrhœa—8. Dyspepsia—9. Gout—10. Infant Feeding—11. Phthisis and Wasting Disease—12. Pyrexia.

These Diet Lists may also be had bound separately, 50 copies of one kind, in cheque book form, 2s.; post free, 2s. 1d.

THE KINGSWOOD COOKERY BOOK.

By Mrs. Wicken (late Teacher of Cookery, Technical College, Sydney).

Fourth edition, revised and enlarged to 372 pages. Crown 8vo, cloth gilt, 3s. 6d.; post free, 4s.

Newcastle Morning Herald: "Mrs. Wicken has long been recognised as an able exponent of the art of cooking, and the success of her book is probably due to the fact that it was written by a practical teacher, of many years' Australian experience."

Sydney Morning Herald: "Her excellent 'Kingswood Cookery Book,' which is handsomely issued."

Sydney Daily Telegraph: "This work may be said to fulfil all the requirements of a practical course of instruction."

Town and Country Journal: "A real boon to Australian women."

Maitland Mercury: "The merit of the book is that it is written by a scientific teacher who has had ten years' Australian experience."

Adelaide Advertiser: "No materials are mentioned which are not easily procurable, while the quantities in every case are concisely stated."

RECIPES OF LENTEN DISHES.

Containing over 250 useful recipes for preparing Fish, Soups, Vegetables, Cakes, Pastry, &c., &c. By Mrs. Wicken, Author of "The Kingswood Cookery Book." Cloth, 6d.; post free, 7d.

SIMPLE TESTS FOR MINERALS; OR, EVERY MAN HIS OWN ANALYST.

BY JOSEPH CAMPBELL, M.A., F.G.S., M.I.M.E.

Fourth edition, revised and enlarged (completing the ninth thousand). With illustrations. Cloth, round corners, 3s. 6d.; post free, 3s. 9d.

Newcastle Morning Herald: "The book is a thoroughly practical one."

Bundaberg Star: "A handy and useful book for miners and all interested in the mining industry."

Daylesford Advocate: "A very useful and valuable work."

Bendigo Evening Mail: "Should be in every prospector's kit. It enables any intelligent man to ascertain for himself whether any mineral he may discover has a commercial value."

Omeo Standard: "Exactly the work required."

Bendigo Advertiser: "To those engaged in prospecting for minerals this book should be invaluable."

PASSAGES FOR TRANSLATION INTO FRENCH AND GERMAN. For use in University and School Classes, Selected by DR. E. J. TRECHMANN. 2s. 6d.; post free, 2s. 9d.

LIVY—Book XXVI.—With Notes by W. H. Nicholls, B.A. 3s. 6d.; post free, 3s. 9d. (The text-book prescribed for the Senior Sydney University Examination of 1900.)

THE AUSTRALIAN LETTERING BOOK.

Containing the alphabets most useful in Mapping, Exercise Headings, &c. (with practical applications), Easy Scrolls, Flourishes, Borders, Corners, Rulings, &c.

Second Edition. 32 pages. Cloth, limp. Price, 6d.; post free, 7d.

THE AUSTRALIAN PROGRESSIVE SONGSTER.

BY S. MCBURNEY, Mus. Doc., Fellow T.S.F. College.

Containing graded Songs—the words by A. B. Paterson (Author of "The Man from Snowy River"), and others—Rounds and Exercises in Staff Notation, Tonic Sol-fa, and Numerals, with Musical Theory. Price, 6d. each part; combined, 1s.

No. 1—For Junior Classes. No. 2—For Senior Classes.

(Prescribed by the Department of Public Instruction, N.S.W., for First and Second Class Teachers' Certificate Examinations.)

ENGLISH GRAMMAR, COMPOSITION, AND PRÉCIS WRITING. BY JAMES CONWAY.

For Use by Candidates for University and Public Service Exams.

Second Edition, revised and enlarged. Cloth, 3s. 6d.; post free, 3s. 10d.

Sydney Morning Herald: "To its concise and admirable arrangement of rules and definitions, which holds good wherever the English language is spoken or written, is added special treatment of special difficulties. Mr. Conway adopts the excellent plan of taking certain papers, and of answering the questions in detail. . . . Should be in the hands of every teacher."

Victorian Educational News: "A book which we can heartily recommend as the most suitable we have yet met with to place in the hands of students for our intermediate examinations, and also for matriculation, pupil teachers', and certificate of competency examinations. We should be glad to see the work set down in the syllabus of the Department so that it would reach the hands of all the students and teachers engaged in studying the subject in our State schools."

(Prescribed by the Department of Public Instruction, N.S.W., for Third Class and Pupil Teachers' Examinations.)

CONWAY'S SMALLER ENGLISH GRAMMAR, COMPOSITION, AND PRÉCIS WRITING.

Second Edition, revised and enlarged. Cloth, 1s. 6d.; post free, 1s. 9d.

N.S.W. Educational Gazette: "The abridgment is very well done. The clearness of the instruction, both rules and examples, is as evident in one book as the other, and by this one would recognise the hand of a man who had had long experience of the difficulties of this subject."

CAUSERIES FAMILIÈRES; OR, FRIENDLY CHATS.

A Simple and Deductive French Course. By MRS. S. C. BOYD.

(Prescribed for use in schools by the Department of Public Instruction, N.S.W.)

Teachers' Edition, containing, in addition to the above, grammatical summaries, exercises, a full treatise on pronunciation, French-English and English-French Vocabulary, and other matter for the use of the teacher or of a student without a master. New edition, revised and enlarged. Cloth, 3s. 6d.; post free, 3s. 10d.

Pupils' Edition, containing all that need be in the hands of the learner. Cloth, limp, 1s. 6d.; post free, 1s. 8d.

The London Spectator: "A most excellent and practical little volume, evidently the work of a trained teacher. It combines admirably and in an entertaining form the advantages of the conversational with those of the grammatical method of learning a language."

The Scotsman: "A pleasant and familiar tone pervades the whole work, and it is to be welcomed as a further step in the desired direction."

GEOGRAPHY OF NEW SOUTH WALES.

By J. M. Taylor, M.A., LL.B.

New Edition, revised. With 37 illustrations and 6 folding maps. Crown 8vo, cloth, 3s. 6d. ; post free, 3s. 10d. (Prescribed for use in Public Schools of New South Wales.)

Queensland Education Journal: "A mine of thoroughly well arranged, perfectly accurate, and, for the most part, interesting information on the general physical and political features of New South Wales."

The Australasian: "The reading is very interesting. . . . . There are any number of excellent and striking photo-prints . . . . commendable features in a school book."

The Queenslander: "The book embraces within its 152 pages all the information that a geography should, presented in an easy, assimilable form."

Sydney Morning Herald: "Something more than a school book; it is an approach to an ideal geography."

Review of Reviews: "It makes a very attractive handbook. Its geography is up to date; it is not overburdened with details, and it is richly illustrated with geological diagrams and photographs of scenery reproduced with happy skill."

FOURPENNY GEOGRAPHY OF NEW SOUTH WALES.

Abridged from the above work.

With folding maps. 40 pages. 4d. ; post free, 5d.

N.S.W. Educational Gazette: "In May last we expressed the opinion that Mr. Taylor had succeeded in producing a compendious and reliable work, well up to date in every particular. The little volume now under consideration is an abridgment of the original work, and contains all that our Standards of Proficiency require for third and fourth class pupils. The work of the teacher will be much facilitated if he can persuade every pupil to provide himself with this excellent little handbook. For senior pupils and pupil teachers we would strongly recommend the larger work."

The Australian Teacher: "We noticed in our last number the excellent work in its larger form by Mr. Taylor. This should be in every teacher's hand; while the present cheap abridgment would be an excellent text-book for his class."

GEOGRAPHY OF AUSTRALIA AND NEW ZEALAND.

With Definitions of Geographical Terms.

Prepared for First Year Third Class Pupils under the New Standard of Proficiency in New South Wales.

With maps of the World, Australia, New South Wales, Victoria, Queensland, Tasmania, and New Zealand, and 21 other illustrations. 64 pages. 6d. ; by post, 7d.

GEOGRAPHY OF EUROPE, ASIA, AND AMERICA.

Prepared for Second Year Third Class Pupils under the New Standard of Proficiency in New South Wales.

With maps of Europe, British Isles, France, Germany, Austria-Hungary, Asia, India, China and Japan, North America, and South America; also 22 other maps and illustrations, showing distribution of animals, mountain and river systems, and other natural features. 84 pages. 6d.; by post, 7d.

HISTORY FOR THIRD, FOURTH, AND FIFTH CLASSES

under the New Standard of Proficiency in New South Wales.

Part I.—Third Class, First Half-year.—From the Roman to the Norman Conquest. *36 pages and a coloured map, 4d.; by post, 5d.*

Part II.—Third Class, Second Half-year.—From William I. to Richard I. *39 pages and a coloured map, 4d.; by post, 5d.*

Part III.—Third Class, Third Half-year.—From John to Richard II. *47 pages and a coloured map, 4d.; by post, 5d.*

Part IV.—Third Class, Fourth Half-year.—From Henry IV. to Elizabeth. *59 pages and a coloured map, 6d.; by post, 7d.*

Part V.—Fourth Class, First Half-year.—From James I. to Anne. *86 pages and a coloured map, 6d.; by post, 7d.*

Part VI.—Fourth Class, Second Half-year.—From George I. to the present time, and History of Australia to 1855. *142 pages, illustrated, 9d.; by post, 11d.*

HANDBOOK FOR TEACHERS OF INFANT SCHOOLS AND JUNIOR CLASSES.

Second Thousand. With colour chart (printed in nine colours) and upwards of 100 illustrations. Crown 8vo, cloth limp, 1s. 6d.; post free, 1s. 8d.

N.S.W. Educational Gazette: "It contains all information on Kindergarten work, object lessons, drawing, drill, form and colour necessary for Infant Schools and first classes in ordinary Primary Schools. . . Junior teachers and teachers in the country who have not had the advantage of training will find the pages of the *Handbook* invaluable."

THE AUSTRALIAN OBJECT LESSON BOOK.

Compiled by practical teachers, and edited by
DAVID T. WILEY.

PART I. For Infant and Juvenile Classes. With 43 illustrations.

Crown 8vo, cloth, 3s. 6d.; paper cover, 2s. 6d.; postage, 4d.

N.S.W. Educational Gazette: "Mr. Wiley has wisely adopted the plan of utilising the services of specialists. The series is remarkably complete, and practically includes almost everything with which the little learners ought to be made familiar. Throughout the whole series the lessons have been selected with judgment and with a due appreciation of the capacity of the pupils for whose use they are intended. The illustrations (forty-three in number) are admirable. Teachers should lose no time in placing their orders for this excellent book of object lessons."

PART II.—For Advanced Classes. With 113 illustrations. Crown 8vo., cloth, 3s. 6d.; post free, 3s. 11d.

N.S.W. Educational Gazette: "The Australian Object Lesson Book is evidently the result of infinite patience and deep research on the part of its compiler, who is also to be commended for the admirable arrangement of his matter."

Evening News: "It gives evidence of the utmost care and of attention to most minute detail in its preparation. It is appropriately illustrated, well arranged, and is eminently practical and contemporary."

THE AUSTRALASIAN CATHOLIC SCHOOL SERIES.

History of Australia and New Zealand for Catholic Schools, 117 pages. Price 4d.

Pupil's Companion to the Australian Catholic First Reader, 32 pages. Price 1d.

Pupil's Companion to the Australian Catholic Second Reader, 64 pages. Price 2d.

Pupil's Companion to the Australian Catholic Third Reader, 112 pages. Price 3d.

Pupil's Companion to the Australian Catholic Fourth Reader, 160 pages. Price 4d.

A. & R.'S AUSTRALIAN SCHOOL SERIES.

Grammar and Derivation Book. New edition, entirely re-written and enlarged to 64 pages. Price, 2d.

Test Questions in Grammar for Third Class, First Year. 64 pages. Price, 2d.

A. & R.'s Australian School Series—*continued*—

Table Book and Mental Arithmetic. 34 pages. Price, 1d. Nearly one-half the book is devoted to Mental Arithmetic.

Chief Events and Dates in English History. PART I. Chief events and dates from 55 B.C. to 1485 A.D. 50 pages. Price, 2d.

Chief Events and Dates in English History. PART II. From Henry VII. (1485) to Victoria (1895). 50 pages. Price, 2d.

History of Australia. The best authorities have been consulted in the compilation of this work, and the information is accurate. 53 pages. Price, 2d.

Geography. PART I. Australasia. This is a geography of the Australian Colonies and New Zealand, together with geographical definitions and three illustrations. 50 pages. Price, 2d.

Geography. PART II. Europe, Asia, America, and Africa. New edition, entirely re-written and enlarged to 66 pages. Price, 2d.

Euclid. BOOK I. With Definitions, Postulates, Axioms, and general terms used in Geometry. 64 pages. Price, 2d.

Euclid. BOOK II. With Definitions and Exercises on Books I. and II. Price, 2d.

Euclid. BOOK III. With the University "Junior" papers from 1891 to 1897. Price, 2d.

Arithmetic—Exercises for Class II. Contains Slate Exercises on the Rules prescribed, Test Questions on each half-year's work, and Typical Problems in Mental Arithmetic. 49 pages. Price, 2d.
ANSWERS to above, 2d.

Arithmetic—Exercises for Class III. Contains graduated Test Questions on the Rules prescribed in the Standard of Proficiency, Exemption Certificate Tests, and Typical Problems in Mental Arithmetic for each half-year. Enlarged to 66 pages. Price, 2d.
ANSWERS to above, 2d.

Arithmetic—Exercises for Class IV. 65 pages. Price, 2d. This book contains over thirteen hundred exercises and numerous "Exemption Certificate" Test Questions and Miscellaneous Examples.
ANSWERS to above, 2d.

Arithmetic and Mensuration—Exercises for Class V. 65 pages. Price, 2d. With the Arithmetic Papers set at the Sydney University Junior Public Examinations since 1885, together with the Papers set at all the Public Service Examinations to date
ANSWERS to above, 2d.

Algebra. PART I. Exercises in Notation, Simple Rules, Easy Equations and Factors. 49 pages. Price, 2d. Contains nearly nine hundred carefully graded Exercises, selected from all sources, and thereby giving a greater variety of questions than is usually found in one Text-book.
ANSWERS to above, 2d.

Algebra. PART II. To Quadratic Equations. 89 pages. Price, 4d. Contains nearly twelve hundred Exercises, including the Junior University Papers from 1888 to 1897 inclusive, and the Public Service Papers of January and June, 1897.
ANSWERS to above, 4d.

THE AUSTRALIAN DRAWING BOOK.

By F. W. Woodhouse,

Superintendent of Drawing, Department of Public Instruction, New South Wales.

(Approved by the Department of Public Instruction for use in the Public Schools of New South Wales.)

Nos. 1, 2, 3, 4—Graduated Elementary Freehand, Regular Forms, Simple Designs, &c.

Nos. 5, 6—Foliage, Flowers, Ornaments, Vase Forms, &c.

No 7—Book of Blank Pages. Price, 3d. each.

N.S.W. Educational Gazette: "This series of drawing books has been arranged by the Superintendent of Drawing for the purpose of enabling teachers and pupils to meet fully the requirements of the Public School Syllabus of 1899. It consists of six numbers, designed for the third, fourth, and fifth classes respectively, and there is also a seventh number containing blank pages only. Nos. 1 to 4 treat of elementary freehand, simple designs, pattern drawing, &c.; Nos. 5 and 6, of foliage, flowers, and ornaments. The copies are excellently designed and executed and carefully graduated, and the books are printed on superior drawing paper. 'The Australian Drawing Books' should be used in every public school in the colony, first on account of their intrinsic merit, and secondly because they are the only books that accurately fit our standard."

Testimonial from a Queensland Head Master holding a South Kensington Certificate.

I have carefully examined the above Drawing Books, and consider they are the best productions I have yet seen as aids for teaching drawing. They are so thoroughly practical in their construction—step-by-step lines, general "get up," and printed instructions—that they are exactly what are needed to help Teachers who have been unable to properly study the subject, and it naturally follows they will afford much self-help to the pupils, and lessen the work of the Teacher—a great consideration, in large drafts especially.

The "matter" is so technically good that Mr. Woodhouse would have been amply justified in styling his books "thoroughly practical."

Not the least part of their value is a well-graded set of corner and border designs, which a boy or girl could make good use of in colouring, woodwork, panels, and design-aids in netting and crocheting.

Most of the copies are new, well arranged, methodically thought out, and printed on excellent paper.

Another feature in the series is the introduction of drawings "off" the upright or perpendicular—an excellent innovation—and in many examples of designs Mr. Woodhouse has introduced their names and uses, the omission of which is a serious defect in technical drawing work, especially in the Colonies. I have no hesitation in stating that the books will improve the drawing of any School; they will be useful in Schools where drawing is systematically taught; and invaluable to those Teachers who have little or no practical knowledge of the subject.

(Signed) WM. WILSON,
Certificated Art Master.

State School,
Howard, Queensland,
November 6th, 1899.

ANNOUNCEMENTS.

Brunton Stephens.

The Poetical Works of Brunton Stephens. With a photogravure portrait. Crown 8vo, cloth, gilt top *(uniform with "The Man from Snowy River")*, 5s.; post free, 5s. 6d.

A. B. Paterson.

Rio Grande's Last Race and Other Verses. By the author of *"The Man from Snowy River."* Crown 8vo, cloth, gilt top, 5s.; post free, 5s. 5d. [*Shortly.*

The Commonwealth Series.

In Picture Covers, 1s. each.

On the Track: Stories by HENRY LAWSON. [*March.*

History of Australian Bushranging. By CHARLES WHITE. Illustrated. In 4 parts. (*Part I. Ready*). *Part II.—April.*

Popular Verses. By HENRY LAWSON.

By the Sliprails: Stories by HENRY LAWSON.

Humorous Verses. By HENRY LAWSON.

Old Bush Songs. Edited by A. B. PATERSON, author of *"The Man from Snowy River."*

The Billy Boils Series.

Cloth, gilt, 3s. 6d. per volume.

Humorous and Popular Verses. By HENRY LAWSON.

By Track and Sliprails. Stories by HENRY LAWSON.

History of Australian Bushranging. By CHARLES WHITE. Illustrated. 2 vols.

www.ingramcontent.com/pod-product-compliance
Lightning Source LLC
Chambersburg PA
CBHW032314280326
41932CB00009B/808
* 9 7 8 3 3 3 7 2 8 7 8 3 2 *